The Tel Aviv Review is published annually in January by *Ah'shav* (*Now*) Publishers, Tel Aviv.

All contributions, correspondence, subscriptions and applications for advertising should be addressed to the *TR* office: 3 Smolenskin St., 63415, Tel Aviv, Israel, Tel: (03)245120.

Unsolicited manuscripts will not be returned unless accompanied by addressed envelope and stamps, or international reply coupons.

Subscribers to *TR* will receive a thirty percent reduction of the cover price.

The Tel Aviv Review will practise catholicity as regards British and American spelling.

Table of Contents

A Statement of Aims

The Tel Aviv Review is an annual magazine which will appear each January. It will be devoted to translations from ancient and modern Hebrew literature; to poetry, fiction and drama of non-Israeli Jewish writers; and to essays on aspects of Judaism, Israel, the Middle East, and other issues bearing on these.

The *TR* will emphasize the pluralism and the unique character of spiritual, cultural, literary and artistic tendencies in Israel. Despite the small number of Hebrew speakers, Hebrew is one of the classical languages of West and East alike, and perhaps the only one spoken today. Its vitality and richness are also manifest in the achievements of contemporary Israeli literature. The *TR* seeks to transcend the barrier of language and to foster a genuine dialogue between Israel and the Diaspora, based on a mutual exploration of cultural issues. Concerning political issues, the *TR* will provide expression primarily for that body of opinion defined as liberal.

In our view, the Jewish intellectual and ethical heritage, as well as a real concern for Israel's democracy and security, should guide our approach to current political agendas. Thus, concerning the Israeli-Palestinian conflict, we believe that its reasonable solution is necessary for maintaining the democratic and predominantly Jewish character of Israel, for developing the country's socio-cultural and economic potential, and also for improving its international political standing.

However, the *TR* will not exclude discussion and controversy. All contributions will be published solely on their intrinsic merits, and will not necessarily reflect the views of the editor.

The *TR* has been launched by *'Ah'shav'* publishers. Among *'Ah'shav'* publications are books by Amichai, Appelfeld, Avidan, Vollach, and many other important Israeli writers, as well as a leading Hebrew literary magazine.

Gabriel Moked

Yehuda Amichai

From Man You Are
and to Man You Shall Return

My Son

Because of love and because of making love
and because the pain of the unborn
is greater than the pain of the born,
I said to the woman: "Let us make a man
in our own image." And we did. But he grows
different from us,
day by day,

Furtively he eavesdrops on his parents' talk.
He doesn't understand but he grows on those words
as a plant grows without understanding
oxygen, nitrogen and other elements.

Later on he stands before the opened
holy arks of legend
and before the lighted display windows
of history, the Maccabean wars, David and Goliath,
the suicides of Masada, the ghetto resistance,
Hannah and her seven sons.
He stands with gaping eyes
and, deep down, he grows a vow like a big flower:
To live, to live, not to die like them.

When he writes, he starts the letters from the bottom.
When he draws two fighting knights
he starts with the swords, then come the hands,
and then the head. And outside the page
and beyond the table – hope and peace.

Once he did something bad in school
and was punished: I saw him,
alone in an empty classroom,
eating with gestures of a tamed beast.
I told him, fight me.
But he fights the school,
law and order.
I told him, pour out your wrath on me.
But he caresses me and I caress him.

The first big real
schoolchildren's outing
is the outing from which
they never return.

I Guard The Children in The Schoolyard

I guard the children in the schoolyard.
The dog is part of me, I hear
the echoes of his barking from within.

And the shouts of children like wild birds
rise up. Not even one shout
will return to the mouth it emerged from.

I am an old father guarding instead of the great God
who is eternally boasting of His eternal youth.
During the Holocaust, I ask myself, did
son rebel against father? Did father beat
son between the barbed wire fences?
Was there a quarrel between mother and daughter
in the annihilation shacks?
A disloyal and defiant son in the transport cars?
A generation gap on the platforms of the abyss?
Oedipus in the Death Cells?

I guard the children in their games.
And sometimes the ball bounces over the wall
and bounces and bounces down from yard to yard
and rolls into another reality.

But I lift my face and see above us,
as in a terrible vision, the bearers of dominion,
the exalted in honor, uprisen and haughty,
the clerks of war, the merchants of peace,
the treasurers of fate – ministers and presidents
decorated with multicolored responsibility.
I see them skipping over us
like the angels in the plague of the firstborns' death.
And the groins yawning, dripping
with the filth of nectars like sweetened motor oil
and their feet trampling like the rooster-footed Demon,
and their heads in the sky, stupid as flags.

A Dangerous Land

A dangerous land. A land full of suspicious objects
and trapped people. And it's all supposed to be
the beginning of a new religion: each birth, each death,
every thorn-brush fire in the field, each wisp of smoke.
Even the lovers have to be careful of what they do and say –
hands outstretched for an embrace, whisper at midnight,
hidden weeping, gazing into the distance, the descent
of stairs in a white dress – all are the beginning of a new religion.

Even the migrating birds know this
when they come in the spring and don't stay in the fall,
like the gods of the land who don't stay either:
and he who says "here was" is a prophet of mercy,
and he who says "here will be" is a prophet of wrath.

And from north to south is an unending summer celebration
and warnings of deep or stormy water
with warnings of water drying up off the face of the earth.
And monuments of memory laid everywhere like weights
so that the history of the land will not fly in the wind, like papers.

Late Wedding

I sit in the waiting room with other grooms
younger than me by many years. If I lived in olden times
I'd be a prophet. But now I wait quietly
to register my name with my love in the big book
of marriage and respond to questions I can still
answer. I have filled up my life with words,
have gathered in my body enough information to support
the secret services of several countries.

With heavy steps I bear light thoughts:
As in my youth when I bore fate-heavy thoughts on light feet
– almost dancing from so much future.

The pressures of my life bring the date of birth closer
to the date of death, as in history books,
where the pressures of history affixed these two
numbers together next to the name of a dead king,
and only a dash separates them.

I hold onto this dash with all my might.
Like a lifeline, I live by it
with a vow – not to be alone – on my lips,
the voice of the groom and the voice of the bride
the voice of rejoicing children in the streets of Jerusalem
and the towns of Judea.

Evening with the Children

The Hannukah candles in a box,
the folded clothes in the closet,
the children in their beds, the rooms in the house.
Rooms sometimes give birth to smaller rooms
dark velvet-padded boxes
for precious vessels and silver goblets of the soul.

And there are people who are soft and open
and there are people in whom all is closed and pressed
like fossilized fish
or fossilized birds.

I am good-hearted, not out of goodheartedness
but from the decay of my long life.

And outside the window the night wind blows
and a large network is unfolded there:
"Relations among men."

My Mother's Death and the Lost Battles for the Future of Her Children

My mother white on her bed in the world
like the black stain
of a bonfire that was once in a field.

On the dresser the comb
that combed her hair
to one side
with the passing days
and left her forehead bare
on the pillow.

And outside,
the lost battles for the future of her children.

And My Mother from the Times

And my mother from the times when they drew
marvellous fruit in silver bowls and made do with that,
and people travelled through their lives
like ships, with the wind or against it,
true to their destination.

I ask myself what is better:
A man dying old or a man dying young?
As if asking what weighs less:
A pound of feathers or a pound of iron.

I want feathers, feathers, feathers.

My Mother Died on Shavuot

My mother died on Shavuot when they finished counting the Omer*,
her oldest brother died in 1916, fallen in the war,
I almost fell in 1948,
and my mother died in 1983.
Everyone dies at some counting,
long or short,
everyone falls in a war,
they all deserve a wreath and a ceremony and an official letter.
When I stand by my mother's grave
it's like saluting
and the hard words of the Kaddish a salvo
into the clear summer skies.

We buried her in Sanhedria next to my father's grave,
we kept the place for her
as in a bus or a cinema:
Leaving flowers and stones so no one would take her place.

(Twenty years ago this graveyard was
on the border, facing the enemy's positions.
The tombstones were a good defense against the tanks.)

But in my childhood there was a botanical garden here.
Lots of flowers with frail wooden tags
bearing names of flowers in Hebrew and Latin:
Common Rose, Mediterranean Sage,
Common Scream, Tufted Weeping,
Annual Weeping, Perennial Mourning,
Red Forget-Me-Not, Fragrant Forget-Me-Not,
Forget-me-not, forget.

*) Sheaf of corn; 49 days between the second day of Passover
and Shavuot (Pentecost).

Now She Descends

Now she descends into the earth,
now she is on a level with the telephone cables, electrical wires,
pure water pipes and impure water pipes,
now she descends to deeper places,
deeper than deep where lie
the reasons for all this flowing,
now she is in the layers of stone and ground water
where lie the motives of wars and the movers of history
and the future destinies of nations and people
yet unborn:
My mother, Satellite of Redemption
turns the earth
into real heavens.

Freed

She is freed, freed. Freed from the body
and freed from the soul and from the blood that is the soul,
freed from desires and freed from sudden fears
and from fear for me, freed from honor and freed from shame
freed from hope and despair and from fire and from water
freed from the color of her eyes and the color of her hair
freed from furniture and freed from spoon knife and fork
freed from the heavenly Jerusalem from the earthly Jerusalem

freed from identity and identity card
freed from the round seals
and from the square seals
freed from copies and freed from staples.
She is freed, freed.

And all the letters and all the numbers
which ordered her life are also free
for new combinations, new fates and new games
of all the generations to come after her.

The One and Only Door

She went out of the one and only door
through which all the dead leave the world.
It is the same one and only door
through which one enters the world.

And her new last name
is the same as everyone's:
Blessedbehermemory.

Her entire name from now until the resurrection:
Frieda Blessedbehermemory.

The Laundry Basement

The laundry basement in a big house. There I love
to be, there the sky is profane, and outside
in front of the high windows, the world is at its noisy evil.

The laundry basement. The meeting place of the raging grey-haired
    man
with the girl naked under the last sheet left her.
The rest of her clothes, outerwear with underwear,
eden and hell, spin together in enthusiastic dizziness
in the drums of the machines, like the games of chance,
for a new distribution of fates and bodies.

The laundry basement. Among the steam of sweet soaps
there rises within me a great desire
to change my life from beginning to end.
I embrace the warm scented basket
and rise in the drunken elevator
like a man who dreams a dream within a dream
and he must wake up
again and again
to return to this world.

In a Rustic Inn in Germany

Rain falls. The rain always falls
from the past to the future, like words.
The Holy Trinity sits opposite me in the inn:
Jesus, Peace, died in Jerusalem –
like me, probably.

Wet coats hang on hangers,
I speak to them as if they were human.
On the heavy wooden table the wine in the glass
remembers its whole life, like a man
the moment before his death, from grapes to now.

Rain falls outside and within vapors and men mingle,
for all mankind are vapors.

Two Poets in Mexico

Claudia is a multitude of Jews
made into one pretty girl in Mexico.
Veronica a multitude of rumors.

I'd like to describe them as in travel accounts
of the last century
with a lot of love and little knowledge.

I don't know what words make them happy
and what words make them sad,
what are their vistas of despair and what their vistas of hope,
deep plantations and deserts,
and distant snow-capped mountains
and what night brings.

Claudia is pretty, like windows open to the sea,
she is a scout of separation.
Veronica is Trotsky's granddaughter,
her lovely hair covers the deep wound in her grandfather's skull.
She lives in a house with a lot of books and a lot of death.

Lately I saw them together in the holy
ceremony of picture-taking at the foot of the stairs
among people, who clustered and scattered
and the trumpet that was summoned to soothe
opened memories, old and painful.

Claudia will carry on her shoulders
her fading face.
Veronica will take with her
all the words I didn't know.
My soul will throb for them
like the skin of a dozing dog.
The hand and the handle both lost.
And the bee drowned in its own honey.

Jerusalem 1985

Pleas stuck in the crack of the Wailing Wall,
crumpled, wadded notes.

Somewhere else, a note stuck in an old iron gate
half hidden in a jasmine bush:
"I just couldn't come,
hope you'll understand."

Cafe Dante in New York – 1

Four waitresses (one lovely eagle)
serve under the aegis of strong thugs.
The girls the soul, the thugs the body.

And one of them is a lovely eagle. On her narrow waist
a wide belt with a silver buckle.
The buckle is the answer.
No, the buckle is the riddle,
the belt is the answer.

Far away in a closed valley
the evening wind blows
from one place to another place.

Elizabeth Swados

You live in your permanent home
opposite my temporary home.
Only the street separates us,
and at night its white lines
like the white of an eye.

When you are not at home, the lights are on in your window,
when you are there, everything is dark.

Your hair is laughter and weeping all at once,
in your soul a tiny hole for stringing,
you wear your soul like a necklace.

Farewell, I must return to my land,
for I begin to know the names of trees
and flowers of your land. Hence I must return.
I gave you flowers smuggled out of Eden
into a world of thorns and the sweat of your brow.
You gave me scented powers
for bubbles in a soothing bath.

Farewell.
You too a knife
that didn't mean to be a knife.

Cafe Dante in New York – 2

Four waitresses talking in the tongue
of the Isle of Malta. In their mouths, resurrection
of mortal enemies, Crusaders and Moslems,
their sweet chatter mixes them, like history,
words make peace.

One wears her hair tight on her scalp
like a helmet. She mixes drinks
ringing spoon and goblet. She knows
the soul is made of glass.

Wineglasses on a shelf,
upside down, quiet
and flashing lies for a fast screw.

With Her in an Apple

You visit me in an apple.
We listen together to the knife
paring all around us, carefully
not to tear the peel.

You speak to me, I can trust your voice,
it holds pieces of hard pain
as real honey holds waxen pieces
of honeycomb.

With my fingers I touch your lips.
This too is a gesture of prophecy.
Your lips are red as a scorched field is black.
Everything comes true.

You visit me in an apple.
And you stay with me in the apple
till the paring knife finishes its work.

Memory of Love – Image

I cannot imagine
how we shall live without each other,
so we said.

And since then we live inside that image,
day after day, far from each other
and far from the house
where we said those words.

Every door closing, every window opening,
as under anesthesia, no pain.

Pains come later.

Memory of Love – Terms and Conditions

We were like children who didn't want to
come out of the sea. And the blue night came
and then the black night.

What did we bring back for the rest of our lives,
a flaming face, like the burning bush
that won't consume itself till the end of our lives.

We made a strange arrangement between us:
if you come to me, I'll come to you.
Strange terms and conditions: If you forget me,
I'll forget you.
Strange terms and lovely things.

The ugly things we had to do
for the rest of our lives.

Memory of Love – Opening the Will

I'm still in the room. Two days from now
I will see it from the outside only,
the closed shutter of your room where we loved one another
and not all mankind.

And we shall turn to the new life
in the special way of careful preparations
for death, turning to the wall
as in the Bible.

The god above the air we breathe.
The god who made us two eyes and two legs
made us two souls too.

And we shall open these days
on a day far away from here, as one opens
the will
years after a death.

From Man You Are and to Man You Shall Return

Death in war begins with
one young man
descending the
stairs.

Death in war begins
with the silent closing of a door,
death in war begins
with the opening of a window to see.

Therefore do not weep for the one who is gone,
weep for the one who descends the steps of his home,
weep for the one who puts his keys
into his final pocket.
Weep for the photograph that remembers instead of us.
Weep for the remembering paper,
weep for the unremembering tears.

And this spring
who will arise and say to the dust:
From man you are and to man you shall return.

*My Son, My Mother's Death and the Lost Battles for the Future of Her Children,
And My Mother from the Times, My Mother Died on Shavuot, Now She Descends,
Two Poets in Mexico, Jerusalem 1985, Cafe Dante in New York – 1, Elizabeth
Swados, Cafe Dante in New York – 2, With Her in an Apple, Memory of Love –
Image, Memory of Love – Terms and Conditions,* and *Memory of Love – Opening
the Will* were translated from the Hebrew by Barbara and Benjamin Harshav.
   *I Guard the Children in the Schoolyard, Late Wedding, A Dangerous Land,
Evening with the Children, Freed, The One and Only Door, The Laundry
Basement, In a Rustic Inn in Germany,* and *From Man You Are and to Man You
Shall Return* were translated from the Hebrew by Karen Alkalay Gut.

Yoram Kaniuk

The Vultures

Then silence fell. The last groans died away and it was only three in the afternoon. A wind began to blow. It blew through the crevices higher up on the hills and echoed like a howl. A row of cactus, an abandoned shack, a few trees and a dirt track winding up the hill. Our last shots had sounded hesitant. The ammunition had run out and it was every man for himself. As the commander maneuvered his driver out of the ambush, someone shouted 'Don't run!' and I knew. Everything was harsh and clear in the bright afternoon glare and the dead lay in a messy row in torn shirts made into bandages; they lay with their eyes open or closed and, from the side, I heard a voice: We're screwed. I looked but there was no one there. The silenced voice lay among the bodies and the commander's armored car got through the barrier next to the other burnt-out cars and there was a rapid burst of fire and bullets whistling at him from the hills. Then there was the brightness in the air that didn't quite fade but was somehow transparent and the little valley surrounded by pines and cactus and low rocky hills embedded in a broader circle of distant purplish mountains; then the defeat was clear. The armored car broke through another barrier. The sound of an exploding mine and shots firing wildly at the commander, wispy smoke rose and in the distance the pine trees murmured in the breeze and there I was, seventeen years and eight months old, brown hair, eyes shut, clothes torn, Sten empty, thirsty, I wanted water, I licked the canteen of the dead man on my left, I didn't know who he was, it was almost empty and then the waiting. Look, I'm writing today a book about what happened long ago. I forgot it; later on, I wanted to shove it off of me. Now that the memory has returned, on a rock on the beach at Apollonia, on a warm day with a breeze sliding softly over the waves and a young couple necking in the bushes below, and the cliff grooved with sandstone and strewn with bits of pale greeen

27

glass plunging down to the sea and the tumbledown mosque on my left, now everything comes back to me with nothing added on, as if it were yesterday, for nothing touched the memory, it lay dormant inside me complete and I touch it and it has none of those things that stick to every memory and interpret it even as it is remembered, now the pictures come rising to the surface as if I'm living for a moment in another place; I can smell, see a torn shirt and know just which side they sewed the pockets on in those days. The pictures well up plain and clear inside me, from where I forced myself to forget and to go on living as if it had never happened; but it did, the armored car did climb the hill and vanished into the woods looming up inside me from the shadows enveloping it a long time ago and I see the birds in formation as if through a transparent theatre screen, the birds gliding silently through the air in their perfect formation, passing over me in an indifferent and mute but not so innocent display.

The faintest sounds began to fade, as if obeying some inaudible command. I stretched out my arms, lay there like that; looking dead, I didn't have to think about it only obey the ancient cunning of the will to live and through my half-closed eyes I saw a golden ray of sun savagely beating down on the jutting rock where a man had been standing before and collapsed after shouting: Take the wounded at least, and the commander replied: No time! Where should I take them? I'll come back soon with help, then the man collapsed, dropped like a stone in water, then a few more fell, like in a silent movie and, if they had been acting, it might even have been funny. Children pretending to be grown-ups collapsing in exaggerated ways, freezing awkwardly in contrast to the graceful birds wheeling above us with a kind of contempt, for us, for the enemy, for the victory or for the crushing defeat, for the pines trying in vain to lend an organized, geometrical air to the little valley, which began to fill with stillness and perhaps even a hypocritical self-pity. A pity that maybe only I could feel without pretense, although it was so clear that I thought that even the ones shooting from the hills must feel it and maybe they saw their victory, for all its overwhelming solemnity, as a geometrical mistake in a game whose rules were only now revealed, a game that made a mockery of the deaths of those who had walked unwittingly into their trap. So I lay. From under my carefully lowered lids I could see the dead. No one prepared me for what a man was supposed to think at a moment like this. No one prepared any of us for anything. I thought about kindergarten, because most of them, or a lot of them, I don't know how many, I can't remember exactly how many of the men next to me had gone to the kindergarten with me once, most of them had started a year before me, and I thought about the kindergarten teacher, Eve, with her baby chicks and all of us standing behind a ship of cardboard or perhaps plywood opposite the village hall; and the ship had two funnels, that's what I thought about, I swear, those two fucking funnels, between the two palm trees and the wall shaded with a gigantic bougainvillea and Eve with her bitter smile too, maybe she knew something she wasn't allowed to pass on to us and we in the sailor suits our tired mothers had made for us after collecting eggs and milking cows and cleaning house, and reciting "Where are you going ship with a funnel, I'm bringing Jews from far away", and me looking really funny, maybe funnier than the rest of them, a year younger, in a pale cap, very thin, wishing I was somewhere else as usual, trying as hard as I could to be happy yet scared to death of the cardboard funnels; yes, that's what I thought about. Now they were lying all around me. I wasn't there when they were born but in our little village and in the villages nearby we really did grow up together, there were things we all said in more or less the same way. Suddenly, at three o'clock in the afternoon, they stopped living, came to an end in postures full of desire, as if to die was all they ever wanted and not to be sailors on a cardboard ship bringing Jews to Eretz Israel with bundles on their shoulders and sticks in their hands.

There were others too, there must have been, not from my kindergarten, not from school, others I got to know later on, and some I never knew at all. I peeped at them with half-closed eyes shaping the moments, all the moments, in a kind of maddening slow motion, with controlled emotion, with unconcealed determination to hate the birds so grandly disdaining the event I was part of, an event crystallizing, becoming eternal, full of children beginning their inevitable crawl into the earth with their frozen hands at this very moment, bodies locked into place forever. All around, on the hills, people were sitting, I couldn't see them, now, I must have been alone, just them and me. Sometimes I caught a glimpse of a gun barrel or of a machinegun muzzle, maybe a Bren and they, the invisible ones, went on shooting at thirty-three corpses, and me. Who could dream up such a thing? Me, after all these years, with the same face, although every minute that passes must age me slyly, astoundingly, unlike the frozen eternity of the thirty-three dead men. All the kids who stood behind that ship, almost all, maybe I'm exaggerating and it was only half but there were other kindergartens so alike, we were all extremely like one another and now they were stone figures growing harder every minute in a field of thorns while, in my breast, a heart was still beating, my blood was still coursing, my hands outspread and playing dead was ridiculous, even insulting, next to the dead. They were dead as they could be and I was only playing, like in kindergarten, then a sailor now a dead man and there is no more kindergarten teacher and now the wind blows, bringing a distant chill; but it was an east wind and the chill was harsh and dry and two twigs hovered with deliberate slowness in the air that now seemed to lose some of its violent transparency.

He should have hated, I said to myself in somebody else's voice. Too bad I don't have a handgrenade to finish myself off with. The game has its own rules and I knew I played it well enough but it annoyed me to be despised by birds that looked like a little cloud of floating question marks in the distance.

They went on shooting at us, having fun after their complete victory. They must have seen the commander running away too, slipping through the barriers in his armored car with his marvellous driver giving the scene a glory it didn't really have. And maybe the sight of our defeat excited them and became real to them when they saw the commander running away and someone shouting and falling off a rock and then absolute silence descending on the bodies that once were children or youths, call them what you like, and so they shot at random like insolent children throwing stones, without any particular malice or system. Maybe that was their mistake, they should have had some system, because even this mass death in the valley should have had some visual logic, maybe even a margin of reflection, indifference and hatred in turn; but they shot lazily, maybe even wearily, and it was only too bad I couldn't see them. They were outside my field of vision, all I could see was an occasional gun barrel glinting in the sun, no people and, after a while, I felt that some impersonal machine was shooting at me, not human beings and, far from making things easier, this made my flight into the game of perfect death even harder, more immoral and ignoble. I had no way of knowing, of course, who they were aiming at and this created some tension, which later may have given way to a rhythmic sense of doom, shots and silence in turn; but this tension was only a human skin covering something and their indifference made it so mechanical it couldn't fill the emptiness of the moments trickling but too slowly. The bullets were sticking into my friends and some of them even jerked when they were hit, as if they were waking up; but what actually happened was that, every time a dead man was hit, he would sink deeper or their faces, their beautiful faces, would be more mangled than before.

The sky was spread out above. I had more sky to myself than ever in my life. I even wondered why I had never seen so much sky before or so many shades in that pale blue. There was an enormous need to find the right formula, something definitive, so as not to budge, because if I did, I would never get up again and maybe even if I didn't move; there was a big maybe here and there was nothing I could do but merge with it and try to help myself by imprecisely decoding the warp-and-woof of life and death, which I could not, of course, fail to see or understand. For a moment I even fell asleep.

Maybe I didn't really fall asleep, maybe I only dozed, we were all tired, after all, we'd been tired for hours. We set out on what was supposed to be a diversionary tactic at four in the morning, they discovered us at six, we fought without much hope of winning till two, two-thirty. The dying started then and ended at three, when almost everyone was dead. The ammunition ran out and the commander ran away and our isolated, stubborn ineffective shots died out one by one. Now it was already three-thirty, maybe four, and that fatigue was overpowering. It lowered my lids, the sun grew dark for a moment, there were stars in my lids, seconds of being merging into non-being, or that's how I see them now, and you can erase these last words if you like because you too could have stayed there forever, like me, in utter oblivion or been there every waking minute, knowing, imagining, deceiving yourself; after all, why should you know less than me, when I didn't even suspect the still indestructible connection between those moments there and all the moments to come, over many years, out of oblivion, out of profound longing, sometimes even out of great denial, unforgivable, although maybe, maybe not understandable to you, so "non-being" is only a late literary description, I know, for shutting my eyes, for the whiff of a distant outdoor oven, for the grumbling of my stomach hungry even at those moments, for merging into the dead as if they were a fortress and I were seeking some impossible closeness, for friends who turned their backs to me with a stubbornness that wasn't in them at all; and I even dreamed short, hypnotized dreams, full of leaps, and in one of them, I remember it with amazing clarity, Baruch Kogan, whose stiff dead foot I could see all the time out of the corner of my left eye, Baruch who was once a friend, maybe not a real friend but whose unique personality you discovered one night on a trip in an armored car, on one of the roads on one of the nights, when all stopped still at three o'clock in the afternoon, drawing a thick, black line behind them, Baruch said to me then: Listen, there's going to be a real war and it's going to be bad. I knew, in the dream I knew, that it was already here, around me, next to me, above me, inside me, but when I tried to talk to him, somehow I couldn't say a word. He went on: Take a gun, you have to have a gun, go home and stay upstairs. Then suddenly I said to him, the words did come to me: Why not downstairs, if they bomb, it's better not to be upstairs; but he said: No, no, it'll be serious and there'll be cases where you'll have to actually shoot at them, and I woke up because I didn't have a gun.

I tried to figure out how much time had passed: minutes, an hour? The sky was almost the same color but instead of the birds that were overhead before, now I saw a few crows approaching. They were still flying over the Sheik's tomb and one of them perched for a moment on the finger of a cypress slightly bent by the wind toward the cactus and those on the hills, the ones shooting at us, now shot at the crows too and suddenly the shots were coming from two directions at the same time, I could hear the difference in the whistling of the bullets and I heard distant laughter and I think I even heard the gurgle of water poured into a pot or a kettle and in fact a light cloud of smoke rose innocently into the air behind the bushes and once again the bullets sprayed into the row of bodies and from my side there was only something still and a distant, blurred picture of a cardboard ship with two funnels and what do they think, I said to myself, how am I supposed to define situations like this to myself, changing from one cardboard cutout to another and what was the connection between the wafting smoke and the advancing crows and I thought of a bullet, I could actually see it, a bullet like the ones I shot before my ammunition ran out, I saw it in sharp, vivid details penetrating my brain, and then I said to myself: you only know you're alive when the high whine of the bullet stops and inside me the tension grew between waiting death and a stay whose length I couldn't gauge and you measure minutes, try to understand the flow of time and your own subjection to it, which I was only beginning to comprehend now, next to the bodies stiffening into eternity beside me but time, that time, was different from other times, much as it was part of you it was also intangible and had dimensions of its own, even though it didn't have a precise boundary, nothing you could hold onto, or perhaps it did, perhaps it was time itself transposing you from one image of the past to another so I could flit from one reality to another and back again until darkness fell, though then, and here I remember exactly, I wasn't waiting for the dark at all, even though something inside me was waiting for it like hell; I waited maybe another minute, another five minutes, but I didn't interpret this expectation as the passing of time. After all, the sky was the same sky, except for a slight, almost imperceptible change and you measure things by distant sounds, by the column of ants passing under your body, a beetle twitching, a few bushes swaying, the wind suddenly sobbing in the pines and then the flock of crows came closer, circling in the sky as if some ceremony was in store for you, would emerge from the ceaseless stirring of all those tiny objects, the beetle, the ants, the smoke hanging in the air, then amid the circle of wheeling, cawing crows, it appears, yes, it was then that the first vulture appeared.

I remember it exactly though I didn't know then that that huge bird was a vulture. My half-closed eyes kept everything deliberately vague, sometimes I could shut them tight and open them again and I would feel an excruciating pain in my temples and scalp, I was hungry and thirsty after all and my whole body – I imagine though I don't remember the pain exactly – was burning and felt like it had been taken apart and patched together again and my eyes must have been red too but if I shut them tight and opened them again I could see things much clearer and sharper, then the vulture entering the prism of my bloodshot eyes would spell out his name, his clear identity, his majesty even, as if he had flown straight out of some awesome epic which had just now been created in some remote, exalted eternity. All I could do was lie on the ground and search for a clue to its meaning among the thorns and the ants; I wanted to understand, of course I did, and everything was really ready, in some way I can't describe, for the appearance of the vulture and then another and another... and I really could have known and I didn't know; but I was in on the secret because of my very small part in what was going on.

The crows were now circling round the vultures with brilliant virtuosity in a weaving, organic formation, ritualistic but not yet terrifying, maybe lacking the dignity of the first solemnly circling vulture but not panicky either; something tightly woven in the formation of their flight seemed precisely and perfectly coordinated with the shots, which now died down for a while as the formation became a tight texture of swift and certain transparency.

The crows were wheeling round what looked like flying gods, the sky was still very clear but the light was softer now and a kind of darkness, a veil of darkness, began to envelop it, everything was dominated by the majesty of the vultures coming as if to some event or even someplace created just for them, where they were lords and masters, not necessarily hostile or even insensitive. They had an immortal beauty, transcending the ordinariness of shots and death, they did not come to death, death came to them, called to them, yearned for them. This was the strangest feeling of all, there was something archaic about them, as if they were sent here by ancient monarchs and were not guests but the owners of the palace which now assumed its proper dimensions in this little valley which had seemed so mean and insignificant so far; an unpretentious palace, full of death and frozen children and twisted limbs and crows and shots and beetles and ants and sobbing winds, which they brought into being with their very presence, so lordly but yet gentle, a gentleness woven into the slow, gliding manner of their flight as they slowly circled and amassed strength with a steady rhythm that seemed deliberate and permanent, set by the ancient, lofty laws that still ruled in this place where I, by contrast, was only a temporary visitor.

Then I became aware of my right eye. Suddenly it was scared for itself, separate from me. Surely it must have grown more bloodshot, moist, full of tears, not of grief or laughter, tears of mighty effort welling up and covering my half-closed lids, I saw pretty colored prisms but my eye was trapped in a splitting pain and perhaps a certain shame. Before this, before I lay down and pretended to be dead, I caught a glimpse of the woods covering the foot of the hill behind me. And as I dropped to the ground I also saw a few shadows higher up on the same hill which faced east, I remembered this later when I tried to imagine the shade of the hill behind me and I even tried in vain to roll my eyes around and see it, and my eyes burned with the effort of imagining how much shade there was behind me relying on meaningless comparisons with the glare of the hills opposite trapped in the harsh light of the sun and now both eyes hurt and my right eye had suddenly decided to become its own master and maybe it was even trying to signal to the vulture in the pathetic belief that the vulture would take its pleas to heart and leave it alone.

But only someone who lay there like I did, and you of course never did, and I myself could not remember the scene for years, only someone who was there himself could understand the irony of the story about the eye. A young man lies among the dead. The enemy does not know that he is pretending to be dead. The enemy shoots at random. A bullet may hit him at any minute. Then the vultures arrive, the vultures who own this vast theatre, for whom this whole drama has been unfolding here since morning, the vultures, the famous "laws of nature" who feed on dead bodies, for whom the bodies die and it is they who live the drama, who own it, who come to it like royalty to a command performance — they knew I wasn't dead. And my eye, that part and product of tens of thousands of years of human knowledge, didn't know what they knew and I thought – but what did I think? Could a child not yet eighteen years old, obliged to construct an endless series of responses to situations for which no one had prepared him, know that the vultures knew who was dead and who wasn't? And my eye, even if it were fifty times cleverer than I was or a hundred times more foolish, was still my eye, and I interpreted its signals in terms of my own ideas and not those of some biology teacher.

So, trapped between the pleas of my eye and a fear so paralyzing I could not even begin to comprehend it and aware of a future pain I didn't know how I was going to endure, I thought about this disgrace given to me a few months before my eighteenth birthday, a gift from a long line of kindergarten teachers and school teachers, the disgrace of dying alone in the middle of a game whose rules I couldn't understand. Perhaps the vulture wheeling above me, who, unlike my eye, knew very well that I was alive was fully aware of the comedy of the situation, and perhaps would swoop down on me even though I was alive, just because I was alive, to show me, even for the fraction of a second when my frightened eye was plucked out by the pincers of his hooked beak, the inadvisability of playing childish games when you don't know the rules. And did I know them? Even the commander who ran away claiming he would bring help – could his ignorance be excused simply on the grounds that he wasn't in possession of all the facts? He was in possession of a lot more facts than I was. ...And now I was facing them all by myself and you try playing the hero to an audience of vultures and gun barrels and crows and beetles and ants and wind.

The vultures were now circling like a ballet. Two of them, or even more, were wheeling round the bigger ones in the middle. My eyes measured shapes and sizes because this was all I could know: colors and shapes and sizes and I knew that this knowledge had no importance or meaning and nevertheless I went on measuring. The crows cawed and croaked and intermittently circled the vultures in a large circle as in some ancient round-dance, cutting figures deeply embedded in their blood, not landing yet, measuring the hills and the valley which was not very impressive and was full of little humps and hillocks of earth and bushes and thorns and which didn't look in the least like a royal amphitheatre but simply like a good place to ambush us from the enemy's point of view, which of course it was, but the vultures had turned it into one; after all they had seemed more important than the enemy from the moment of their appearance, not only because the enemy fire had died down for a while by the time they appeared but because, in taking the measure of their kingdom, they made no distinction between us and the enemy and, if there were any enemy dead – and perhaps there were dead men there that I couldn't see, in fact, how could there not be after such a long battle? – they would have swooped down on them if they could and perhaps they would swoop down on the dead enemy later in just the same way as they would swoop down un us. It made no difference to them, they were too far above us, from their point of view death was one and this produced a special attitude toward them because they had a godlike ability or the ability of a fly to be neutral and as annoying to your enemy as to you.

Children sometimes think about a country of their own, with stamps and a king, who is them... Facing the lords of the valley I thought about the children who had not grown any older in the hour that had passed but no longer in connection with them and I thought about Eve the kindergarten teacher behind the cardboard ship with the two funnels, who taught us to hate in an orderly way, the Greeks at Hanukkah, the Persians at Purim, the Egyptians at Pessach and who wasn't there now to help me orchestrate the row of corpses which belonged to her, which came from her, into a choral recitation of some heroic poem; no, she wasn't there to organize and supervise and I thought with the bitterness of the boy I had been up to then, why aren't you here with your hard eyes and lined face, you who may perhaps have suffered real suffering that you didn't know how to teach us instead of Hannah sacrificing her seven sons and Haman's children hung on a tree, in three voices, although of course I was a child then and I didn't know what real suffering was, but even now, you have to understand, in the face of everything that was happening, there was something quite simple that I didn't know – I knew that something terrible was happening but I didn't know who it was happening to, I didn't know that it was happening to me, only my eye bore witness to the fact that I was fighting against something, that I was surmising something that may have included me too.

Lying among the dead; don't forget that I was taught to define nations, hatreds and plants and to press wild flowers – and there wasn't a flower to be seen where I lay – I never learned a thing about vultures or about children who would be pushing up the wild cyclamens that would bloom here in the spring; I still find it hard to say corpses, I think about them in abstract terms, their death is still no more comprehensible to me than my own life; but the circling of the vultures gives these things a certain reality, documents them so to speak, and you of course know how important it is to define things, even if later I silence these definitions for many years to come and look for a way to evade any personal responsibility, and after all there is an enormous responsibility here that I can't not sense, the responsibility for what you see, what you think, what the vultures are going to do to the children nurtured like me by Eve the kindergarten teacher and others like her.

My friends were now in a state of perfect defeat; next to them I was still a living potential and so I dreamed of kingdoms and a ship with two funnels and I was a child again wearing his father's cap and thinking how sad it was to see the barn flooded with water after the singing in the night and of that evening when the bull mounted the cow next to the cowshed and Miss Chestahova freaked out and laughed for three weeks running and said who needs a flag when something has a natural flagstaff like that? I remember the words now and it's all so out of place, the blind laughter of Miss Chestahova who had been made to stand in front of national flags all her life, in sandstorms, in howling gales pouring rain and made to listen to bombastic speeches, especially in front of the founders' well by the water-tower, the local tourist trap which the head of the village council enlarged every year, secretly on Yom Kippur when everyone was in synagogue praying and it isn't as if they didn't bring her marriage brokers and suitors from the surrounding villages – but all she could see was flags, what she apparently never saw was the flagstaff, until that night next to the cowshed...

The enemy began firing again, more frequently now. The crows clustering around the vultures were playing an organized game, even though it didn't have the same weight, the same discipline or masterful authority. One of them would circle slowly, caw, fly up to reconnoiter the terrain, and then the rest of them would swoop, wheeling round and round the vultures who were still gliding with the same calm, restrained power and land with a series of rapid, uncertain hops. The man whose stillness touched mine was hit by a bullet. He vibrated like hard rubber and I tried to turn my eyes to see what had happened to him and I didn't even know who he was. At the beginning I didn't take too much notice of exactly who was lying next to me and now it was so important for me to know and my hand groped, my eye failed to fish up his face, the cold blood trickled onto my hand – maybe it was Menachem? I saw him before, when he yelled at the commander who had disappeared long ago in his armored car with his tame driver taking him far away from us. In a moment of pity for him or maybe seething rage, I thought: maybe he really will bring help? But I remembered Menachem's face when he yelled at him: Take the wounded at least! And the commander said: How can I? I'll be back soon with help! Menachem, I wanted to say to him, the man's afraid! We had no chance to feel fear but the commander who was older who knew the roads and the plans and the risks, he must have known the fear a long time before. But was it Menachem whose cold dead blood was trickling onto me? I don't know. My eyes are concentrated now through half-shut lids on the birds. Dimly I see the scalpel-shaped feathers, the great wings gliding, the restrained power, the hooked beaks, the huge claws which look like they belong to some prehistoric creature. Then one of the birds dips and rises right in front of my eyes and I see them up close and they are very sharp and the bird looks like he's hiding behind a giant pair of iron talons and suddenly, like a magnetic command on the nerve centers, a colorful event takes place, full of vitality and the savagery which has so far existed only in vivid potential. The operation begins; murderous but acrobatic at the same time; the vultures land with a speed out of all proportion to their slow, aristocratic glide, as if they are parachuting without a parachute, a free fall full of joy, they cling to the corpses for a moment and I say "corpses" here though I didn't think in those terms then, and they soar.

Soar into the sky which is now a deeper blue, its radiant film or aura changing in response to some hidden event, like arrows shot from a bow. With supersonic speed, perpendicular and then with a cunning suddenness the rapid ascent stops and again the vultures circle, leisurely, gliding, then the crows fall to like a band of brazen, impudent boys hopping among the men and the soaring vultures and an activity emerges whose relationships are set by the silent, murderous contempt of the vultures, the lines drawn between the vultures and the crows. Someone is having a lark here and someone is performing an essential mission. The absolute of the vulture opposed to the capering beggar of the crow. On the ground the crows look more elegant, but in this event they are only the entertainment corps of the celestial department. The vulture circles slowly, beats his wings with self-absorbed, indifferent power and dives with the pounce of a flying panther onto his prey. Then he soars into the sky with his knife-like glide and the crows follow him, aping him, cawing around him, but not daring to intrude upon his circle. And I don't know what to ask for any more, cold blood drips onto my hand, the birds fill the sky, bullets whistle, the wind blows, a beetle crawls over me. I'm thirsty, my body's shriveling up, part of a row of twisted monuments – what can I possibly ask for? What can I think? My mind's empty, the only possibility is fear and that's not a practical proposition.

So I lie there inside something designed to fit measurements I can't even begin to comprehend, among the youths I can't even miss yet, haven't buried yet, haven't said my last farewells to, haven't cut myself off from, haven't made myself known to their loved ones; I haven't grown older by a single day and they're already returning to some primordial grayness that was buried within them, frozen at the same age forever, wearing the expressions of three o'clock in the afternoon in the month of May, nineteen forty-eight.

The birds of prey up there, wheeling above me, I know they can see my game, I can sense the contempt and maybe even the pity they feel for the lone survivor, and the bullets that know nothing somehow don't hit me, as if something is stopping them and the uncertainty creates a kind of suspense and I live in it for a few seconds and then, for another few seconds, I am filled with an almost absolute happiness when the firing stops for a minute and you think: Another minute! You've gained another minute! A minute for what? What the hell do I need another minute for? Why is it so important, this mental effort I'm not even properly aware of, to stay alive for another hour, another half hour? For even in these little eternities between the wheeling of the vultures and the firing of the unseen enemy's bullets, I experience a celebration of awakening to things happening inside me, secret and hidden, coming closer to the surface, crystallizing into shape as I begin to pay attention to them, things going on inside me but coming from unimaginably distant places.

Fifty thousand years of human experience have been devoted to the evolution of every gesture of your body, says something inside me which did not know how to say such things before today or to think them even today, at half past two in the afternoon.

Precise and sophisticated systems are now busy working computers inside my body, calculating distances, estimating dangers, trying to bring nerve centres up to date, sending urgent messages, broadcasting frantic transmissions, and, for a moment, I sense all this activity going on inside me, suddenly conscious of a new-born ability to listen in to the pulsing of the parliaments in my bloodstream; but as I become conscious of myself, the voices I hear are not those from within. I hear the roar of a distant truck. I don't know where it's coming from or where it's going. Another convoy on the way to Jerusalem, fighting for its life, perhaps. The birds screech, the shots become more sporadic or maybe I'm only imagining it, the wind grows dense, as if it's trying to blot out a radiance in the air whose brilliance is now subdued. There is, my dear, a certain happiness here; time passes somehow; there are certain changes in the air; the light has not failed or dimmed but grown more transparent, a thin veil over shapes like shadows trying to break through. The delicate wisp of smoke has already disappeared behind the cactus; but beyond the hills there is a haze of dust with a different radiance. It shines more brightly on the backdrop of the sky whose tint seems to be changing too. Can it be five o'clock already? I hear a distant bell and the bleating of a goat, something innocent and I begin to think about the organs of my body.

If I hadn't painted a little at the age of sixteen in that old studio next to the village hall under the instruction of the art teacher who came from the city every week wearing a corduroy suit and a broad-brimmed hat, if I hadn't tried then, because of certain doubts which had begun to gnaw at me, to paint red and blue pictures in a desperate, perhaps even ridiculous, attempt to be a momentary, transient painter of non-existent things which seemed more real than anything in actuality, if I hadn't painted then, maybe I wouldn't have thought now, lying in the gradually dimming valley, about my limbs as if they were something outside myself. But I had painted hands in that studio with the high, old-fashioned windows and seven ugly farmers' daughters and two boys from the kibbutz next door and I knew some facts about my hands and feet that a lot of other people might not know. My head and arms too. My eye is really an exception because so far it was known to me only in its external appearance, while I would have been aware of my muscles even without the paintings in that funny little studio stuck onto Villabovitch's dove-cote made of rusty tin sheets pieced together like a hive, with the cooing white doves flying in and out and leaving their droppings with infinite delicacy. At most, my eye was a sophisticated, highly efficient optical instrument. But I was trying then to paint something mystical, elliptical, something whose delicate lines did not define but lent expression to a face which was supposed to reflect a reality whose physical existence was unknowable. In other words, as far as I was concerned the eye was an ornament and I was not overly interested in its wonders and workings and the delicate lines that composed its form. So I was completely ignorant of the negotiations of my eye with the vultures. In the silent, elegant ballet of gouging and plucking and cruel grace which I witnessed, my eye acted as an independent agent and I did not understand its forms, structure or laws. But my hand was something I was familiar with, I knew it as one who had painted real hands, copied the hands of the Arab from the village of K. who sat in an armchair smiling and smoking a cigarette and served as our model. His name was Abu Shaluf, I even remember his name and, as for his hand, I knew it as one who knew how it looked in different positions and perspectives, sculpted in three dimensions and looking different from the front than it looked from the side, whereas you can't see the eye from the side except as a silhouette, a triangular nail inserted into an equation of lines and broken ellipses.

So I could think about my hand or foot, I had the data; but I couldn't think about what I would say later when I came to Nilly's tent or when I met my teacher Mr. Halkin. I couldn't know my final role as a limb of a frozen kindergarten pressed between the pages of the book kept specially for pressing flowers by our Nature Study teacher whose name was Ferber and who was sympathetic to the child I was when I brought him the first squill that bloomed in the fields or the blue anemones. Yes, it was only later, at the moment of getting up, the getting up which would come later after hours that must have been the longest in my life, with the sudden gush of bitter hatred I felt then, with an almost impossible intensity, for the vultures and the crows and the invisible enemy shooting at me, shooting at random at the dead children who could have grown into men in a direct relation to the growth that would take place in me, whether I wanted or not, it was only then that I would be able to think of the moments when the turning point occurred. The turning point when these children would be left forever at the one, final age set without pity and without malice by what people in the village used to call "nature" and by which they meant wild flowers in the winter, the rains in season and the bull mounting the cow. But was it really necessary? Human? Natural? I wanted to think about it. For when else would I be able to think about war lying prone, taut as a tightrope between possible death and lightning pardon? Could I ever again think about things that were apparently simple but buried deep inside me – inside all of us in fact, even you, though I never say the things I think to you, as if I talk to you without really talking – would I ever be able to think like this again from inside the event but outside it at the same time, lying on my back, pretending to be dead, measuring seconds like light-years, celebrating a moment of life after the vulture rises or while the anonymous enemy reloads his gun behind the cactus or the bush whose name I don't even know. Yes, this is the moment for thinking. But they all dissolve, the flowing life, the laws of nature, the dead children at my side, the cold blood dripping onto my hand and I think instead of the future, sometimes a future of an hour, sometimes of a ripe old age and of course I'll always be older than they are even though all of them are one or two years older than me, even Menashe, kept back a year at school and in the class below me, will still

41

be a boy when I come here full of the echoes of all this death as an old man, with a gray beard maybe or a furrowed face... will I be able to say hello then, or drop some hint, maybe light a pipe so they can smell the tobacco from vast distances? Will I be able to smoke it for them, have the children they'll never have?...

So I could reflect on the echoes that would fill my life in the years to come and not on their frozen agelessness here in the valley, in a grace composed of encircling hills, in the weakening light, yes, the somehow lessening light in the long intervals between one closing of my eyes and the next, and think about some hand, the position of a foot. I wondered abstractly, although not without anxiety, about the sweat of the bodies embracing death with a hostility full of yearning. I thought about the flesh that had once been my friends and was now gouged by the beaks of the vultures, I saw eyes, real eyes and each of them had seen me during the long hours of fighting when we were still shooting, when we were hiding behind the burnt-out armored cars,eyes lifted into the sky by beaks become hostile, full of a fury that was programmed rather than passionate. I was overcome by a dread that drew pictures of limbs and organs, a dread feeding on the accurate, intimate knowledge of the torn off limbs, the plucked out organs, which later, thank God, turned for a minute into the most terrible rage I have ever known in my life, a rage that would fade and dissolve into my life like hidden poison.

But the eyes were different, the eyes were the worst: there was something particularly vicious about the way the eyes were plucked out and borne aloft in the beaks of the vultures and the clownish crows, like savage little warlords flaunting their victory and I closed my eyes and thought about the tissues of my hand mauled by iron beaks and bullets cutting shrilly through the air.

I don't remember ever reading anything in all the encyclopedias I read so tirelessly for a year or two before the war, stuffing my mind with information useless to me now when I needed to know, so that the only place I could look for a source of knowledge was inside myself, in the body and brain whose workings were a mystery to me – I don't remember ever reading anything about the vultures' love of eyes. But then we all spent years and years learning things and yet not knowing how to behave in the most crucial moments of our lives, terrible moments of love or birth or death or sickness... They plucked out the eyes and I didn't know why they were so crazy about eyes and why it was just the eyes that made me sick to death and then came the flesh, whose? Maybe Menachem's, whose blood was dripping onto my hand? I heard the vulture, I saw it swoop and what kind of face did he have left now? I didn't know. Then the vulture landed on the hill, came to rest on a jutting rock, a magnificent creature, and the enemy, I want to say something to his credit, began to shoot at them too now, at the vultures; but the vulture's contempt for the enemy's bullets was even more absolute than his dominance of the valley where he was lord and master. The enemy is satiated, the vulture contemptuous, the enemy shoots apathetically, drinks coffee, the victory is his, for how long? The vulture knows perspectives that are perhaps eternal – life is not someone shot or a chance enemy drinking coffee today and dead tomorrow in another battle; life is a text including him as well as what my eye has been hinting about him all this time, that there is a broader time, things that are only beginning to happen, now the shots sound as if the enemy is also no longer so sure of just who is the victor here, and the vulture's contempt says: who is the true victor? Human bodies or the light already fading and bringing the tomorrow when the shooters will themselves be dead flesh rotting in some other valley or on some other hills, flesh for crows to sport with.

Perhaps this is why later, two days later, people would see in the camp behind the wood eight heads of my friends stuck up on poles, a symbol of the futility of the victory already beginning to erode in the face of the vulture cleaning his wings with elegant discretion. The word "cruelty" at the sight of all this, even the impaled heads, came to me later. Words too had to be reborn and know their place and I thought in the words with which I had been equipped like the empty canteen or the magazines with no bullets left in them and this enemy too, who would die tomorrow or the next day in the hills and was drinking his last cup of coffee now, not knowing that the vulture would be here after him, but perhaps I would be here after the vulture and I lay on the ground and wondered who was indeed the victor in the eternity between one barrage of bullets and the next.

For the avenger of this victory would surely come and revenge would be silent and sad. But did I know then what the other price would be? The price of the echoes that would fill my life and the symbols they would make of you, my sweet friends lying next to me, vague, forgotten symbols of mystery, twisted out of shape, who brought some salvation – but whom did they save? Not me, or maybe they had ? And the crows, despised even by the vultures, were cawing now, capering and cavorting, a gray-black entertainment troupe against the background of the changing light and the church bell speaks again of the crucified god and you lie there, changing color, searching for words, born again every minute and the vultures rest and clean their feathers.

I don't know when I decided to get up and make a run for it. It must have been dark by then; but not dark enough not to see and be seen, but I did get up and at the very same second two others rose from the row of dead men and we looked at each other and shouted something and a hail of bullets rained down on us and the crows went crazy and the vultures started swooping as if something had gone wrong in the rules of the game, something had been spoiled and we began to run toward the wood we had all been holding in our hearts all this time, the wood we had seen behind us before we fell flat on our backs.

And we all got up at exactly the same second and how the hell do you account for that? This was after long hours of short silences and crows and vultures and a slow sinking of the pale bright light into a kind of dull transparency and twilight and after that a kind of gleeful dusk and I don't know what the word "gleeful" is doing here but there was something full of glee in the suddenness of the darkness descending and offering itself as a refuge, a kind of planned end of the day and you really could rely on some order in nature, on changing and eternal systems, on the day coming after the night, on a vulture knowing its place, on the enemy and on the chance you were given to flee and anyway there was this one moment when the three of us all knew together that we had to get up and it took us completely by surprise because each of us was aware only of his own presence alive in the row of the dead and then yes it was then, at the moment of escape, that we all felt together, perhaps because suddenly we were three and we could hate something together and hating together is always more exciting and more plausible than hating privately and in secret, it was then that we sensed that dull, heavy hatred replacing the glee, a hatred whose timing may be hard to understand in the light of all this but which was so very understandable to me and my friends, a hatred for the vultures.

It's hard to say with any certainty that our hatred was equal; we felt it for a moment and then, of course, right after, we parted. During the flight out of the darkness into the woods all three of us were trembling with violent loathing, then we lost each other... and later on we met and talked about it. We talked, or rather they talked and I kept quiet, about the vultures and the crows. They spoke with contempt. I should explain something here: I didn't speak not because the hatred suddenly stopped working in me – on the contrary it intensified and devoured me – I didn't speak because I couldn't understand what they were talking about.

Because, you see, I didn't remember and they did. They tried to remind me and I said I didn't remember and I really didn't. Three whole days had been wiped out of my mind and the story I'm telling you now, a story that you, of course, will never read because I'll never show it to you, is the result of sitting on the cliff opposite the beach in Apollonia and suddenly remembering it years after it happened. But they spoke and what they said found an echo in secret stirrings inside me and I knew they were talking about my own hatred but I didn't know then that it was the hatred born in that specific moment of flight.

But they spoke and I found an echo inside me of a hatred and contempt that only a few felt then: what a fuck-up, the bloody bastards, fuck them, the cunts, the pricks, and here, where, next to, why, boy, who, on the roof... And afterwards, the wars, which, me... You, war, which... Don't know, all one, when did this one start and the next one finish, the other one begin and all over again, boy and you, not him, maybe your son, you from the village, the one the old woman said the psalms for and you're alive and what, don't know and then. Don't touch the bandages, draw yourself on the plaster cast, I'll be silent and I in myself, the ceiling comes down lower and lower and then the blow which is me. Who. Me, no? Not you. Trust me and he screams, shoot the shits and there aren't any bullets and afterward billiards in the night, how long and who's dead, don't know, who's alive, the kindergarten, remember, the kindergarten teacher, she's alive, they're dead, the children, see them in the kindergartens, what happens to them the last minute before. What happens. What grows stronger in them. What makes them steel and rubber and they stop death with their bodies and then they freeze like the people in Pompeii, they filled in the holes with plaster and thousands of years later they took out people frozen in positions of mating or living, what happens to them at the moment of the Olympian gesture, like a steel napkin, and they never said who they were, what they thought, love your father and your mother, say hello nicely and they smiled and then froze and saved me. Why me. Me of all the shitheads, me of all people, on the monastery roof, before the bloodletting and afterward next to the wall in the valley of death, with the bullets in your leg you do it to your fathers and afterward they'll do it to you and generation to generation with bullets and jokes and why do they make you with teaspoons and why do they feed you with teaspoons and why don't you get up and run and why don't you scream and why don't you scream and why don't you say who you are you bastards, you suppurating shits, you prickless scared-shitless useless hasbeens who who.

I didn't talk. They did. There were echoes. I'll tell you about them later after I'm dead. To engrave on my tombstone: Here lies a man who silenced his beauty and tried to make his ugliness live with uncompromising force.

Today I tried to think about the crows. Today they seemed grand. I thought about them because I was writing something about a woman who stood in a graveyard dressed in black and she looked like a stunningly beautiful crow. Animals should be isolated from each other. Next to the vultures the crows were nothing but a crew of fools. The vulture needs no definition. He is a law unto himself in any case, with the eccentricity, the splendour of an old-fashioned carriage, a stuffed tiger, a lonely aristocrat who has dynamited all the roads leading to his palace so you have to reach him through the fir-trees and the nettles, riding on a horse.

The vultures who wheeled above us during the flight wanted revenge. The enemy fired at us but the sanctuary of the descending darkness saved us. Then we went our separate ways. I don't remember now why we didn't run through the wood together. Was it because we knew something we weren't supposed to know? It took me two days to get to our camp. I don't know what happened to me during those two days. I don't know why I got to the camp naked, starved, parched and filthy and fainted at the gate. Did I kill anyone? What did I do with my clothes? Then I rested for a day, went home for a day and came back and went to do what I had to do again.

I laid mines, shot when I had to and felt no special hatred for the enemy and no special love. But the vultures, at that moment of detachment from their world, from their sunlit valley, the vultures we glimpsed once when we looked around for the last time and saw the bodies sculptured into the landscape, we hated the vultures then with a passionate hatred. In my own hatred there was apparently also some cunning, for as I have already said, it dissolved into me and became something I became too and no longer depended only on them...

When we were shooting from the monastery roof, for instance, and a few vultures suddenly showed up they couldn't have been the same vultures or maybe they were – and everyone was shooting at the enemy, my two friends aimed their guns at the sky and shot at the vultures, they forgot all about the enemy surrounding us, but I went on shooting at the enemy. My friends shot wildly and of course they missed and they knew how ridiculous they were. But they had to shoot at the vultures and I shot at the enemy I didn't hate just because I hated the vultures with a profound hatred, because when you hate something so much you respect it too and you know it deserves something bigger and greater than your puny revenge. They cried, my friends, they cursed but they didn't hit them. Did the vultures know them, did they smell the end of their lives? Because one of them was killed right there on the roof and the other one disappeared later, after he went after the commander who ran away, who knew the chances and assessed them correctly and maybe really hoped he could bring help. My friend went to find him and didn't, and later I saw him there on the roof with me, then he disappeared.

Is he drying swamps in Brazil now? Selling shirts in New York? Driving a truck in Chile? I don't know. All I know is that he's finished with the cursed land that hates landlords and loves vultures. I think about those two boys my friends, I don't even know their names, the one who was killed and the one who disappeared, they shot at the sun gods with the splendid, eternal laughter of the vultures who had such contempt for them and I saw it in the iron beaks and understood it, for how could a couple of boys reverse the order of creation and change the nature of the world? Earlier I said "cunning" because I felt I was a chosen sacrifice and I felt the hatred of someone who acknowledges the absolute superiority of the object of his hatred. For the vulture soars like an arrow, floats like a feathery cloud, he is gentle and fierce, rapacious and fine and if I feel a cunning hatred for the lightly gliding bird of prey that plucks out children's eyes, I feel it with the passion of the victim who chooses the enemy of his heart's desire. So I can't hate other vultures without feeling that a vulture in a cage is a hypocritical vulture, a dead vulture, not my enemy. My enemy is up there in the sky seeking my body among the rocks and he'll find it, one day he'll find it... In the last reckoning, he'll win, he has to. Without passion or desire, out of a necessity I'm part of too.

The hatred I felt for them I felt at the moment of gathering darkness and the astonishing knowledge that perhaps I was not doomed to die like the rest of my friends. Hey, kids, what do you know, I'm not going to die with you today after all, in fact I'm going to abandon you, with your permission of course. If you died for me, who am I going to die for? But the bullets that hit you were aimed at me too and I haven't got a private god in my pocket, no divinity reports to me and no one in the village would believe that I'm the favorite over all the other, more deserving kids and you were all more deserving, weren't you, all of you who went to kindergarten with me and school, from our village and the neighboring ones, we all knew each other, we were all hatched from the same eggs and now I'm leaving you next to the vultures, I did my bit, I did what I could, for four hours I lay next to you, playing dead and now you're staying here, I'll have children for you, you won't have your children, you won't milk your cows... There was something skeptical and mocking in this poetry and pathos, but a man lies on his belly, a snake on the rocks, helpless, facing thousands of years of hostility and the Cossacks of all the generations don't shoot at him, the birds of Satan don't guillotine him or burn him at the stake. I'm a little loophole for myself, for the son I may bring into the world one day, if he wants to be brought into the world that is. And you here, with your boldly sprawling postures, you I'll have to forget, because remembering is forbidden, remembering the naked moment when, with your bodies, you stopped my sorrow, their hostility, the fundamental workings of nature and saved a nation, maybe you saved me too and I can't even say thank you, how can I, why should I, did I ask you for anything? Whom should I thank? The vultures' claws didn't dig into me not because I respected them but out of indifference, out of a lack of challenge and maybe it was my eye that made them ignore me and treat me with contempt? Or maybe they wanted me to see things through to their bitter end, because time really crawled interminably there, like a maimed, crushed creature and I was half frozen into myself and my blood seeping through my body was like a secret, hidden death, a death that wanted to show itself, that knew it had to manifest itself in the beak of a vulture, the beak of a sun god and there was a determination pulsing in me, perhaps, a will to live whose nature I cannot comprehend, to live in a world where the true victors are the vultures, for they are the real beneficiaries of all the battles, all the events led us all, on both sides, into that valley of death.

Have you ever seen fish nibbling at a sick fish? Nibbling and nibbling until it's dead? And doves, the symbol of peace, don't they kill the weak, the wounded, the maimed? What passion for perfection lies behind this pecking to death of these birds of silence?

The enemy was there. He fired his guns. He was there because of me. Because of us. He was there for motives that can be grasped by words but not by life. The vultures came there from the domain of the gods, where death precedes life and your existence is a justification in advance, a retroactive journey from the death which precedes everything to an unneeded and unnecessary birth, while this death, these eye-gougings are necessary until, until

The hands that killed. The children who will never grow up. The grandiose postures of the monuments to defeat, children whose heroism will later be taught in schools for the benefit of other children destined for other wars, to demonstrate in death and in life the idea of the unnecessary words invented by human computers and not the elusive ingenuity of nature.

The vultures didn't hide. They ripped and plucked and gouged. The crows tried vainly to amuse them. They devoured dispassionately and methodically, obeying a strict pattern of laws, they soared into the sky without excessive pride and without joy. They did not flatter themselves like the crows, who preened and pranced, they were profound, quiet, ominous, gliding, immeasurably powerful and utterly lacking in greed. They were full of glory and I hated them so much. I forgot them.

When I reached the gate, the sentry said, here's Asa and I managed to say, Not Asa, Asa-el and then I fainted. Later on I woke up. They were drinking tea. Listening to Arab music on the phonograph. The wind was blowing. Someone gave me a cigarette, I don't remember who. It was round, not flat. Later on, I didn't speak, even though some people say that in the last conversation between us, the three of us, I did speak. But I swear I didn't say a word against the vultures, so deep and full was my hate.

So I became what you have to put up with, a kind of non-man who can't forgive himself. What can't I forgive?

That I was there, a joke lying flat on its back and death swarmed around and I was sick with loathing for all my teachers who had failed to provide me with the means of coping with that day, for kindergarten teachers and parents, friends and uncles, acquaintances and mentors. I didn't even forgive the dreams I dreamed until that day, I didn't forgive the officer and the officer's officer, the enemy, the enemy-lovers, I didn't forgive them for the possibility they instilled in me of loving, something whose desirability and necessity I doubt and of saying, I want, saying here I am, a man who loves the rain and not being able to be a man like that and to love the rain, a new car, never mind what, some act, street, house, whatever and what does it mean to be minutes strung on a string stuck together with safety-pins in the past and the present and to be superfluous not to say the right things to go from war to war and seek their beaks and they me until the day comes when and didn't I know other things then? And if I did, have I forgotten them?

Something deep inside me keeps me from knowing what happened. The vultures' revenge. They sowed in me the seeds of that profound knowledge which one must never be allowed to know.

Translated from the Hebrew by Dalya Bilu and Barbara Harshav.

Ya'ir Hurvitz

Fifteen Poems

The Words as is Their Way

"The poems, as is their way, reveal nothing
except what can be said in words".

David Avidan, *Power of Attorney*.

Suddenly the cold poem comes over me,
words like sands of the sea in a soul-seeking sea,
when the departing vision surrounds me
in multitudes of the sea sets folds in sea mirrors
agitating assembled birds in an answerless whirl
and I record words as motion and the words like sand
near a sea gouging its flesh, a sea is not consumed
and behaves like a sea and the words as is their way are nothing
but rain from a heavy cloud or sand on
a sea shore, driven or sinking and are naught
when a sea rages and its place of rest is some-where

A Scattered City

A scattered city its eyes children,
from brilliance of eastern arcs to yearning of western rainbows
a scattered city its heart-of-heart
celebrates anointed in oil of seven branched winds.

A scattered city, from sights of its journeys
birds embroider honey paths
and the smell of fruits of the waters accompanies
journeys of a scattered city to fountains of the sea.

Its journeys grew heavy as flight in captivity.
Gusts confused its sights and colors of the orange and smell of
    innocence.
Light that passed circled from fountains of the sea
is weighted in scales of waves.

From shadows its soul burned like a fruit.
It said: a soul to a soul speaks.

And in fountains of the sea, waters and dimmed.
Smells of fruit of the waters are washed like seaweed beside
skeletons of small fish.
A scattered city its gift a marvelous calm
its darling-child death watches her
from that place.

Envy

Tree. Envy the tree.
Stone. Envy the stone.
Thing. Envy the thing.
Ephemeral. Who adds knowledge adds pain, from the fruit he adds.
Hence we blew the soul of silk into seeds, toiling, toiling.

★

The great river crosses me in my dream,
a sun sphere of the moon runs it and wheels of fire whip it.
I come with it till here and save a kiss.
A white sphere of the moon runs it and sea wheels whip it.
I come with it till here and save a kiss.
From here on it goes north and south.
My thoughts go with it north and south,
turn it over on its face
and the great river rises fathoms to chimes of sky.
As I turn it on its face the sky touches fathoms of water.
In my dream there is the great river and I am here
my thoughts go north and south
and from across comes a wind waking a kiss
in the sails waking to the wind
and my eyes are as the great lakes.

I Envision

By the frame, close and hazy, wind fibers twist.
By the frame, wind fibers blow wind in a new frame.
I cannot see, I cannot see:
A forged and rigid frame casts blindness over me.
All I see, without light, are meditations of a pencil erasure.

They Look at Me

From the valley they look at me from crystal planes.
Multicolor frozen winds from the crystal planes look at me.
In the valley, the instruments become wind and again I envision.
I see multicolor winds there in the valley in the crystal kingdom.

A Plank of Air

Four walls, a door, a ceiling,
the door is fixed, windows, blinds,
they say a dwelling. Each wall
each ledge and every outward lattice
steeped in consolations, joys,
ascetic sickness, viewing grief
a moment as belongings that may be and are not only belongings,
if they would, belongings are recorders of histories.
One day a new wall,
new walls, floor, ceiling
(it all sounds like a bad scene
or at best a departure).
Four walls, floor, ceiling,
the door is fixed, windows, blinds,
they say a dwelling, painted,
everything moves
nothing but an empty hand
moving and removing belongings
but leaving somewhere consolations, joys,
sickness. As of itself,
ledge after ledge will move an inch
an awe-stricken wall will also move,
a ceiling also disappears to a clear horizon,
walls will stand like a heap on a plank of air,
and only the floor that hopes and the table
will see us putting out consolations, joys
and asking questions what
will be the garden's fate and where.

★

I want to say it simply:
love caused pride in her.
I want to say it more simply:
her heart swelled with pride to the depths of love.
No.
I want to say it still more,
still more simply,
the height of love was an ornament to her:
I don't remember anything,
I want to say it simply.

For My Love, as She Rises

Silently silently the evening passes
in tree and heart. The earth
abandons face to heaven's grace and the wind
blowing cool will scatter
the magic graying in autumn leaves and herald
seeds awaiting the coming
of water in thirsty roots. Silently

silently in my love. Return
return to your magic my love, return
veiled in angels' faces, angels' faces are love to me,
alighting on islands angels and flower
light opens, coming and going, in their pleasure sailing
on seas, vanishing,
and only the heart confabulates envy in angels alighting
on islands, on islands evening

passes silently silently. The earth
abandons face and gusts of wind cool in lucid air for my love
as you rise.

★

And still I love. And still I sit hidden.
And still I don't know. And still I don't know what.

Nothing like amazement. I saw a face in sudden amazement.
And still I love. And still I'm held captive.
Still I don't know. Still I'm not there and I

saw wonders in the look of a face. Fabulous corruption I saw
and still I love and still in fabulous embroidery I'm her captive,
and still I love wonder that bears her corruption o great
as suffering and still I love and my mother
from out of my dream bursts forth, my mother from out of my house.

And still I love and still my hands like blossom
and the wind caresses me in its sweetness and is gone and still love
and still kingdom.

★

Now their hair grows into their happiness and their happiness revives;
I sit and think of their hair that grows
while they prepare the book
that tells how their love disappeared. I
sit and am consoled and all this comes to me
like blessed water and this too
like a passing cloud, while they
grow marvelous hair from the buds of their happiness.

★

I was left alone with the pictures; once I
loved a young girl. I don't remember
her for good or bad. Once I loved
a poet's poems, that no longer
move me, indifferent. The horizon line
like a knife
cuts in me ropes of desire
which cut me, shakes
the parchment of days. I feel
inside me the knight who returns to his scabbard
swords, daggers;
barefaced the horizon dwells near me like strength.

Spring Song

Early riser moves like dew –

Yomtov dug and carried
two pails full of earth, innocently
thought two pails full of sun, said
to himself: I want to live.

He'd hear a bird sing:
well I'm higher
and your land
isn't heaven's land.

Yomtov dug till deep deep down
he said to the bird: well
a spurt of water isn't heaven
and the tree is a hollow stump.

"A fly got in your head," the bird
sang on, "A bird's in my head," said
Yomtov who innocently dug.

At the Hour of Brightening

At six o'clock on the Spring clock
Louise child of dreams hand
in hand with her love will cross the avenues
and compare, she'll compare everything
to the sun.
At the corner of a main street in a city
in a small kiosk
she will drink and compare
to a glass of sun. But
if she moves down a few buildings
I'll show Louise child of dreams
the land of shadow,
I'll show Louise girl of dreams the land of shadow
at the hour of brightening.

And not Wind from There

And Ya'ir asks Ya'ir where, where are you going Ya'ir
and Ya'ir to Ya'ir replies I don't expect anything and I'm happy that
I'm here Ya'ir free of stress and don't ask, no,
don't ask about how I don't expect aside from my not expecting,
you understand, I'll go out, you see Ya'ir I speak,
go out, air myself out, you remember I was here with me
woman five foot three, you know, Ya'ir
I parted from a woman five foot seven,
height of heels and not depth of stride, you understand, Ya'ir,
I've been here before Ya'ir
and not a wind from there washes over me and not a wind from there,
don't ask about the broken thing, cut down, Ya'ir
you know, regenerates. And thereupon, Ya'ir asks
Ya'ir where will we go Ya'ir, how long will the consoling strength flow
consoling all that comes in its way
rising bright and fresh from darkness
if not Ya'ir asks
Ya'ir, just you
Ya'ir

The above poems were translated from the Hebrew by Harold Schimmel, except for *Envy* which was translated by Barbara and Benjamin Harshav.

Solomon Ibn Gabirol

Four Poems

The Garden

Ah, come, my radiant friend, along with me,
Let's lodge us in the villages. For, see,
The winter's past, and now on every hand
We hear the voice of turtles in our land.
We'll linger in the shade and take our ease
Neath pomegranates, palms and apple trees;
We'll stroll amid the vines, and peer to see
The gentle folk who live in luxury
Within a palace set upon a height,
Built of the finest stones, a splendid sight,
On strong foundations firmly fixed, and bound
With fortress-walls and turrets all around,
With level galleries above, which show
The fine display of courtyards far below.
The chamber-walls are intricately wrought
With carvings and reliefs of every sort,
While many-coloured marbles pave the floors,
And who could count the number of the doors,
Of reddish hue, as though of algum-wood,
Like those which in the Halls of Ivory stood,

Solomon Ibn Gabirol (c.1020 – c. 1057) lived in Spain.
He was a Hebrew poet and Neoplatonic philosopher.

And set above the doors are windows bright
Whose clear transparent panes let in the light.
The dome is like a royal palanquin
On which suspended ornaments are seen
Revolving in a multicoloured whirl
Of onyx and of sapphire and of pearl —
That is by day, but when the sunlight dies
It seems that stars hang in the darkened skies.
It is a sight to sweeten bitter minds,
And here the troubled spirit comfort finds:
I looked at it, and soon forgot my care,
My heart was freed from pangs of deep despair,
My joyful body seemed to float on high
As though an eagle bore me through the sky.
A brimming pool recalls the molten sea
Which oxen bore aloft, but here there be
No oxen tame, but lions in fierce array
Along the margin, roaring for their prey;
The gushing water issues from their maws
And from their mouths in constant streams it pours.
Along the channels there are hollow fawns
Which sprinkle purest water on the lawns
And spray the plants and flowers in the beds
And shower gentle raindrops on the heads
Of myrtle bushes, which release their scents
Upon the air like clouds of frankincense,
And singing birds are glimpsed among the bowers
And in the beds below are fragrant flowers,
As spikenards, roses, henna-plants and balms,
Which vie each with the rest to vaunt their charms,
Though all are passing fair. The hennas claim:
"Our brightness puts the moon and sun to shame,"
While pigeons coo and murmur, and declare:
"Our song is for the doves, that we may snare
Their hearts, for they are precious past compare."*
Then up there rise the pretty boys and maids
Whose glory all the others overshades,
And they too vie their splendors to disclose,
For they resemble young gazelles or roes.
But as the sun began to sing their praise

I answered: "Silence, sun, deflect your rays,
And praise instead the man who, with his light,
Has darkened you, and hidden you from sight.
Before him kings and ministers give way,
By him kings rule and ministers hold sway:
They have appointed him their overlord,
They are like cattle when the lion has roared;
He guides them like an angel from above,
A shepherd who protects his flocks with love.
And surely no more lavish spirit lives:
Where others merely promise, this man gives;
His undimmed eye is never sought in vain,
His cloud has not withheld its needed rain,
His actions fit his words, it may be said,
As close as golden crown fits royal head.
All rulers flock to him as eagerly
As mighty rivers rush to join the sea.
In truth, he is the lord of all the earth:
He equals the entire creation's worth."

*) or: "We are princesses, we have necklets fair,
Which capture every heart, they are so rare." (Text unclear)

I am a Man...

I am a man who, once his loins are girt,
Will not relent until he has achieved
His aim, whose mind is troubled by his mind,
Whose soul is sick of dwelling in his flesh,
5   Who from his youth has chosen Wisdom's path,
Although Fate's furnace test him seven times,
And Time demolish all that he has built,
Uproot what he has planted, breach his fence,
Yet will he reach, despite misfortune's blows
10 And the frustrating troubles of this world,
The highest pinnacle of Wisdom's mount
And plumb the deepest treasures of the mind.

Know that no man, before his body fails,
Can bring to light the hidden mysteries.
15 But yesterday I gained a modest meed
Of understanding, and already Time
Demands his due; yet while I live I'll ride
In search of Wisdom's path, although the day
Make no attempt to saddle up his ass;
20 My mind shall not be weakened by my time,
But I shall keep my word, and not renege.
I only fear, dear friends, what is to come –
Although it only comes to him who fears.

I saw one night, within a stainless sky,
25 The moon aglow with perfect innocence;
She beckoned me to follow Wisdom's path,
Leading me onward with her guiding light,
Which, with forebodings of dismay, I loved
As any father loves his firstborn son.
30 Then suddenly the wind hoisted his sails
And spread a veil of cloud across his face,
As though he longed for showers of soothing rain
Which he might bring by pressing on the cloud,
And all at once the sky was clad in black

35   As though the moon were dead, as though the cloud
         Had buried her, and all the mists of heaven
         Were weeping tears of mourning. Then the night
         Put on black armour, which the lightning lance
         Of thunder pierced, and played across the sky,
40   And darkness spread his pinions like a bat
         And at the sight his ravens flew abroad.
         So God shut up my thoughts and blocked my mind
         And bound it fast with cords of darkest night,
         An ambushed warrior struggling to escape:
45   I longed to see the radiance of the moon,
         But blackest darkness reigns instead, my friends,
         As though the clouds were jealous of my soul
         And therefore hid her brilliance from my sight.
         But when I see her face I shall rejoice
50   As slaves do when the master smiles at them.

Notes:

l.1) Cf. Lamentations 3:1, "I am the man..."
l.18f) "the day" – i.e. Time. He has not saddled his ass to accompany me on my journey.
l.24) "I saw one night": or "I slept and saw" (text uncertain).
l.31) Cf. Job 36:29, "the spreadings of the clouds".
l.37) The Hebrew also has "...as Aram wept for (Balaam) son of Beor".

The Forsaken Lover

She's gone away and left me,
She's flown beyond the sky.
(How gracefully her necklace
On her dainty neck would lie!)

She loved to make men suffer,
They grovelled at her feet;
She caused them bitter torments,
But oh! her lips were sweet.

Her eyes were polished lances
Or swords to slay the foe;
She stabbed me with her glances
And cruelly laid me low.

She eyed me and she panted
As the heart pants for the brooks:
Her face was like the rainbow,
There was lightning in her looks.

And when the love-thirst took her
Her features clouded o'er
And little crystal droplets
Upon her cheeks did pour.

Let not her tears amaze you,
For I, in deep dismay,
Wept bitter tears for you, my friends,
So near, though far away.

How can man live without his friends
Or how forbear to weep?
How can he rest upon his bed
When night-time murders sleep?

May God look down upon me,
A robbed man smitten sore,
And what was taken from me
May He lovingly restore.

A Gift of Roses

Bear my fraternal greetings to thy lord,
Who has no peer, in this land or abroad,
For all the many lavish gifts he gives
My heart shall render thanks while yet it lives,
And for this latest gift of fragrant scents
My God reward him with rich recompense.
Their outward form, of red encased in green,
Suggests a girl whose fevered flesh is seen
Beneath her ragged clothes, a reddish gleam
Such as a man may clutch at in a dream.
Their flesh within its outer garb recalls
A path of russet earth within stone walls,
Or mingled shame and fear upon the cheeks,
Of a son who to his father rudely speaks.
Some are exposed, their charms to all revealed,
Others, more virginal, are tightly sealed:
They hide their faces from the gaze of men
Behind a veil of finest gauze. But when,
The veil removed, they show their visage fair
To the suspicious husband's angry glare
Their cheeks appear to blush for guilt and shame,
Although their hearts are pure and free from flame,
Their faces radiate a brilliant light
As when the sun pursues his upward flight,
And, though bereft of sense, each perfect flower
Speaks to mankind of Wisdom's wondrous power.
Their beauty terrifies the watching eyes
As when a fallen warrior strives to rise,
Or like a prince ensnared in hostile schemes,
Or like a sleeper startled by his dreams,
Or like a trapped bird struggling perplexed,
Or like a student wrestling with a text.
I know them when I see them, but my mind
In seeking to describe them cannot find
The fitting words, like men I know by sight·
Whose name I never can recall aright.
Time raised them on green stems, with coats of red
Embroidered with a blazing crimson thread,

And time will gnaw their skin and waste their flesh
Till they, like sin-purged souls, are born afresh.
The breeze will waft abroad their sweet delight
And summer clouds will dapple them with light.
They'll blush for shame before men's longing eyes
And wave in time to grieving spirits' sighs.
Their fragrant perfume will enchant men's hearts
As when the mind some new-found science charts.
Their scent would make the thought of sleep forsake
The restless man who nightly lies awake;
Even a corpse would clutch at them, and crave
To have them lie beside him in the grave;
And in the harem they would far outshine
The fairest votaress of beauty's shrine.
Cut from the garden-bed they could not walk:
There's little strength in such a slender stalk.
They came to me, a present from my lord,
Like royal letters, sealed and tied with cord,
And when I loosened the confining bands
And held them heaped together in my hands
They separated, freed now from restraint,
And vied to bring before me their complaint.
Theirs is a perfect loveliness, which needs
No ornament, as flawless as thy deeds,
A simple innocence, like thine own heart's,
Guileless and pure of all deceptive arts,
Attesting their affinity with thee
Whose power is raised aloft for all to see,
Whose virtues slap time's daughters in the face
And leave upon their cheeks a lasting trace.

My God, the source of blessings, fill thy hand
With all the wealth that thy heart may demand;
May he confound thy foes, and make thee stand
Above the highest princes in the land!

Translated from the Hebrew by Nicholas de Lange.

Amos Funkenstein

Theological Interpretations of the Holocaust

An Evaluation

1.
The Meaning of the Meaning

The extermination of the Jews of Europe obviously merits the attention of theologians. That it does indeed hold their attention, especially during the last decade, is a fact. But the *meaning* of an investigation of the "meaning" of the Holocaust is far from obvious. For some, it is the meaning *of* catastrophe in traditional theological terms and is an attempt to salvage a theodicy from the rubble left by an eruption of evil behaving like an apparently autonomous force. For others, it is the meaning of the catastrophe *for* theology: as polemics when the target is the failure or even complicity of rival theologies, or as criticism when one questions the legitimacy of one's theological heritage in the shadow of a phenomenon of the systematic destruction of human life and dignity. I call these tendencies, respectively, the direct mode, the polemical mode and the critical-reflexive mode of theologizing on the Holocaust. I maintain that the first is insulting, the second hypocritical and the third insufficiently radical even in its most radical manifestations.

2.
The Holocaust as Punishment and as Sign

Let us begin with the position of one of the rare interpreters who dare to maintain that the Holocaust can be explained perfectly well in traditional theological terms. This extreme case allows a better understanding of seemingly more reasonable attempts in the same direction.

Shortly after the establishment of the State of Israel, a book was published with a typically rabbinic title: *And It Pleased Moses, Vayo'el Moshe.*[1] The author, Rabbi Yoel Taitlbaum, was the leader of an ultra-Orthodox, anti-Zionist movement whose Israeli branch is known as Naturai Karta, "The Keepers of the City." After summarizing all the traditions that support passive messianism (a term I shall elucidate presently), Taitlbaum concluded that the Holocaust was the inevitable consequence of and punishment for a terrible sin: the transgression of the divine prohibition against the Jews seeking redemption by their own power, by human initiative. Here is his reasoning:

"Because of our sins, we have been exiled from our country." The dispersion of the Jewish people and the oppression it experienced in the Diaspora has a punitive-cathartic function; only God can put an end to the punishment. Those who want to "hasten the end" and force the hand of God by human action are rebels, whether they are aware of it or not. In the Song of Songs, one phrase is repeated three times as an oath: "I charge you, O ye daughters of Jerusalem, by the roes, and by the hinds of the field, that ye stir not up, not awake my love, till he please." An ancient exegetic tradition justified the introduction of these patently profane love songs into the canon of sacred texts by maintaining that they must be read as purely allegorical, seeing them as the dialogue of God with the spirit of Israel (or elsewhere, with the *ecclesia*). The three oaths, as we learn in the tractate *Ketubot* of the Babylonian Talmud, have a special allegorical significance.[2] The triple repetition of the formula refers to the three oaths imposed on Israel and the nations of the world after the destruction of the Temple. Israel was bound by oath not to revolt against the nations where she was held captive as a "prisoner of war" and not to try to "hasten the end." In exchange, the nations of the world were bound by the third oath not to oppress Israel *too much*.

From these premises, Taitlbaum draws an insulting conclusion. Because, in the development of the Zionist movement, an ever increasing number of Jews had broken their oath and taken their destiny in their own hands – according to Herzl, they wanted to stop being "a political object and become a political subject" – the nations of the world, in turn, also considered themselves freed from the oath not to oppress Israel too much – and in fact did oppress her. But why did they behave like that? Taitlbaum considers it self-evident that "Esau always hates Jacob," inherently and relentlessly. The Holocaust is the inevitable consequence of the spontaneous efforts of the Jews to gain sovereignty and even autonomy. It is not even the ultimate catastrophe: the sin continued to be committed with the establishment of the State of Israel. A disaster is imminent and only a small number of Jews will survive it, the "remnant of Israel" who will be witnesses to the true redemption. Taitlbaum's reasoning is, in fact, completely anchored in the presupposed apocalyptic according to which real redemption, accomplished by a divine miracle, is at hand. In traditional imagery, the times preceding it are times of war and extreme tribulation, an era filled with false hopes and false messiahs.

Curiously, Taitlbaum shares his faith in a Messiah close at hand with his adversaries in the interior of Orthodoxy, the "Bloc of the Faithful" (Gush Emunim).[3] The latter also take for granted that hatred of Jews is natural to the nations of the world because Israel is the chosen of God or, in the more secular version of Uri Zvi Greenberg, because Israel is "the race of Abraham which has taken the road to become mistress."[4] For Gush Emunim, the Holocaust and the establishment of the State of Israel which ensued and the wars it fights are divine signs that invite an active preparation in the "dawn of our redemption." As our age is a time of the messianic war and redemption has already begun, it is up to the Jews to conquer and defend the frontiers of their holy land, to make it a *civitas Dei*. For Taitlbaum, the Holocaust occurred because the Jews were too active; for Gush Emunim, because they were too passive. To both, it announces the coming of the Messiah.

Two distinct traditions in Jewish messanism collide here in exaggerated form: passive and utopian messianism is opposed to active and realistic messianism. The first tradition is by far the dominant tendency: established rabbinic power has used it as an antidote to dangerous messianic eruptions. The second tradition, though in the minority, has never ceased to exist. It has the authority of some important figures: Maimonides, Jacob Berab, Zvi Kalisher. Maimonides, for whom the history of the world is the history of the continuous monotheization of the world guided by God's *List der Vernunft*, "miracles in the category of the possible," also considered the messianic age as a period inside history, with no changes in either cosmic or human nature.[5] He believed that there are means of hastening the approach of this period by human initiative, for example the reconstruction of the ancient system of justice in the Land of Israel. Jacob Berab, who wanted to realize this plan by renewing primitive ordination, incurred the reproach of the head of the Jerusalem court, for whom the time of the Messiah could come only at one fell swoop: it was not possible to isolate one element of that miraculous whole to realize it here and now.[6] In the nineteenth century, Kalisher, who spent his life encouraging the settlement of Jews in Israel and even the renewal of certain sacrifices, was impelled by the same reasons as Maimonides and Berab. Notably, this "active messianism" is not a precursor of Zionism. On the contrary, Zionism is part of an antimessianic demand, the will to gain a sovereignty independent of messianic hopes. Taitlbaum and Gush Emunim both express pre-Zionist mentalities. Both are fossils, each in its own way, but poisonous fossils.

The passive messianism that Taitlbaum inherits must not be confused with the myth of the physical passivity of the Jews of the Diaspora. Why did the Jews not resist extermination? In the preface to his monumental work, Hilberg refers to a spirit of conciliation that had been shaped by two thousand years of conditioning.[7] According to him, passivity constituted an intrinsic mental characteristic of Diaspora Jews. That is a myth as widespread as it is dangerous; it is dangerous because it creates an artificial cleavage between the mentality of the Diaspora, which is seen as passive, and that active and sane mentality of the Jews of the new species, of Israel. Neither in Antiquity nor in the Middle Ages did Jews refrain from physically resisting persecution whenever possible. They resisted the pogroms of the Crusades, the pogroms of Chmielnicki and modern pogroms as well. Their resistance under the Nazi occupation was no less than that of most other occupied populations. At best, we can wonder why the German Jews did not play a more active role in resistance movements before 1939 or why, later on, cooperation with these movements did not go beyond necessity. But, if there was passivity, it was not a heritage of the Diaspora mentality but a product of modern times. For the modern European Jew who identified himself with the country he lived in, resistance against that country seemed outside the universe of discourse; he could no longer imagine a State acting against the purpose of the State. On the other hand, prior to emancipation, the Jew considered himself a stranger, a "prisoner of war," always on the alert. The legal principle according to which "the law of the kingdom is the law that obliges," quoted by some reformers of the nineteenth century to prove the priority of the law of the land, originally had an opposite meaning, even in a Jewish perspective. It only concerned property and defined a *Widerstandsrecht*, a right to resistance: it is only if the government acts in harmony with the law of the land that it must be obeyed.[8] The only genuine origin of the myth of passivity is the ideology of passive messianism: it served to reveal the absence of any strong political aspirations. In a way, the political emancipation and the acculturation of the Jews of Europe opened the way to two new and extreme possibilities: total passivity and total affirmation of the self. In Sartre's words, one can say of the post-emancipation Jew that he lives constantly in a "situation of 'being-seen'": he flees this situation by identifying himself with the aggressor or he defies it by becoming a Zionist.[9]

Passive messianism was, at best, an ideology, not a legitimately constraining position. It was once predominant but has now been discarded even among Orthodox Jews. Why, then, should we honor Taitlbaum's insult to decency and good sense with a detailed discussion? Because, in theology, as in law, limited cases are highly instructive. Better an obvious absurdity than a concealed one. Less extreme Jewish theologians than Taitlbaum or Gush Emunim ideologists – e.g. E. Fackenheim or E. Berkovits – recognize that they cannot provide a theological explanation for the Holocaust.[10] The Holocaust is incomprehensible, they say, and defies all theodicies. But they do find a theological meaning in survival: the survival of every man or of the nation and in the rebirth of the State. In these two phenomena they find a confirmation of the divine presence and of the promise to save Israel.

Even in these sweetened versions, a theodicy is insulting. To have survived when others – friends and relatives – died is a heavy burden for most survivors. Haunted by horrible memories, many refused to speak or to remember during the years that followed their captivity; some talk today only because they fear that the memory of what really happened will be lost within a generation. It may be that the State of Israel owes its birth, in part, to the Holocaust; that, too, is a horrible burden, not a sign of election or of divine grace. Whatever one may think of his taste, George Steiner's recent book was perhaps a product of such feelings.[11] There is only one example of theological reflection in Primo Levi's account of his life in Auschwitz:

> Silence slowly prevails and then, from my bunk on the top row, I see and hear old Kuhn praying aloud, with his beret on his head, swaying backwards and forwards violently. Kuhn is thanking God

because he has not been chosen.

Kuhn is out of his senses. Does he not see Beppo the Greek in the bunk next to him, Beppo who is twenty years old and is going to the gas chamber the day after tomorrow and knows it and lies there looking fixedly at the light without saying anything and without even thinking any more? Can Kuhn fail to realize that next time it will be his turn? Does Kuhn not understand that what has happened today is an abomination, which no propitiatory prayer, no pardon, no expiation by the guilty, which nothing at all in the power of man can ever clean again.

If I was God, I would spit at Kuhn's prayer.[12]

3.
Anti-Judaism and Antisemitism

Whether it has a theological meaning, it is absolutely certain that recent history does have a meaning *for* theology – more concretely, for Christianity. Jewish and Christian theologians devote a good deal of energy to condemning, expiating or reformulating past and present attitudes of Christians with regard to Jews and Judaism. How extensive was the role of Christianity in the establishment of conditions that permitted the genocide of the Jews? Can Christianity revise its anti-Jewish attitudes without endangering its very foundations?

No honest historian has any doubt that the anti-Jewish attitudes of Christianity have constituted determining factors in the persistence of anti-Jewish feelings since ancient times and that it is the old theological alienation that partially explains the silence of the Church in the face of the treatment inflicted on the Jews, the deprivation of their rights, then deportation and finally extermination. This silence contrasts with the firm and effective resistance of the German clergy to euthanasia. However, if it could be proved that the antagonism between Church and Synagogue was not part of original Christianity, then – some theologians claim – one might excise it from the principal corpus of Christian doctrine without any damage.

That is a fallacious argument for logic as well as for history. For logic, it is simply not possible to recreate in Christianity the conditions of the *primitiva ecclesia*: an apocalyptic Jewish sect withdrawn from the world. The very program of "reform" is inaccessible. At best, one might arbitrarily choose certain elements of Christianity and declare them essential and, thus inevitably, dismiss others. But, in this case, there is no reason to exclude the rest of the history of Christianity and to distinguish clearly between *Christentum* und *Kultur* (Overbeck). The same arguments which have produced a crisis in Protestant theology for the last hundred years also apply to its attitude toward Judaism. Nevertheless, we must distinguish the various ingredients and vectors of force that constitute the anti-Jewish doctrines of Christianity. If the anti-Jewish ideology of the Church does not depend entirely on social, political or economic conditions, it is also true that it was not the product of hatred alone. The Jews have always been and still are a *mysterium tremendum et fascinosum* for the Christian church. The investigation of the phenomenon of Judaism and the eternal nature of Jewish existence is part of the self-definition of Christianity and of its very essence as an historic religion. But, contrary to popular opinion, I hasten to add that this ambivalence – fascination and rejection – is also characteristic of the Jewish attitude toward Christianity, more than toward any other religion, including Islam. We will also see that certain Christian attitudes were theological by nature while others were not, even when they were made to assume this guise. This last distinction will perhaps allow us to clarify the contemporary theological situation. Here is how I see the evolution of Christian attitudes toward Jews and Judaism.

3a. The Pagan Attitude[13]

Christian anti-Judaism appears in a stronger light when it is compared with what preceded it. Christianity did not inherit grievances against the Jews from pagan antiquity: these were grievances of political and national origin, born partly from measures hostile to the Greeks in the land of Israel imposed by the Jews in the Hasmonean period and partly from a rivalry over privileges in Egypt. Under the Roman Empire, the revolt of the Jews and the fears engendered by the missionary influence of Judaism combined to perpetuate anti-Jewish propaganda and attitudes.[14]

If, from the second century, Christianity has perhaps inherited some of the anti-Jewish feelings of the pagans, the arguments of pagan anti-Jewish propaganda would hardly be useful to her. Christians have never denied, for example, that the land of Israel belongs to the Jews, at least until the emergence of Christianity, a time when God's choice passed from "Israel in the flesh" to the "true Israel" *(verus Israel)*, "Israel of the spirit," i.e., the "Church among the nations" *(ecclesia ex gentibus)*. The nimblest of pagan polemicists used a characteristic technique: they manipulated and twisted the meaning of biblical passages to construct their own version of the history of Jewish origins; they built a counter-history, just as the Jews did later for Christianity in the *Sefer Toledot Yeshu*. The Bible itself provided pagan polemicists with arguments in their attacks on the Jews. Is it not admitted that the Canaanites were driven out by force?[15] More seriously, is it not admitted that the people of Israel were banished and lived apart in the Egyptian province of Goshen? That Moses was raised as an Egyptian? That what came out of Egypt was a mixed multitude *(erev-rav)* of rabble *(assafsuf)*? In fact, the Hebrews are not an ancient and venerable nation and their constitution is not authentic and does not deserve to be preserved. On the contrary, they were originally an Egyptian colony of lepers, isolated and scorned, until they called for help from the Semitic tribes of the Hyksos and established a reign of terror that lasted a hundred years (the historical reversal of Joseph's rise to power). Thrown out by Ramses I, the Hyksos, accompanied by the exiles, left Egypt, led by a renegade Egyptian priest called Osarsiph (Moses). He gave them a constitution which was, from all points of view, a plagiarism, a mirror-image of Egyptian customs. Or, as Tacitus was to say later on: "Moses... introduced new laws, contrary to those of the rest of humanity. All that is sacred for us is profane for them; and all that they authorize, we regard as sacrilege."[16] They conquered the land of Canaan by force and established the type of community suitable for exiles – separated and concealed by a sense of election – made to perpetuate their spirit of revolt and their hatred of mankind *(misanthropia; odium humani generis)*.

It was an ingenious piece of propaganda. Thus, in Manethon, the description of the way the exiles maintained the sense of their own worth by constructing a counter-ideology where the discrimination they suffered is interpreted as a sign of election is similar to modern descriptions of the formation of a "counter-identity" in sociologies of awareness.[17]

This tradition of pagan anti-Jewish propaganda is remarkable for what is present as well as for what is absent. It would be useless to search for a religious polemic against monotheism: the pagan intelligentsia was also monotheistic, for the most part, if one can use such terms. From Xenophon to Plotinus, through Aristotle, Greek philosophy had developed an image of God that was less anthropomorphic and more purified, a natural religion *(theologia naturalis)*.[18] Xenophon had already proposed the argument that dominated the history of the criticism of religion down to Feuerbach and Freud: man makes his gods in his own image, that is, he transfers or projects onto the transcendent his own virtues and vices and those of the society he lives in. The educated Greco-Roman intellectual believed, roughly, that, except for the "political cult" *(theologia politica)*, if cults are numerous, religion is one.

Augustine puts such expressions in the mouth of Porphyre;[19] our own Sages make a pagan philosopher conversing with Rabbi Akiva say: "We both know in our hearts that there is no reality in idolatry."[20] In other words, the Church Fathers and the *Tana'im* knew very well that they were not the only monotheists in the midst of polytheism. What distinguished Judeo-Christian theology from pagan theology was not the number of gods but the nature of the unique god. For the Greek mind, God was the principle of cosmic harmony, a passive and self-contained principle: the notion of a god as a moral persona acting in history, an omnipotent busybody, was repugnant to it. That God might abandon the care of the cosmos to concern himself exclusively with the affairs of a filthy little nation was for Celse an idea worthy of "frogs and worms on the ground."[21]

Nevertheless, for the pagan mind, monotheism was one of the most seductive characteristics of Judaism. Was it not a truly philosophical religion, venerating a philosophical principle rather than anthropomorphic images? The initial reaction of cultivated Greeks to contact with Judaism was admiration.[22] A pagan polemic could not attack the monotheistic idea as such. But it could venture to show that there was nothing original among the Jews or in Judaism; nothing, in Jewish laws and customs, that was venerable and deserved to be preserved. The missionary success of Judaism and later of Christianity showed how hopelessly ineffective this pagan propaganda was.

3b. The Christian Attitude

Christianity, as we have said, could not use the arguments of pagan anti-Jewish propaganda. However, the Christian/Jewish antagonism goes back to the era when nascent Christianity was still only an apocalyptic Jewish sect. Christians shared with other sectarian movements – for example, the one that gave us the Dead Sea Scrolls – the hatred for established Jewish power. The sectarians of Qumran had already defined themselves as a "holy community" *(adat kodesh)* and saw established power as a "false city" *(ir shav)* – *civitas dei* against *civitas terranea*. They were the sole remnant of Israel; they alone possessed the key to the eschatological "decoding" (pesher) of the Scriptures; in brief, they were the vanguard of a new and magnificent cosmic order inside the old and corrupt order. Sometimes they make it clear that they alone, "the eternal descendants," will be saved at the end of time, which is at hand. They put established power in the category of the "children of darkness" and are exhorted to "love all the children of light, each according to his fate, and to hate all the children of darkness, each according to his guilt in the vengeance of God."[23] The first Christians, who resembled them in many respects, considered themselves the *verus Israel* and thought that other Jews were damned. Faith in Christ, as earlier at Qumran faith in the "Master of Justice" (moreh zedek), was the true sign of salvation. Like the community at Qumran, early Christianity hated the established power of the "Pharisees and Saduccees."[24]

Early Christianity was soon to enter into competition with established Jewish power in the missionary efforts carried out by both, first among "God-fearing peoples" (yire'ei shamayim in Hebrew, hoi sebomenoi in Greek), those large groups of Jewish proselytes that surrounded several communities of the Diaspora, and later among genuine pagans. This mutual hostility was reinforced by that rivalry in conversions as it was by the internal conflicts in Christianity between Jews and Gentiles who had become Christian. The antagonism was sealed by the absence of Christians in the second revolt against Rome (132–135 CE), which, unlike the first one, seemed to have been unanimous. However, after that revolt and Hadrian's persecution following it, Judaism lost its missionary spirit and, in the end, Christianity became the dominant religion in the Roman Empire. "The kingdom becomes heretical," as the phrase runs, and the Judeo-Christian elements, which had once been important in the Church, disappeared.[25]

What use, later on, were the anti-Jewish doctrines of the Christians? Why was there not one generation that did not leave anti-Jewish pamphlets behind? What logic is hidden behind this enormous corpus of writings which are both insipid and repetitive? For these writings soon stop being a record of living polemics and increasingly become the stereotypical enumeration of veiled allusions to the Old Testament proving the truth of the New.

The function of anti-Jewish propaganda was not external – not aimed at converting the Jews – but internal. Precisely because the Church had not succeeded in converting them, their very existence became a theological paradox of the first magnitude. It was different in Islam: unlike the Church, Islam did not consider its raison d'être to be the conversion of all infidels one by one. Certainly, the world must be made "safe for Islam" by means of political hegemony; but in countries ruled by Islam, monotheistic peoples who have not had an authentic revelation, like Jews and Christians – the legal term is "people of the book" *(ahl al kitab)* – can maintain their political and religious autonomy as a second-class but protected minority *(dhimmis)*.[26] Quite the contrary, the Christian Church proves that its truth is unique by making itself universal: it is an *ecclesia militans*. But the conversion of the Jews, who were originally the chosen people and who still clung to the Old Testament in its original language, was as impossible by persuasion as by force.

They were called "Israel in the flesh" *(Israel secundum carnem)*. Christianity and Judaism shared the fiction of a Jewish people descending from Abraham in the literal sense; they differed only on the value accorded to such an ethnic community. *Secundum carnem* also refers to the mentality of the Jews: they interpret the Scriptures and the laws "according to the letter", not through a spiritual comprehension *(spiritualis intelligentia)*; hence they are "blind" to the veiled allusions of the Old Testament to the truth of the New; they are a living anachronism – "these Jews refused to change with the time" – a fossil.[27] They have not been able to understand that Judaism (circumcision) was only "good for its time" and that it must be replaced by a new covenant, for which it had prepared the way (Hugh of Saint-Victor).[28] In sum, the Jews are a fated people.

But was this very fate not also worthy of admiration? Saint Augustine thought so and wished for the Christians of his day a little of that obstinacy in the face of persecution and temptation.[29] Moreover, Jews and Judaism continued to fascinate Christians because of their antiquity – that very antiquity for which they were reproached in theory. Throughout its history, the Church has feared Judaizers *(judaizantes)* in its midst. We must not forget that, by appealing to a *new* covenant, the Church introduced a change in the system of values in the classic world as well as among the converted Germanic tribes of the Middle Ages: both were suspicious of novelty, age alone was a sign of authenticity and quality. In the political vocabulary of the classical period, a dangerous revolutionary was a *homo rerum novarum cupidus*; in the High Middle Ages, legal awareness considered the ancient law *(altes Recht)* as the only good law *(gutes Recht)*.[30] Pope Gregory VII shocked his Germanic adversaries by proclaiming his right to establish new laws *(novas leges condere)*.[31] Thus, an internal tension was introduced into the European mind between worship of the ancient and glorification of the new. The antiquity and existence of the Jews and Judaism were used by Christians as an argument in their propaganda against paganism – to prove the authenticity of the Bible. The Jews, too, maintained that Judaism was the true monotheism because it was the oldest – that is demonstrated in the *Kuzari* of Judah Halevi; in the Middle Ages, the rare cases of conversion to Judaism that we know of originated in such sentiments.

Finally, the Church Fathers elaborated a doctrine to justify the persistence of Judaism in the economy of salvation as well as a practice of anti-Jewish legislation within that conceptual framework.[32]

The Jews filled a triple function. Their physical existence proved the authenticity of the Scriptures against the pagans; they guaranteed the preservation of the authentic revelation and had to continue to play this role. In the second place, their humiliation in dispersion constituted an eternal proof (*testimonium aeternum*) of the right of Christians to maintain that, with the coming of Christ, "the sceptre was withdrawn from Judah" and that God's choice passed from "Israel in the flesh" to "Israel of the spirit." The present condition of the Synagogue, "slave" to the Church, bears witness to the superiority of the latter. Lastly, the Jews had an eschatological function. At the end of days, the remnants of the Jewish people would convert *en masse* to Christianity and perhaps even save Christianity from the Antichrist. Such was the explanation of the existence of the Jews and of the relative tolerance they had to be granted. It rested on the firm belief that the Jews had not changed; that they adhered, now as ever, to the letter of the Bible. Even their clothes had perhaps not changed: to Anskar, his biographer tells us, Christ appeared "tall in stature, dressed like a Jew, handsome in appearance."[33]

3c. The Twelfth Century: New Models

Thus, the Jews were tolerated by the Church on the double condition that they play the role of slaves and of fossils. They refused both. In reality, they constituted a privileged minority and developed tastes that were clearly aristocratic. In legal status as in mentality, they were very close to the ruling classes, "belonging to the royal palace." In Germany, even in the twelfth century, a young Jew could dream of becoming a knight. Much later, Shlomo ibn Varga, reflecting on the Spanish expulsion of 1492, saw the desire to reach the highest ranks of society and the vanity in it as one of the major causes of the disaster. Throughout the

Middle Ages, the Jews were considered "prisoners of war," in foreign territory, and that was how they saw themselves; but that was hardly how they behaved. They did not accept the role of fossil either. On the contrary, they developed an imposing system of adaptable laws and institutions and created a vast corpus of interpretive and speculative literature. The distinction between image and reality and the ever-present reserves of popular hostility against foreigners (especially Jews) could constitute sources of tension.

It is in the twelfth century – a decisive moment in the life of the Jews of Europe – that the history of the anti-Jewish doctrines of Christianity assumes a new direction. Several factors contributed to the deterioration of the situation of the Jews at that time: the independence and increasing power of the Church; the Crusades; the rise of popular religious movements; and the fact that, since the Spanish *Reconquista*, most of the Jews of Europe lived in Christian countries. Anti-Jewish doctrines were then modified both in quantity and quality. Not only did they multiply; the models themselves changed as well. The models created in that period were to last until the eighteenth century. Next to the old categories of stereotypes, the new ways of propaganda stand out clearly.

Sometimes the new image could be adapted to ancient stereotypes. The image of the greedy, exploitative, "usurer" Jew was born of new circumstances: in Antiquity, Josephus was only repeating a commonplace when he regretted that the Jews, compared with the Greeks and the Phoenicians, were not gifted in trade. Once born, this new image could easily be adapted to old theological stereotypes. Even when she observes the precepts, "Israel in the flesh" is preoccupied only with earthly rewards and, even more, with the secular realm. But the new stereotypes could also conflict with the old ones or replace them. This last process, leading to the alienation and demonization of the image of Jew at the end of the Middle Ages, merits closer examination.

A totally new stereotype belongs to this category, the one associating threat and secrecy with the image of the Jew. Henceforth, it operated on all levels, from the theological to the popular. From the twelfth century on, increasing numbers of clergymen became acquainted with Jewish doctrines and with the imposing corpus of post-biblical literature. Some of them turned to the Hebrew Studies for the sake of exegesis of the Holy Scripture. Others found in them a new kind of argument against the Jews.[34] The Talmud especially served to prove that the Jews were not those simple preservers of the Bible to which they had been thought faithful "according to the letter." Wasn't this new law a heresy, even from the point of view of Judaism itself – as the Church understood it? Wasn't the tolerance granted them based on the axiom that they did not change – but if they did change and were in quest of a new law, should they not seek only the True Law? Instead of turning to the Bible of the *lex caritatis*, they seemed to have created a new law of their own invention. And they observed it secretly, pretending to remain the bearers and preservers of the Old Testament.

The first pamphlet of this sort was written in the middle of the twelfth century by Peter the Venerable, abbé of Cluny. This specialist of conciliation promised to "reveal" the secrets of the Jews: they had stopped obeying divine law and were in fact obeying a diabolical legislation shaped by humans.[35] He took sections and fragments of the Talmud out of context to prove that, far from being a simple literal interpretation, the Talmud maintained that God Himself had to bend to the decisions of human tribunals, that God Himself was bound by talmudic law. From then on, Judaism no longer looked like a religion that was certainly anachronistic and perhaps even ridiculous but at least transparent; its image was transformed and became that of a religion of secret and diabolical traditions. Such accusations had the Talmud condemned and burned in Paris in 1240.[36]

This dehumanization and demonization of the image of the Jew was not limited to a few polemical pamphlets. First and foremost, it characterized all popular sermons and imaginations.[37] It is in the twelfth century that the Jews are accused of ritual murder for the first time. Thomas of Monmouth refers the tale of that supposed murder to a converted Jew who had revealed to him that the "ancient Scriptures of the Jews" stipulate that Christian blood must be shed at least once a year if they want to be saved. Hence, a secret synod of rabbis from all over Europe gathers once a year to decide which community will have a turn to commit the ritual murder.[38] There is a clear line from this story to the images evoked by the unfortunately famous *Protocols of the Elders of Zion*.[39]

Thus, unwittingly, the twelfth century revived elements of pagan propaganda against Christians and Jews: accusations of dissimulation, secret habits and beliefs engendered by Jewish "misanthropy" (Tacitus's *odium humani generis*). Jewish "secrets" (*arcanae*) endangered the healthy social texture around them. Originally, Christians had not been able to use such arguments: they too were the target of these accusations and they claimed a part of the Jewish "secrets." But, at the end of the Middle Ages, from the twelfth century on, the Jews once again become mysterious, incomprehensible and dangerous. The popular image of the demonic Jew, accused of murder, never became the official theological position of the Church: she neither denied nor confirmed those deceitful allegations and, when she had some interest in them, she used them. Nor was the attack against the Talmud carried out in the ways that it had originally assumed. Indeed, how could the Church, always on guard against heretics who wanted to return "to Scripture and Scripture alone," eliminating the authorized ecclesiastical tradition, demand that the Jews hold to the Scriptures "without commentary"? Not that the Church would not have been able to justify such inconsistency; but, in every period, certain figures of thought become untouchable. Other reasons for attacking the Talmud would be found – it would be said, for example, that it contains blasphemies and that, at least, must be suppressed.

However, the renewed contact of Christian theologians with Jewish writings did not only produce repulsion or new polemical possibilities. It also reinforced the fascination we have already mentioned, a fascination for Jewish exegesis (*veritas hebraica*) and, later, a much more intense fascination for the Kabbalah.[40] In its own way, the Kabbalah is an example of the dialectic of repulsion and attraction on both sides. It manifests the Jewish fascination for emanentist, even trinitarian, speculations; and the first Kabbalists were quickly accused of Christianizing tendencies. The Kabbalists discovered profound mysteries in the Bible and in interpretations considered heretical until then – like the one that makes "God" in Genesis 1:1 the object and not the subject of the sentence. For the Humanists and the Platonists of the Renaissance, the Kabbalah seemed to reveal an ancient, secret, pre-Christian, pre-Jewish tradition in touch with the most profound truths. Thus, the "mystery", the "secret traditions" of the Jews did not only have pejorative connotations – those in the word "cabal" in various European languages. This mystery also attracted people who conferred an inestimable value on it.

Certainly it is true that, in every society, people are quick to attribute secrets and hidden traditions to minorities, to accuse them of conspiracy. Perhaps in Christian society of the late Middle Ages, such popular terrors served to externalize fears and guilt that were unexpressed otherwise. It may also be that the Church in the shape of the majority of serious theologians did not create such images. Nevertheless, it did sometimes appropriate them. It is also true that in Spain, in the Middle Ages, even converted Jews were not safe from suspicion. Far from being experienced even by the Church as the realization of a burning desire, the massive influx of *conversos* into Spanish society in the fourteenth and fifteenth centuries engendered fears: the Jews were suspected of heterodoxy or of secretly falling back into their error. An unprecedented social and legal effort to expose the secret elements of society poisoned Spanish life for more than two centuries, made Spain a society sick with suspicion, made it the first State in the history of modern Europe to be governed by racist principles. In the name of purity of blood, the *marranos* were excluded from public functions and lost their position in society. In this process and similar ones, originating in the twelfth century, I see not a religious antagonism but rather antagonisms hiding behind religious differences.

3d. Toward a non-Christian Attitude

Despite Luther's venomous attacks, why was the obsession with Jews and Judaism not so strong in the Protestant world?[41] First, there were few Jews left in the Protestant regions of Europe; most had been expelled in the Middle Ages. However, this situation had not prevented anti-Jewish propaganda from arising in the past: it filled internal functions. Perhaps Protestant theology itself holds the key to the increasing indifference of the Protestant world to the Jews.

For the Catholic Church, Jews and Judaism constituted, *mutatis mutandis*, a living example of a life *sola scriptura*, of the wretched fate of those who believed only in the letter of the Scriptures; they showed the necessity of the mediation of the Church, that Church of which Saint Augustine had said that, if its authority did not force him, he would not even believe the Scriptures. But, at the same time, the Church feared, not without reason, the influence of that very example. From the start, ambivalence was at the heart of the Catholic attitude toward the Jews.

Protestantism could go beyond this ambivalence even if it did not always do so. Protestant theologies oscillated – and still do – between two poles. According to the characteristics they lend to the early Church, they want either to revive biblical ways and institutions – hence an abundant literature on the "Jewish Republic" – or on the contrary to emphasize the division between the Old and the New Testament. Either way, their relationship with the Jews and with Judaism was freer, for it was less immediate. For them, there was no *auctoritas sanctae ecclesiae* which Jewish existence threatened to destroy or, on the contrary, promised to confirm. In some cases, as H.H. Ben-Sasson has shown, certain sectarian minorities even developed a tendency to identify with the fate of the Jews *in partibus infidelium*.[42] In other cases, the Protestants reproached the Jews as well as the Catholics for obscuring the word of the Lord – but the Catholics evidently constituted a more dangerous adversary for them.

The rationalists of the seventeenth and eighteenth centuries were the heirs of this fundamental Protestant indifference, for better and for worse. Fossil or not, Judaism was no longer at the core of discussion.[43] At best, the fate of the Jews served to illustrate Christian – i.e., religious – intolerance. At worst, they used Judaism to exemplify ethnocentric religious parochialism. Sometimes, attacks against Judaism were nothing more than a circumlocution allowing an attack on Christianity. In all cases, historic and cultural curiosity conquered theological uneasiness, as seen in Schudt's *Merkwurdigkeiten*.[44]

Hence, we must ask how far modern antisemitism is rooted in the Christian tradition.

Whether extreme or moderate, antisemitic propaganda has one remarkable characteristic.[45] Its target is not so much the traditional Orthodox Jew, recognizable as such, but rather what the antisemite believes to be the disguised Jew: that emancipated, assimilated Jew who is about to break the healthy web of the new nation to which he claims to belong. Assimilated or not, the Jew is and remains a foreigner, a danger, a force of disintegration. Jewishness is a *character indelebilis*, which can be changed neither by baptism nor by other external signs indicating a change of identity. The first political goal of the antisemite, therefore, is to make up for the original sin of nineteenth century Europe, to revoke the legal emancipation granted to Jews and to make them recognizable again through discrimination. Certainly, moderate ideological antisemites concede that the Jews are subjectively sincere in their desire for assimilation but, they add, they are in fact incapable of assimilating. More extreme antisemites maintain that the external signs by which Jews seem to indicate that they identify and assimilate into the society around them are only a dangerous ruse, even an international Jewish plot aimed at seizing power; the most enraged antisemites demand not only the annulment of emancipation but also expulsion and genocide.

In broad outline, this is the phenomenology of antisemitic manifestations. They presuppose emancipation and are directed against it. For this reason, they constitute a radically new phenomenon in Jewish history. Of course, antisemitic hatred here is again the other side of the coin of fascination. The antisemite appeals to those categories of the population who are least adapted to a modern, industrialist, capitalist and mobile society. For right or wrong, antisemitism is fascinated by the image it makes of the adaptability of the Jews and proposes a sinister interpretation of it. Whatever its motives, however, antisemitism seems far from the anti-Jewish attitudes of Christianity.[46]

Theoretically, at least, a converted Jew, on the theological level, was a Christian in every respect. No doubt, certain Protestant tendencies, which demanded a complete rupture of Christianity from Judaism and even with the Old Testament, need only be secularized a bit to be more antisemitic than any Catholic doctrine. There is not much distance between Adolf von Harnack with his adoration of Marcion and Chamberlain proving that Jesus was an Aryan. But perhaps these are only exceptions. In general, the *ecclesia militans* fights the visible Jew and Judaism; the antisemite fights the invisible Jew who hides in society (and which he hides in himself).

However, theological anti-Judaism and ideological antisemitism both draw from the same base of popular prejudices accumulated over centuries; the theological positions of Christianity, because of their very continuity, provide a framework for these prejudices. Some recent theologians, Ruether or Baum for example, have recognized this dependency. Moreover, since the twelfth century, theological doctrines have adjusted to popular prejudices and have increasingly reflected them. They reinforce the image of a secret and dangerous Judaism, more than is demanded by religious antagonism. Certainly, antisemitism is a secularized phenomenon; but here, as elsewhere, the secularized phenomenon is not the pure counterpart of religious attitudes. It develops within the framework of the religious mind and institutions long before it wins its independence.

3e. Theological Consequences

These are the broad lines of the development of anti-Jewish doctrines, positions and images. While it is certainly not our task to reformulate or modify theological doctrines, we can however draw attention to two possible errors in the interpretation of the historical diagnosis, one of which emanates from an overestimation and the other from an underestimation of the power of history.

First of all, a theologian can maintain that anti-Jewishness is so intrinsic to Christianity as a historical phenomenon that only an absolutely new departure could prevent it from once again becoming a vessel of anti-Jewish sentiments. Anti-Jewishness, says R.B. Ruether, is "the left hand of Christology."[47] Baum's self-criticism emphasizes "the ideology of substitution" as a source of the heritage of "contempt."[48] E. Berkovits goes further: only Christianity, with its insistence on a salvation that can come only from Christ, produces an anti-humanist ethic; Judaism is exempt from such abuses.[49] *That is a hypocritical argument.* The Jewish religion, like the Christian, subordinates man to God. Judaism has always approved of war *deo auctore*, ordered by God (*milhemet hova* as opposed to *milhemet reshut*) just as Christianity spent more than a thousand years finding an appropriate formula to make war a sacred mission. Until the Crusades, it was necessary to obtain absolution for killing an enemy even in a just war (*bellum justum*).

In the case of the Amalekites and the seven nations of Canaan, biblical exigency is very close to genocide. The Edomites were converted by force; the Karaites persecuted; the distinction betwen Israel and the "nations of the world" is no less discriminatory than the principle of *nulla salus extra ecclesiam*. Berkovits claims that, according to Jewish law, even a non-Jew can be saved: that is true but in the same way as with the Christians, i.e., with conditions. "All those who obey the seven laws of the sons of Noah," Maimonides teaches *ex cathedra*, "are among the Righteous Gentiles" and can obtain a portion of the world to come. But he adds: "When is this the case? When they obey the commandments because those are the will of God. If they obey them only out of a rational intuition (*hechra hada'at*), they are not among the Righteous Gentiles or their sages." Maimonides goes even further and underlines the obligation to kill all genuine pagans who refuse to submit to the seven precepts of the sons of Noah, according to him, they constitute the veritable equivalent of the Moslem *ahl al maut*.[50] And this obligation is not just theoretical; it resembles the obligation of exterminating the Amalekites or the "seven nations" who lived in Canaan (which he believes are extinct today). Both religions can lend their language to discrimination and contempt and have done so. To claim that only a Christian world could lead to genocide is at best hypocritical.

In the second place, the underestimation of history can be just as prejudicial or at least lead to arbitrary choices. F. Little thinks that, in Christianity, anti-Jewish attitudes begin only after Paul, after the large-scale arrival of proselytizing non-Jews.[51] Even if he is right – and our historical remarks suggest the contrary – it is hardly important whether Christianity was defined by opposing itself to Judaism before or after

Paul. The opposition is an historical part of its self-definition. Similarly, it is hardly important whether the origin of the antagonism is pagan or not: a good part of the philosophical and dogmatic language of Christianity is borrowed from the pagans. But the opposition – on which, let us not forget, orthodox Judaism insists no less than Christianity – must not necessarily be judged by its uncontrolled exaggerations. It is not inevitably malevolent: even if my neighbor detests music, which is the essence and meaning of my life, I will not hate him for it. With a little training, I will perhaps even learn not to despise him for it. If our analysis of the development of anti-Jewish attitudes in history is correct, there are factors external to religion that determine the change produced at the moment when Judaism stopped appearing simply as an anachronistic and false religion and was transformed into a threatening secret society, fomenting plots. Although incontestably part of the history of Christian anti-Judaism, this evolution can be separated from it in theory as well as in practice: not because it comes later but because its sources have nothing to do with religious images or doctrines.

It is a claim to be the sole owner of the holy truth that opposes Judaism to Christianity (and, sometimes, to Islam), precisely because it is a claim common to all of them. At least in their *historical* manifestations, the three monotheistic religions claim the exclusive possession of the revealed, whole, authentic and absolute truth. Each one recognizes in the two others at best an incomplete, erroneous or even falsified version of authentic principles. To the Christians, the Jews have remained fixated at a previous stage of revelation. For Islam, Christians and Jews are "People of the Book" who must not be converted by force as with pagans. For the Jews, Christianity and Islam seem to be more or less monotheistic religions – "nations enclosed within the limits of religion" (*umot hagedurot bedarche hadatot*) though the first was founded by a heretic and the second, says Maimonides, by a madman.[52] However, each of these religions is persuaded that it alone possesses the complete truth. That is what distinguishes them from classical, Greco-Roman paganism which was tolerant of other cults because *una est religio in varietate rituum*. An intellectual pagan ordinarily despised what Varron called *theologia mithica*; he paid allegiance to *theologia politica*, the gods of the city, and he believed only in *theologia naturalis* – philosophical truth superior to all positive religions. It is mainly monotheistic religions that imagine and introduce intolerance, although to varying degrees.

Can Christianity or Judaism abandon their claim to possess absolute truth without completely losing their identity? I do not know; but when some Christian theologians propose that revision, it seems to me that their position is very close to the conscious syncretism of late Antiquity. It is strange that Baum, who recommends the abandonment of the principle *nulla salus extra ecclesiam*, simultaneously holds the "pagan mentality" which spread throughout Europe in the twentieth century responsible for the Holocaust. These rather common theological prejudices are not free of hypocrisy. In its historical manifestations, "paganism" – whatever meaning the term has – was certainly no less human than Christianity – or Judaism.

Implicitly or explicitly, "paganism" often functions as a synonym for "secularism." Several theologians hold irreligion and the triumph of "secularization" responsible for the horrors of our century. This proves that even the most sincere theologians have not pushed self-criticism far enough. The Holocaust was not the consequence of irreligion any more that it was the product of religion. In fact, there are good reasons to suspect theology – Jewish, Christian or Moslem – of having been one of the factors that contributed to the ideological relativization of purely human values. The very claim to possess an absolute truth and the devotion to values beyond the human serve as paradigms for more profane ideologies. This *honor dei,* which man must serve without conditions, can be and has been made into *honor patriae*. If Christians and Jews put God above man, other priorities can also be constructed on this model: the working class, race, progress or other abstract reifications. Of course, we cannot make a religious attitude responsible for the erroneous or caricatured imitations that are made of it. That Hitler often chose to use a language saturated with religious images (*Vorsehung* – Providence – was the most common) does not prove he was Christian: Rauschning's *Conversations with Hitler (Gesprache mit Hitler)* and other documents rather prove the contrary and testify to violent anti-Christian sentiments. But theologians are the last to have the right to assign responsibility to irreligion for ideologies and practices of "absolute dependence" and submission to abstract principles – the terms, let us not forget, by which Schleiermacher *defined* religion. We will return to that later.

Reading Basnage's *History of the Religion of the Jews from Jesus Christ to the Present* (Rotterdam, 1707), the first attempt by a Christian author to describe the development of the Jews and post-biblical Judaism in a coherent and nonpolemical way, Heinrich Heine reacted with a poetic "reflection," titled "To Edom" (1804). ("Edom" is the traditional

Jewish metaphor to designate Rome and Christianity.) Written shortly
after the pogroms led by shouts of *Hep-Hep-Hep*, this poem seems to
sum up our discussion.

An Edom

Ein Jahrtausend schon und länger
Dulden war uns brüderlich
Du, du duldest dass ich atme,
Dass du rasest, dulde ich.

Manchmal nur, in dunkeln Zeiten
Ward dir wunderlich zu Mut
Und die liebefrommen Tätzchen
Farbest du mit meinem Blut!

Jetzt wird unsere Freundschaft fester
Und noch täglich nimmt sie zu;
Denn ich selbst begann zu rasen,
Und ich werde fast wie du!

To Edom

For millennia now, as brothers,
We've borne with each other an age;
You bear the fact I'm still breathing,
And I – I bear your rage.

But often you got in strange tempers
In dark times since the Flood,
And your meekly loving talons
You dyed in my red blood.

And now our friendship grows firmer
And daily increases anew,
For I too have started raging –
I'm becoming much like you!

4.
The Theological Dialectic of Non-Meaning

For the bravest of recent theologians, it is the very non-meaning of the Holocaust that constitutes its theological meaning. According to them, to lose faith before the Holocaust is another manner of faith, a positive religious act. In the eleventh century, when Anselm of Canterbury proposed his ontological proof of the existence of God, he also gave a new meaning to the verse of the psalm: "The fool has said in his heart: there is no God." As the existence of God necessarily results from the concept of Him, anyone who thinks of God, even to deny His existence, cannot be mad (evil). The modern theologians I refer to – Rahner, Baum, Rubinstein and others – have reversed Anselm's argument. "He who, deeply troubled by the Holocaust, has become incapable of affirming the presence of God is caught up in an essentially religious problematic and thus is already under the influence of the grace of God. A superficial or purely pragmatic man or a selfish man or one who cares only for his personal interest would not be troubled at all. The one who is troubled is he who is religious."[53] Even the atheist, as Vatican reminds us, can be touched by grace.

To admit that God – or ethical theism – died at Auschwitz because Auschwitz defies all meaning leads, as we have said, to a radical revision of the most fundamental premises.[54]

> What has emerged in our theological reflection based on Karl Rahner is a rather different religious imagination: Here God is not conceived of as lord ruling history from above, but as the vitality at the core of people's lives making them ask the important questions and moving them toward their *authentic* existence. God is conceived here as the *ground* of human existence, as the summons operative in their lives, and as the *horizon* toward which they move. God is not so much lord of the universe as heart of the world. What is emphasized in this theology is what theologians call Divine immanence, which in ordinary language [!] means God's being *in-and-through* the world... God's presence to people changes them, severs them from the destructive trends, and moves them toward a more creative future... But the in-and-throughness of God does not leave the world as it is; it judges the world and summons it to new life.

However, even where theologians are most courageous, false notes are inevitable. The important expressions we have underlined lead us without any possible error toward a well-defined philosophical source. If we replace "God" with "Being" (*Sein*), the rest of the vocabulary is Heideggerian. Seemingly without ethical judgment, Heidegger distinguishes two modes of human existence, the inauthentic and the authentic. This is what is done in the passage we have quoted. The *Dasein*, the "being-there" or existence is the only form in which the ungraspable *Sein*, the "being" (unlike *Seiendes*, a being) is concerned with itself: "*Das Dasein ist ein Seiendes*, dem es seinem Sein um dieses Sein selbst geht."[55] However, in its original and ordinary appearance, it is alienated from itself, lost in the world (*In-der-Welt-sein*) so that it uses things in the world (*Zuhanden sein*) and is absorbed in it. Each man is inseparable from other men with whom he shares the care (*Sorge*) of the things in the world. The *Dasein* is inauthentic in this state, it is *man* – "one," "anyone at all" – characterized by the *Seinvergessenheit*, forgetting of the genuine self. He flees anguish (*Angst*) rather than confronting it, confronting his fundamental nature of *Geworfen-sein*, of "cast-thrown" (*geworfen*) into the world. Only the authentic self, unlike the inauthentic "one" (*man*), moved by anguish and trembling (*Angst*), is capable of posing the question-of-the-being (*Daseinfrage*), the question to which there is *ipso facto* no answer because the answer is for that particular being no longer to be. Here, too, the non-meaning of the question constitutes its very meaning. Here, too, the characteristic of the authentic me, the one that is not "lost in trivial cares," is to pose questions to which there is no answer. More than the "chattering" (*Gerede*) of the "one," of "everyone" (*man*), the authentic self allows the Being in himself to speak for himself by his very futile question about being.

Few readers of *Sein und Zeit* have escaped the fascination of Heidegger which is similar in many respects to that of Spinoza's *Ethics*; each work provides an incomparable consolation. In each, the ultimate meaning of everything that exists resides only in that thing. Spinoza's *Deus sive natura* reifies the logic of the Megarians to the extreme: only what is is possible! What is not is impossible and even bereft of meaning. Like Spinoza's God, Heidegger's being is always expressed by beings (*Seiende*), always incapable of expressing "itself" in an immediate way and without their intermediary; it illuminates without being seen, just as (to borrow a metaphor from Wittgenstein) a picture never draws itself. However, in contrast to substance in Spinoza, Heidegger insists on the necessarily temporal structure of the being. For he who accepts the total immanence of the meaning of the world – including, for Heidegger, the temporality of the being – there is nothing more in the life of the subject than that life itself; it cannot be endowed with transcendent meaning or value; when individual life comes to an end, its meaning will be no more and no less than *what* it was. Annihilation does not deprive it of its meaning: on the contrary, it is an integral part of that meaning.

Now, let us return to that appeal to authenticity which some of the boldest theological reflections on the Holocaust have borrowed from Heidegger.

It is precisely this point – the distinction between authentic existence and inauthentic existence – that must serve as a point of departure for moral criticism from the point of view of ethics. Heidegger assures us that this distinction does not bear any moral judgment.[56] In an almost Hegelian manner, he even sees the movement with which the *Sein* departs from itself in a *Dasein* by flight into an inauthentic existence as a stage necessary for its return(*Kehre*) to itself. Let us consider, however, the other attributes of inauthenticity. Only the authentic self possesses consciousness; only it can be said to be capable of "sinning." The "one," the anonymous "anyone at all" lives in a continuous degeneration and fall (*Verfall des Daseins*), a fall "into the world" (*in die Welt verfallen*). "Anyone at all" is, literally, interchangeable with anyone else.

Without getting into a lengthy discussion about the nature of the moral discourse, I would posit that, in this type of discourse, it is necessary to proceed from some "concrete absolutes" if one wants to avoid the double reef of relativization and formal and empty abstractions. Grant me that human life and the dignity of man constitute such absolutes – either in the cognitive or axiomatic-thetic, descriptive or normative sense. They deserve a respect that nothing can undermine; they are the "infinite right" of each individual. One can imagine situations – legitimate defense, for example – that justify violating it: but, even justified, such an act remains evil.

In Nazi Europe, human life and the immeasurable value of each individual were violated in an infinity of ways. But an ethical perspective as suggested above must necessarily be very narrow, rigorously one-dimensional. It cannot make any concession to greater gods or to higher values and it does not allow the establishment of distinctions between individuals by basing itself on higher values. It forces the consideration of life, the life of each individual as always significant in and of itself. From the point of view of one-dimensional morality, the daily reality of the

Heideggerian "anyone-at-all," the man who has never reflected on the question of being but is "lost in the world," assumes as much intrinsic dignity and value as the life of someone who seeks fundamental existential truths. The life of the man who cultivates his garden and accomplishes everything as he must cannot be said to be inauthentic except by its author. From an ethical point of view, *every life is authentic*, every life is a value in and of itself, is not interchangeable with any other human life, is *sui generis*. As soon as one admits a discrimination, even in theory, the consequences are difficult to foresee. If the person of "anyone-at-all" is interchangeable with anyone at all – not to mention if "one" is classed among the non-persons, that is, considered as bereft of personality – then that person has less value. If he has less value, he is perhaps not indispensable. Or, in a Heideggerian perspective, isn't crisis – war and destruction, for example – a good thing since it "calls" man to his true self? Heidegger himself came to such conclusions after 1933.

But, it will be objected, one could not reproach a theory for the abuses that are committed or may be committed upon it, even if that abuse is done by the author himself. That was my reasoning in the last chapter. However, my criticism goes deeper. Even the distinction between authentic and inauthentic existence – and not only the developments to which it might give rise – is an attack on *dignitas hominis*, the integrity and value of each concrete individual life in whatever fashion it is lived. The total respect of this *dignitas*, with all its difficulties and all its paradoxes, must constitute the absolute center of every humanistic moral theory, even if this attitude emerges in a one-dimensional and philosophically flat anthropology. At best, Heidegger's distinction deviates from that position; at worst, it destroys its foundations.

I still think that it is possible to preserve most of Heidegger's central theory on the immanence of being which we spoke of earlier, without introducing redundant discriminations. One can conceive an ethical monadology in which the life of each individual is a unique point of view signifying human potentials for the best and the worst. Each situation, both individual and collective, is significant and one can learn something about man from it. Even if human history ends without leaving any trace, its meaning would be what it was, filled, as it will have been, with good and bad, beautiful and ugly.

Mutatis mutandis, the defects of Heidegger's thought also appear in the dialectical theologies that borrow the Heideggerian language. Why, for example, is he who "poses important questions" concerning the presence of God in the depth of evil more "authentic" than he who does not pose such questions? Why are the questions of *homo religiosus*, broadly as we may define him, more important than the purely human questions posed by others about their experience in the concentration camps? For example, let us consider the most moving and profound account of survival at Auschwitz, Primo Levi's *Se questo e un uomo*. This book poses many question, none of which is theological. Levi refuses to consider the concentration camps as bereft of meaning: "We are absolutely persuaded that no human experience is empty of meaning or unworthy of interest. One can, on the contrary, draw fundamental (even if negative) values from the description of the world we lived in then." And in fact, religious-theological questions, if they were posed, would take away some of the force of Levi's reflections centered on man, not God.

The reality of the concentration camps taught Levi other distinctions than that between authentic and inauthentic existence, between an existence with grace and one that lacks it. There, he learned distinctions centered solely on man, such as the distinction between "the drowned and the saved":[57]

> We do not believe in the most obvious and facile deduction: that man is fundamentally brutal, egoistic and stupid in his conduct once every civilized institution is taken away, and that the *Häftling* is consequently nothing but a man without inhibitions. We believe, rather, that the only conclusion to be drawn is that in the face of driving necessity and physical disabilities many social habits and instincts are reduced to silence...
> This division is much less evident in ordinary life, for there it rarely happens that a man loses himself. A man is normally not alone, and in his rise or fall is tied to the destinies of his neighbors; so that it is exceptional for anyone to acquire unlimited power, or to fall by a succession of defeats into utter ruin. Moreover, everyone is normally in possession of such spiritual, physical and even financial resources that the probabilities of a shipwreck, of total inadequacy in the face of life are relatively small. And one must take into account a definite cushioning effect exercised both by the law, and by the moral sense which constitutes a self-imposed law; for a country is considered the more civilized the more the wisdom and efficiency

of its laws hinder a weak man from becoming too weak or a powerful one too powerful.

But in the Lager things are different: here the struggle to survive is without respite, because everyone is desperately and ferociously alone. If some *Null Achtzehn* vacillates, he will find no one to extend a helping hand; on the contrary, someone will knock him aside, because it is in no one's interest that there will be one more "musulman" dragging himself to work every day; and if someone, by a miracle of savage patience and cunning, finds a new method of avoiding the hardest work, a new art which yields him an ounce of bread, he will try to keep his method secret, and he will be esteemed and respected for this, and will derive from it an exclusive, personal benefit; he will become stronger and so will be feared, and who is feared is, *ipso facto*, a candidate for survival.

Thus, among the "saved," one finds the noble (like his friend Alberto) as well as the ignoble, the wicked and the good. Levi uses the theological vocabulary ironically: a way of saying that salvation is not a theological or otherwise transcendental characteristic, but a fundamentally human property. From the experience of the concentration camp, Levi crystallizes materials to construct a genuine philosophical anthropology, more authentic and more precise than Heidegger's or any other recent theologian's. The force of his reflection, I repeat, lies in the fact that it is centered on the concrete man, not on the chimera of an authentic self or on God.

Even more seriously, religious questions can prejudice the moral care of human life. In my terms, that prejudice is this: even the most self-critical theologians pose a special virtue in devoting oneself to values higher than life and human integrity and claim that one who lives his life *veluti pecora*, without asking existential-religious questions, lacks "grace."

But things can be seen in reverse. Devotion to values higher than the sanctity of the individual does nothing but divert one from the study of man: he can commit abuses and crimes that are much more serious than those ever committed in the name of selfishness and personal interest. No doubt this is not a necessary consequence of the devotion to absolute values but it is a too-frequent consequence. It hardly matters whether these superior values are transcendent or immanent: God, homeland, race or the ideal society of the future. In the name of all these ideals, crusades have been launched, genocide committed, the human being degraded. To my knowledge, no great religion has remained unscathed. Hence, perhaps dialectical theologians do not go far enough. Perhaps theology itself is one of the sources of that danger they contemplate. William of Ockham, who recognized very clearly in his ethical theory the necessity for a concrete absolute to avoid the Scylla of relativism and the Charybdis of formal, empty abstractions, maintained that it was false to say that God wants what is good. It must be said, instead, that this is good because God wants it. The God of the Bible wanted a kind of genocide of the Amalekites and their wives, children and flocks. A few centuries later, a more refined God wanted heretics to be "forced to enter" or destroyed. An even more refined God can demand the self-sacrifice of the faithful for the sanctification of His name. A secular age translated these demands into immanent and intra-worldly terms, among them, race. *Tantum religio portuit suadere malorum.*

Once more, I do not claim that religious commitment necessarily leads to abuse. But let it no longer be said that it is irreligion (the "explosion of paganism," as they say) which made the concentration and extermination camps possible. I maintain rather that, when the essential aspect of the interrogation is brought to bear on the religious-theological significance of the Holocaust, an intrinsic error is committed. To know what it teaches us about God or any other value or superior norm is hardly important; what matters is to know what it teaches us about man, his limits, his possibilities, his cruelty, his creativity, his nobility. In human terms, the Holocaust was not bereft of meaning. To claim that it was seems as insulting as to maintain that it had a theological meaning, that is, that it carried out God's design.

For similar reasons, we should oppose defining the Holocaust as "incomprehensible." This is one of its most frequent attributes in theological literature on the Holocaust – and not only in theological literature. Quite the contrary: historians, psychologists, sociologists and philosophers should not spare any effort to understand the catastrophe and should be guided by the reasonable hope that such comprehension is possible. The crime committed by the Nazis reached immense proportions; the horror and suffering go beyond the capacity of our imaginations; yet it is possible to understand them rationally. Even if those who perpetrated that crime were madmen who had lost all contact with reality, it would be possible to reconstruct their mentality and their models of behavior. But they were not madmen, at least not in the clinical sense of the term: if madness entails the loss of the sense of reality, then no society is mad, for reality is an entirely social construct. The prehistory of the genocide, the conditions that made it possible can become clear. It is possible to follow the mental mechanisms by which Nazi ideology justified mass murder step by step. Germany was fixed in the illusion of a "total," apocalyptic war. There was no doubt that the Jews were not only an inferior race, like the Slavs or the Blacks; they were also more dangerous, a universal and destructive parasite which, unlike other races, skillfully adapted themselves to melt into the host society with the aim of destroying its healthy texture from the inside. They spoke of the extermination of the Jews as a question of hygiene: they were considered a dangerous germ. *Entlausung*: delousing, the ideological metaphor that covers the terrible reality of the concentration camps. To degrade the prisoners of the camp, to strip them of their personality was to make them what Nazi ideology maintained that they had always been: subhumans. This mechanism of degradation functioned to concretize and visualize the reasons that justified extermination. Nor is it true that the extermination of the Jews was accomplished to the detriment of the war effort, as Hilberg and others once believed. We cannot avoid the duty of understanding the Nazi mentality if we want to condemn it, even more if we want to prevent such crimes from happening again.

It seems that the theoreticians put the accent on the "incomprehensibility" of the Holocaust and on the "madness" of those who perpetrated it because they cannot find any theological meaning in it. Perhaps it is also because they do not dare to say that, if it is necessary to believe in transcendent forces, the Holocaust would prove the autonomy of evil, an evil manifested not only – or principally – by the number of its victims but by its inexhaustible inventiveness, by the almost infinite number of methods it discovered to produce murder and degradation systematically. If, on the contrary, abandoning God, we turn to men, the Holocaust is neither incomprehensible nor bereft of meaning. It was neither bestial nor pagan. It was, on the contrary, an eminently human event in that it manifested the extreme limits of what only man and human society are capable of committing and bearing. It designated one potential of human existence, unknown perhaps until then, a potential as human as the most beautiful examples of creativity and compassion.

The original French text was delivered as a lecture at *Colloque de l'École des Hautes Études en Sciences Sociales* of Paris and published by *Le Seuil* in 1987.

Notes:

1. Yoel Taitlbaum, *Vayoel Moshe*, New York, 1952, 2nd ed. 1957.
2. Babylonian Talmud, *Ketuba* 111a; *Cont. Rabba* 2.7. Literally, the formulation is an oath but a ridiculous one and that is why the invocation of God (*el Shaddai, el Tseva'ot*) is replaced by words that are phonetically similar (*aylot ha'sade, tsviot*). Cf. R. Gordis, "The Song of Songs," in Mordechai M. Kaplan, *Jubilee Volume*, New York, 1953, pp. 281–397, especially p. 309.
3. Menachem R. Kasher, *Hatekufa Hagdola*, Jerusalem, 1969, who polemicizes as explicitly against Taitlbaum.
4. U.Z. Greenberg, *Rehovot hanahar, Sefer hailiut veha'koah*, Tel Aviv, 1957, p. 7; "father of the superior race," p. 31 *passim. Gesa* is the accepted modern word in Hebrew for race: a racial ideology will be called *torat geza*. In 1957, the word had different connotations than in 1920 when Jabotinsky promised: "With blood and sweat / A race will be formed for us / Proud, magnanimous and cruel."
5. A. Funkenstein, "Maimonides: Political Theory and Realistic Messianism," *Miscellanea Medievalia*, II, 1977, pp. 81–103.
6. R. Levi ben Habib, *Responsa*, Venice, 1565; appendix (*kuntres hasmicha*); on the ideological background, cf. J. Katz, "Mahloket hasmicha ben Jacob Berab vehaRaloah," *Zion*, 17, 1951, p. 34; Funkenstein, *op. cit.*, p. 102.
7. R. Hilberg, *The Destruction of European Jews*, Chicago, 1967. I have developed some of these ideas elsewhere (*The Passivity of Diaspora* ✔ *Jewry: Myth and Reality*, Aran-Lecture 11, Tel Aviv, 1982).
8. Babylonian Talmud, *Nedarim* 28a; *Gittin* 10 b; *Baba Kama* 111; *Baba batra* 54b–55a. Cf. S. Shiloh, *Dina demalchuta dina* (Hebrew), Jerusalem, 1974.
9. J.-P. Sartre, *Reflexions sur la question juive*, Paris, 1947.
10. E. Fackenheim, *God's Presence in History*, New York, 1970; *The Jewish Return into History*, New York, 1978. E. Berkovits, *Faith after the Holocaust*, New York, 1973.
11. G. Steiner, *The Portage of A.H. to San Cristobal*, New York, 1981.
12 Primo Levi, *Survival in Auschwitz*, New York, 1986 (trans. Stuart Woolf), pp. 129–130.
13. The following chapter develops my remarks in *The Jerusalem Quarterly*, 19, 1981, pp. 56–72, from which I also take notes 15–46.
14. Johanan Hans Levi, *Olamot Nifgashim*, Jerusalem, 1960, pp. 115–189; and A. Tcherikover, *Hellenistic Civilization and the Jews*, Philadelphia, 1959 (trans. S. Appelbaum).
15. For the following, see M Stern (ed.), *Greek and Latin Authors on Jews and Judaism*, Vol. I: *From Herodotus to Plutarch*, Jerusalem, The Israel Academy of Sciences and Humanities, 1976, pp. 62–86 (Manethon) and pp. 389–416 (Apion); I. Heinemann in Pauly-Wissowa, *Encyclopedia*, Supplement, "Antisemitismus" (coll. 3–43); J.H. Levi, *op. cit.*, pp. 60–196.
16. Tacitus, *History*, V. 4.
17. P. Berger and K. Luckmann, *The Social Construction of Reality*, Garden City, 1967, pp. 166–7. By a curious coincidence, the authors chose an imaginary leper

colony as an example.

18. W.W. Jaeger, *Die Theologie der fruhen griechischen Denker*, Stuttgart, 1964, p. 1ff., p. 50ff (Xenophanes).

19. Augustine, *De civitate Dei*, X, p. 9ff (in *Corpus christianorum. Series latina*, vol. 47, p. 281 ff.)

20. Treatise *Abodah Zarah*, 55a in I. Epstein (ed.), *The Babylonian Talmud*, section 4, *Seder Nezikin*, Vol. 7, London, 1935, p. 281.

21. See H Chadwick, *Origen: Contra Celsum*, Cambridge, 1965, p. 199 (trans. with an introduction and notes by H. Chadwick); V. Andresen, "Logos und Nomos: Die Polemik des Kelsos wider das Christentum," *Arbeiten zur Kirchengeschichte*, 30, Berlin, 1955, p. 266 ff.

22. J.H. Levi, *op. cit.*; M Stern, *op. cit.*

23. Rule of Qumran, I, 10–11; see J. Licht, *The Rule Scroll (IQS, ISQa and IQSb)*, text, introduction and commentary (in Hebrew), Jerusalem, 1965, p. 61; V.G. Vermes, *The Dead Sea Scrolls in English*, Harmondsworth, Penguin Books, 1962, p. 72; see also Theodore H. Gaster (trans.), *The Dead Sea Scriptures*, New York, 1956; J. Licht, "The Plant Eternal and the People of Divine Deliverance," in C. Rubin and Y. Yadin (eds.), *Essays on the Dead Sea Scrolls* (in Hebrew), Jerusalem, 1961, pp. 49–75; D. Flusser, *Jewish Sources in Early Christianity: Studies and Essays* (Hebrew), Tel Aviv, 1979.

24. IQPHab, VII, 1–5 (G. Vermes, *ibid.*, p. 239).

25. Tractate (Mishnah) *Sotah*, IX, 15, in H. Danby (trans.), *The Mishnah*, London, 1933, p. 306; see M. Avi-Yonah, *The Jews of Palestine: A Political History from the Bar-Kokhba War to the Arab Conquest*, London and New York, 1976, ch. IV, "Judaism and Christianity to the Accession of the Emperor Constantine," pp. 137–157 (especially pp. 145– 150).

26. E.G. von Grunebaum, *Medieval Islam*, Chicago, 1953, pp. 174–185.

27. Joachim de Flore, *Tractatus super quattuor evangelia*, 105 (edition by E. Buonaiuti), Rome, 1930; see H. de Lubac, *Exégèse médiévale. Les quatres sens de l'Écriture*, studies published under the direction of the faculty of theology of Lyon-Fourvière, Vol. III (II, 1), 1961, p. 144, n. 2.

28. Hugh of Saint-Victor, *De sacramentis Christianae fidei*, II, 6, 4, in Migne, *Patrologie latine*, vol. 176, col. 450A; *idem., De vanitate mundi et rerum transeuntiu usu*, IV, in Migne, *op. cit.*, vol. 176, col. 740C. See A. Funkenstein, *Heilsplan und natürliche Entwicklung: Formen der Gegenwartsbestimmung im Geschichtsdenken des hohen Mittelalters*, Munich, 1965, p. 52 and 165, n. 5. Hugh was perhaps influenced by Rashi in Hen 6:9.

29. B. Blumenkranz, *Der Judenpredigt Augustins*, Basle, 1946.

30. F. Kern, *Recht und Verfassung in Mittelalter*, Darmstadt, 1958, p. 23 ff.

31. Erich Caspar (ed.), *Das Register Gregors VII, Epistolae selectae in usum scholarum*, vol. II, fasc. I: *Gregoris VII registrum libri*, I-IV, Berlin, 1920 (1967), p. 202 ff (see especially p. 203).

32. For this and the following, see: A. Funkenstein, "Changes in the Patterns of Christian Anti-Jewish Polemics in the XIIth Century" (Hebrew), *Zion*, 33, 1968, pp. 124–144.

33. Rimbertus, *Vita Anskari*, 4, in G. Waltz (ed.), *Vita Anskari*, MGH, ser. Germ., *In usum scholarum*, Hanover, 1884, p. 24.

34. B. Smalley, *The Study of the Bible in the Middle Ages*, Oxford, 1952; H. Hermann, *Rashi and the Christian Scholars*, Pittsburgh, 1963.

35. Peter the Venerable. *Tractatus adversus Judaeorum inveteratam duritiem*, V. in Migne, *op. cit.*, vol. 189, col.. 649 ff. See my article (*supra*, n. 32.)

36. Y. Baer, "The Disputation of R. Yechiel of Paris and of Nachmanides," (Hebrew), *Tarbitz*, 2, 1931, pp. 172–189; J. Rosenthal, "The Talmud on Trial 1240," *JQR*, 47, 1956–1957, p. 58 ff; S. Grayzel, *The Church and the Jews in the XIIIth Century*, Philadelphia, 1933, p. 29 ff; C. Merchavia, *The Church versus Talmudic and Midrashic Literature (500–1248)* (Hebrew), Jerusalem, 1970; Jacob Katz, *Exclusiveness and Tolerance: Studies in Jewish-Gentile Relations in Medieval and Modern Times*, Oxford, 1961, and New York, 1961, pp. 106–133.

37. J. Trachtenberg, *The Devil and the Jews: The Medieval Conception of the Jews and its Relation to Modern Antisemitism*, New York, 1961, is an excellent anthropological study but lacks historical analysis.

38. Thomas of Monmouth, *De Vita et passione Sancti Willelmi martyris Norwicensis*, II, 9, in A. Jessop and M.R. James (eds.), *The Life and Miracles of St. William of Norwich by Thomas of Monmouth*, Cambridge, 1896, p. 93 ff (Latin and English).

39. Norman Cohn's study. *Warrant for Genocide*, London, 1967, traces the literary threads of the *Protocols* but not the origin of its *topos*.

40. Ch. Wirszubski, *Three Studies in Christian Kabbalah* (Hebrew), Jerusalem, 1975. And see also Ch. Wirshubski, *A Christian Kabbalist Reads the Law* (Hebrew), Jerusalem, 1977.

41. For the following, see Shmuel Ettinger, *Modern Anti-Semitism: Studies and an Essay* (Hebrew), Tel Aviv, 1978, especially p. 29 ff; in *Dispersion and Unity*, 9, an 1970, pp. 17–37.

42. H.H. Ben-Sasson, "Jews and Christian Sectarian," *Viator*, 4, 1973, pp. 369–385.

43. See Ettinger, *op. cit.;*, A. Hertzberg, in his *The French Enlightenment and the Jews: The Origin of Modern Anti-Semitism*, did not see that the motifs that he discusses had a more ancient origin.

44. Cf. J. Katz, *Antisemitism, From Religious Hatred to Racial Rejection* (Hebrew), Tel Aviv, 1979; J.J. Schudt, *Jüdische Merkwürdigkeiten*, Frankfurt and Leipzig, 1714.

45. For the following, see U. Tal, *Judaism and Christianity*, Ithaca and London, 1975.

46. On the explanation proposed by Sartre in his famous *Reflexions sur la question juive*, see Menachem Brinker, "Sartre on the Jewish Question: Thirty Years Later," *The Jerusalem Quarterly*, 10, Winter 1979, pp. 117–132. In a striking fashion, Sartre confronts the antisemite and the Jew as twin forms of inauthentic existence. His description of the antisemitic mentality is the best I have ever read. Proposing that the Jews persist because they are seen as such, he revives Spinoza's affirmation in his *Tractatus theologico-politicus* (ch. III). Moreover, he translates the psychoanalytical category of Being and Nothingness in terms of

historical analysis: the fundamental situation of "being-seen." But Sartre knew only the Jews of his personal biographical experience, emancipated and assimilated Jews.

47. Eva Fleischner (ed.), *Auschwitz: Beginning of a new Era?*, New York, 1974, p. 74. I owe this reference to my student, Priscilla D. Jones, with whom I have had several discussions on the subject of this chapter.
48. G.G. Baum, *Christian Theology after Auschwitz* (Robert Waley Cohen Memorial Lecture), London, 1976, especially pp. 7–15.
49. E. Berkovits, *op. cit.* (see *supra*, n. 10).
50. Maimonides, *Mishne Tora, Hilchot Shoftim*.
51. Franklin H. Little, *The Crucifixion of the Jews*, New York, 1975.
52. Cf. Funkenstein, *supra*, n. 5. The expression, "nations enclosed in the limits of religion," which J. Katz attributes to Hameiri is in fact taken from Maimonides, *The Guide to the Perplexed*, III, 50. Cf. J. Katz (*supra*, 36), *op. cit.*, p. 115.
53. Gregory G. Baum, *Christian Theology after Auschwitz*, *supra*, n. 48.
54. *Ibid.*, p. 19.
55. M. Heidegger, *Sein und Zeit*, Tübingen, 1957, p. 12.
56. *Ibid.*, p. 175: *"Der titel (des Verfallen, etc.) der keine negative Bewertung ausdrückt..."*
57. Primo Levi, *op. cit.*, pp. 87–88.

Translated from the French by Barbara Harshav.

Aryeh Sivan

Five Poems

Knowing Joseph

In a process impossible to reverse
arose a generation
which knew not Joseph. And really,
how was it possible to know Joseph? And what
was Joseph? A basket of undeciphered
dreams? The humidity
of a dungeon? It was
always possible to find him in one pit
or another.

On the Nile's bank grew the sheaves,
lean cows, fat cows, feeding on leaves,
between heaven and earth hovered shadows.

But what about Joseph, who left
his clothes behind in the hands
of a woman warm and dreamlike, on whose
soft thighs he, naked, would slide nightly,
to a bottomless pit. Strange:
His brothers waited for him there, but never
could he look up
to see them. Weariness,
perhaps, mysterious fatigue,
blurred them into an obscure and dim solid

whose eyes alone shone like
hyena eyes: What a Joseph
naked, what a Joseph, orphaned.
And who'd have dreamt
of a time his fingers would snap behind
the hairy faces
propelling everyone about,
back and forth, stonily.

A boy building sandcastles,
a boy totally absorbed in shaping
gated fortresses and silo roofs,
setting on every side
camel caravans laden with corn and grain.

A boy whose heart cries for his father to come,
to restore at last to their true size
all the things grown immeasurably
from the moment he touched them, the moment his eyes
sought vainly, vainly, a glimpse of his father,
his tranquil profile in the massive expanse
gaping indifferently on every side.

A boy on whose head the sun rests
and whose eyes the stars celebrate and guard,
those eyes so lovely in their confusion and their dread,
their desperate knowing
that the water games and sand castles
will nevermore be dreams –
he'll have no escape from them
in a land mindful of its inhabitants.

Something Else Touching Joseph

Falling into the pit, he knew he was dead. And truly,
you can't expect this dreamy boy
to survive falling into a dry well.
Only in a dream does one fall into wells and survive.

And in full awareness, with a pure heart, he made himself ready
to step down into the barque of death, which would transport him
across the black waters, the waters joining
the bottoms of wells with the dwellings of his mother.

But in that place, instead of putting him to sleep
in the singing white vessel, a woman very much alive
lay hold of his limbs, with demanding hands,
and our innocent Joseph had need of another pit
and of imprisoned men, that he might know
the true appearance of a man into whose dreams death comes.

The above poems were translated from the Hebrew by F.F. Chyet.

The Return to Zion

1.
Speakers with thirsty tongues
come to a dry land.
Lowered into its earth they remove
their feet on their way to the water pits.*
And on high skied nights
great birds come into their
dreams, wrestle with their hair,
weave crimson threads with their bills
at their navels, pull them down in a
long, soft fall toward the abyss teeming
with waters inscribed in
ancient stone.

2.
Suntanned children of the waters
giggling in green shadows.
Like unruffled acrobats
they walk on towers of
water, like stilts,
to hand-feed the songbirds and the
first morning breezes
like hammocks, tied
to trees that have grown,
so incredibly fast,
roots stronger
than stone.

*) See *Jeremiah 14,3.*

Looking for a Shirt to One's Taste

On Allenby Street between sunlight and streetlights
even old shopkeepers leave
their bolts of cloth to get a breath
of fresh air in side-streets.

A man looking for a shirt to his taste
suddenly, in the sea-mirror, sees his nakedness,
he inhales his parents' fecundity, like a delicate fabric
whose design has faded, in rooms
of high ceilings and windows.

A man looking for a shirt to his taste
pauses and thinks about changing his taste,
and suddenly he finds himself in a side-street of sand
enclosed by iron fences, like his bed
in rooms of high ceilings and windows.

They close at seven. He must
find his taste. Or else
goose-necked salesladies will rise
from the moon-washed sand at the shore, like the pictures
on the walls of rooms with high windows
and they'll dress him for his parents' consolation,
in a shirt of black mail
woven of their hair.

Herzl as a Railroad Man

Herzl. Basel. On the bridge. Alone.
A man gasping. Hard.
On the Street of the Last Hussars
uniforms aglitter
kissing the hands of fat ladies.
Furs and passions.
Seamstresses with faces pale
as cellar walls
stitching with their lungs' blood
with scraps of torn uniforms
banners which will rise up
in time like mushrooms.

Eleven more years
and these uniforms
will yield to the rhythm
of sewing machines, turn into
multicolors, scraps of colors,
variegated colors at the throats of plunder.

Herzl. Basel. On the bridge. Alone.
Behind him, rooms of weighty delegates
belching words from
thick featherblankets:
say what you will about the Germans,
they have the trains. Punctuality.
You can rely on it one hundred per cent.
Maybe even more. Even more.

The Orient Express
cattle herders set their bells
by it
speeding through orchards and fields
toward a black chimney forest.
In an unheated sleeping car
the slaughtered body of a spy
journeys eastward,
his papers left behind in the West:

with finest brushes
they'll paint red stains
on a background of snow melting
too soon, too soon.

Herzl. Basel. On the bridge. Alone.
A man gasping, silent.
Tomorrow he'll rise early to put on his uniform –
A clown's costume, a conductor's garb? –
A coachman in brimmed hat, he'll open the
coach doors for throngs of passengers:
women with pillows and puffy featherblankets
and children screaming for no reason.
For no reason.

And in rooms of dreamy smoke
they picture a goat wearily
pulling a cart loaded
with figs and carob
down a twisting path
to the rhythm of an ancient sun
on blue mountain heights.
And the rushing of trains
like a lullaby for little goats.

A titan is dying, Basel, on your bridge,
a titan, your bridge is his leverage: Watch,
with his left hand he'll stop the world –
This round globe rolling
toward purple sundown in a deranged horizon
and with his right he'll gently push
and raise the car
onto the tracks known only to the secret maps
of his inner reflections
and then he'll die.

The above poems were translated from the Hebrew by Warren Bargad.

A.B. Yehoshua

Mister Mani

Jerusalem, 6 April 1918

The Speakers:

Lieutenant Ivor Stephen Horovitz was born in Manchester in 1896. His father, Joseph Horovitz, a native of Russia, came to England with his family as a fourteen year old boy and went to work in the textile industry. His mother, Dina Eliash, was born in Manchester. She belonged to a Jewish family which emigrated to England from Algeria at the beginning of the nineteenth century. Ivor was educated first at a primary school but because of his outstanding promise he was transferred by his parents to a prestigious boarding school in the region of Chessfield, not far from Manchester. In 1913 he finished secondary school and was accepted at King's College, Cambridge, where he first studied Law and English Literature. During his first year he couldn't make up his mind which of these to follow, but at the end of the year, he consulted some members of his family and finally decided to specialize in Law.

At the outbreak of World War I in August 1914, he hadn't yet been drafted but, in the middle of his second year, he passed the medical examinations and a preliminary selection process. In the middle of his third year, in January 1916, a full conscription was announced. He became a soldier and, after basic training in southern England, he was sent with his regiment to the front.

Ivor, who was of medium height, plump and bespectacled, tried unsuccessfully to be transferred to an administrative job. At the beginning of April 1916, the regiment was sent to the Somme front, to the forward line between the villages of Dompierre and Maricourt. There he stayed for nine weeks, fighting bitter battles, twice barely escaping mortal injury. At the end of June his application to an officers' course was accepted and he was sent to Normandy to a makeshift training centre for new officers. Meanwhile his regiment, which had suffered severe losses, was withdrawn from the line for rest and reorganization. In early September 1916, Ivor returned as an officer to his regiment which was bivouacked around Compiègne but because of the serious depletion in manpower there was no command for him and he was appointed to headquarters, as liaison with the French and with responsibility for order and discipline. The whole time he was worried about returning soon to battle.

On November 1916, he chanced upon one of his professors from Cambridge, Major Harville Shapiro, who was in charge of the military provost's office of the 37th Division, a legal department, which was expanding because of the growing number of cases of indiscipline among the troops after more than two years of pointless battles. At Ivor's own request and after some effort, he was transferred to this department which was a branch of the Military Police, and, when the entire brigade was moved up to the Verdun Front in December 1916, he accompanied Staff Headquarters to Lisle, an area within range of the German artillery.

In February 1917, major changes took place in the High Command. After General Murray's defeat in Gaza at the end of March, General Sir Edmund Allenby (nicknamed "The Bull") was given command of the 52nd Division in the Middle East. Allenby took a number of staff officers to organize the Division for the offensive against Turkey.

In May 1917, Ivor sailed for Egypt and was attached to Allenby's forces for the entire Palestine campaign as military advocate. In January 1918, after the capture of Jerusalem, he was promoted from Second to First Lieutenant.

Colonel Michael Woodhouse was born in Wales in 1877. His father, Sir Ashley Woodhouse, was a Tory Member of Parliament and Deputy Attorney General in Disraeli's government. Michael was sent as a boy to a military school in Sussex and joined the army in 1896. He served in the Far East, India, Malaya and Ceylon and rapidly climbed the ladder of command. In 1912 he returned to Britain to command the 3rd Battalion of the Royal Welsh Regiment. In 1914, as major, he reached France with the British Expeditionary Force and his battalion was one of the first to enter the fight against the Germans. He fought in the rearguard action on the Marne in September 1914 and later in the rearguard action on the Somme. Promoted to Lieutenant Colonel he became operations officer of the 6th Battalion in the battles of the Somme. He was captured, escaped immediately and returned to his regiment; but in the trenches of Verdun, at the end of June 1916, he lost his right arm and suffered permanent damage to his sight. For three months he lay in the Cheroneaux château in the Loire Valley which was turned into a military hospital. In early 1917, after he had been discharged from the hospital with a promotion to full Colonel and had received a medal for bravery, he refused to return to England and insisted on staying in active service. He was first attached to Staff Headquarters of the 62nd Division but, after a series of acrimonious disagreements with his superiors, resulting in fits of depression and bouts of heavy drinking, he asked one of the generals on Allenby's staff to transfer him overseas. In September 1917, he arrived at Allenby's headquarters in Cairo and was given a staff appointment in the Military Police. Shortly thereafter he was asked to serve as Presiding Judge in courts martial. Although he lacked any legal training, the new appointment appealed to him greatly.

[His text in the following dialogue is missing.]

— Colonel, Lieutenant Horovitz Ivor Stephen of the Military Advocate's staff, 52nd Division, reporting. I'm grateful to you for agreeing to discuss with me the clarification of...

— Horovitz, Colonel, H.O.

— British, naturally. I was born in Manchester, sir.

— 1896, sir.

— Yes, sir.

— My father unfortunately was not privileged to be born in the United Kingdom, sir, but arrived there at a very early age. But my mother...

— From Russia, sir, but at a very early age. This weather really is deplorable.

— We too were surprised, Colonel, we did not expect to find such a stormy winter in Jerusalem, which in the imagination of us Britons, in mine anyway, is always a city baked by the sun. But it is now several months since the conquest and the rain has hardly stopped and the city fathers swear that there has not been such a winter as this in the whole century. But even on days that begin as gloomily as today for example, sir, a few pleasant clearings are always guaranteed. This isn't the eternal rain of Glasgow or Leeds...

– Even today, Colonel, there is hope...

– No, sir. We do not yet have proper, reliable forecasts here. The weather balloons of the Royal Meteorological Service in Cairo are not strong enough to include Palestine in their observations. But the barometer on the façade of the French Consulate gives us a moderately dependable forecast for a few hours and, before I came here to see you, sir, I checked it thoroughly and I am pleased to inform you, sir, there is hope for clearer weather at midday...

– Horovitz, sir.

– Precisely, sir, H.O. I trust you slept well, Colonel.

– Oh...

– Oh...

– Oh, I am sorry to hear that, sir. After all, this is considered the finest hotel in Jerusalem. General Allenby himself stayed here after the conquest and as far as I remember there were no particular complaints from his retinue. I am most distressed to hear your complaint, sir.

– Well, sir, I do know that. The cook has not been taught to prepare British food and we all know how hard it is to get proper bacon in Jerusalem. Our Governor's wife, Lady Humphrey, also complained to the Brigadier but, on the other hand, it is said that in this very hotel the chef has learned to cook excellent porridge in the traditional British manner. I recommend you try it, sir.

– I see, Colonel.

– The city itself, sir, is small and devastated and, after a few months here, I would state without hesitation – utterly boring. The population is extremely heterogeneous, a ragbag of small and enclosed communities. Poverty and ignorance on the one hand, messianic arrogance on the other. As usual, there is little resemblance between its world-famous name and the marvellous texts written about it, and the miserable reality here, sir.

– What does it have to offer? Not a great deal, Colonel. A single famous and impressive mosque. As you are doubtless aware, sir, it is called the Dome of the Rock. A few important churches, the first being the Church of the Holy Sepulchre; it is, if I may be permitted to express my own opinion, sir, extremely disappointing. I much prefer the small churches outside the walls which have some harmony and charm. Whenever you would like a tour, sir, the Advocate's department will of course place an excellent guide at your service.

– The Jews, sir, have as usual little to offer other than themselves. To our amazement it turned out that they constitute the majority of the city's population, although during the war they were expelled and many fled. From an architectural point of view, they have only a few poor synagogues and of course this white wall, the remains of the wall of their Temple and they are accustomed to come and stand in front of it.

– Yes, sir, they just stand there and pray, they just stand there.

– Half a day would be quite sufficient, sir, for a convenient tour around all the Holy Places. Everything is jumbled so closely together that the distances are ridiculous, I might almost say tragic.

– Outside the walls, sir, there are a few new settlements scattered on the hills. There, even in this gloomy winter, I have found a few accessible corners, even though their charm is not immediately apparent...

– The surroundings, sir, are very poor. If you are familiar with Greece, sir, the area is reminiscent of the southern Peloponnese.

– No, sir, unfortunately I have never visited Greece but people who do know that country have spoken of the olive groves and vineyards, the rounded hills and the poor villages and the black-clothed shepherds. Of course, we mustn't forget Bethlehem a few miles away. It's a nice and pleasant place, rising gently among the hills. The famous Church of the Nativity is there as well as a friendly Anglican cleric who tells his story in the language of the Bible. This is most entertaining. I would also recommend, sir, a visit to Jericho, to the Dead Sea, in the Jordan Valley where the Australian troops are stationed. If Baedeker is correct and this is the lowest place in the world, you really should get there. You shouldn't give up the lowest place in the world since it's not so easy to get to the highest place, ha, ha.

– I beg your pardon, sir, I did not catch the precise name.

– I have made a note of it, sir. Is this a new brand?

– We have an Irish officer who is an expert on liquor. He has established excellent relations with the Armenian Church and its well-stocked wine cellar. I shall have a bottle sent to you at once.

– Five bottles, sir, of Chivas, sir. I have it noted down. Is any other brand acceptable?

– In that case I shall make every effort and guarantee delivery today. Anything else, sir? Cigarettes? Tobacco?

– Very good. Well, sir, the trial will begin tomorrow morning. At exactly eight o'clock your transport will be waiting at the hotel. It's about a five-minute drive. A small hall has been prepared next to the Officers' club outside the walls not far from the so-called Damascus Gate. The hall is in fact the prayer-house of the Dutch Mission and it seems to me, sir, that it has the space and facilities we are accustomed to.

– I beg your pardon, sir, I didn't hear.

– Oh, although I have not checked this in detail, I am convinced there will be no problems on that score. There will be few people present, and the prosecution intends to request the court to hold part of the proceedings in closed session, so as not to expose the identity of our sources who have served our interests so well behind the lines. In any case, sir, if there are no unforeseen developments, I don't expect the trial to last more than a few days.

– The names, Colonel, are known to you. I am sure. They are recorded in the file my sergeant delivered to you yesterday and I believe that tonight at the reception the Governor is giving in your honour you will meet your judicial colleagues. On your right is Lieutenant Colonel Cooper of the Australian Battalion who came up specially yesterday from the Jordan and on your left Major Jahawallah of the Intelligence Branch of the Indian Army. As for the defence, the accused has no defending counsel and as yet it has been impossible to persuade him to take one. Not a Jew or an Arab or a Briton or anyone else. The accused claims to have studied law in Beirut for a year or two in his youth and he considers himself capable of defending himself. In any event, I have asked Lieutenant Brian Oswald to be ready to take the defence if need be. That is all, sir, I think, except of course for the witnesses.

– Oh yes, of course, excuse me. The prosecuting team will consist of two. I myself shall lead for the prosecution, assisted by Lieutenant Harold Grey.

– Yes, sir.

– That is correct, sir.

– Well, sir, Major Clark is the head of our department.

– Actually, Colonel, I assumed that the business of Major Clark's absence was already known to you. After all, his personal letter to you is included in this file.

– I see. Well, sir, to put it briefly, Major Clark sailed for England three weeks ago. He is going to Blenheim for purposes of matrimony. With the Brigadier's permission, of course.

– There is very little I can tell you, sir. I only know that the young lady in question is the daughter of Lord Barton and that, to spare the noble Lord embarrassment, it is essential that the marriage take place without delay. I presume further explanations are superfluous, sir.

– He became acquainted with her in Paris, I believe. Have you had the opportunity of meeting Major Clark, sir? A most charming man.

– I regret that this is as far as my knowledge extends, sir. But I can inquire as to whether it is the younger or the older daughter of Lord Barton who is involved.

– As you please, sir. Anyway, Major Clark is thus prevented from serving as prosecutor in this case and I am his substitute.

– That is correct, sir, there are, indeed, more senior officers than myself in the department, but Major Clark preferred to entrust the task to me.

– I studied Law at Cambridge, sir, between 1913 and my conscription in January 1916.

– King's College, sir.

– I was unable to graduate, sir, because of the war.

– No, sir, at first I was in France.

– No, sir, in the 38th Infantry Regiment, the 42nd Division.

– In 1916, Colonel, from March to August.

– No, sir, at the front itself, in eastern France.

– No, sir, as a private.

– Yes, of course, sir, in the trenches and in actual combat. I had my share of action, sir, and I would not have chosen otherwise.

– April and May 1916.

– On the Somme front, Colonel, between the villages of Dompierre and Maricourt.

– In the northern sector of the front.

– Indeed, sir, the night of the 17th of May I remember only too well, it was a terrible time.

– Speaking of my own experience of course. In only two hours we lost three hundred men and two platoon commanders were killed.

– Indeed, sir, and you actually knew him! What a surprise!

– I was fortunate, sir, just a few splinters.

– Thank you, sir, I should be glad to sit down, that is most gracious of you. But if you do not object, sir, I would prefer to sit next to you so that I may show you some documents.

– Thank you, sir, there is no need for a table. The issue is short, please do not trouble yourself. Now that the basic contents of the file are clear to you, I should like... I should like to raise one point... that is before the actual trial begins... because then I shall obviously be obliged to confine myself to the evidence presented in court.

– I beg your pardon?

– Oh, I was afraid, sir, you might not have time to read the whole file.

– Oh...

– Oh...

– Oh, Colonel, we didn't know anything about this. I am stunned.

– Sir, I really am sorry, I am most distressed. Of course we knew about the wounds you received at Verdun, your name has been famous throughout the Division since the battle of the Marne.

– Sir, I am truly sorry. They didn't tell us anything about it. If we had known, I would have come and read the file to you myself.

– Now? Why not? As you wish, Colonel, my time is yours. I am ready and willing to read the file to you.

– That too is perfectly possible, sir. A kind of résumé as the French call it. This would be more agreeable and also quicker.

– Thank you, sir, with pleasure...

– A small glass will be quite sufficient, sir, in the morning... thank you...

– Excellent whisky... No wonder you insist on it, sir.

– Quite... this, sir, is... precisely the point... you have put your finger on it. The prosecution will demand the death sentence in accordance with the provisions of military law in time of war and we... this is what I wanted to discuss...

– I beg your pardon?

– Of course it is best to begin at the beginning. But where is the beginning, sir, allow me to think for a moment. Let us say it began on the 28th of February on a cold, rainy, misty night, a night of snowflakes that turned into a real snowfall next morning, perhaps the first time of the year, striking fear into the hearts of the local population. That was the night the accused was arrested. And the place – about ten miles north of Jerusalem, a little to the north of a small town called Ramallah, meaning Hill of God, in a remote village called El-Bira, which, I believe, is the Bethel of the Old Testament. It's a poor hamlet of olive groves and small vegetable patches. Allenby's forces got there during the conquest of Jerusalem in mid-December and halted there for no obvious reason. Perhaps they wished to rest for awhile, they were excited by the conquest of Jerusalem, and their decision to rest here was to lead to grim and fateful consequences. It became the front line, with the Turks out of sight just over the hills. The line divided this village so that some of the houses on the slope are in no-man's-land. The inhabitants are poor shepherds used to roaming the area at will and a certain enterprising officer has given them a sort of permission which entitles them to move freely between the hills and the armies. Based in this village is an Irish platoon, jovial fellows commanded merely by a sergeant-major from Ulster. They dug trenches and set up machine-gun and rifle emplacements and they breathe the mist of the winter floating from the sea to the desert and recall their Ulster and from time to time make bleating noises at the goats or call to one of the shepherds in the valley to check his "license," but since they don't speak Arabic and have no interpreters, they have no real contact with the inhabitants who look like black shapes moving around, so it is amazing that they observed him in the dim light of dawn and that they arrested him, and strange that, having arrested him, they would go on holding him, but now, on second thought, it seems to me that he may have *wanted* to be caught, it may be he did everything only in order to be caught and tried and thus have the opportunity to speak out...

– Thirty-one years old, sir, lean and dark-haired and of average height and, though he's only some ten years older than me, he looks like my grandfather, his face is so wrinkled. As if the traces of perverted thoughts and cunning have burst out of his skull and spread over his face. Thirty-one years old, but he looks fifty or sixty, old and intense in his movements and behaviour. When he was caught on that misty dawn wrapped in a broad black cloak, he was dragging three black goats as a symbol of a flock he never had, climbed straight up to the command-post, waking the Irish sergeant-major and his men.

– Correct, sir, so in the mist of the last hours of night, they demanded to see his "license" and because he didn't have it, they decided to hold him until morning when they could examine him properly. But before long he tried to escape under cover of the last vestiges of darkness and they caught him and put him in a small room along with his goats. For a whole day he sat with them as the rain turned to the first snow-flakes, refusing to eat, sullen and angry and cursing in Arabic, waiting for them to get sick of him and let him go and he had some basis for this hope because he sat hunched in his corner, listening to their conversation and understanding every word but without opening his mouth. They wanted to get rid of him because the snow and the storm kept them from taking him to Headquarters in Ramallah but the Irish sergeant-major was determined to hold him until the military police arrived to question him.

– Indeed, sir, I too was curious. Two weeks ago when we went through the whole episode of the arrest with Sergeant-Major Maclean with a view to promotion and mention in dispatches, I again inquired what aroused his suspicion and he replied simply that the goats didn't like the prisoner. Because of their anxiety and nervousness he knew this wasn't a shepherd at all but something else. Ha-ha. Intuition indeed. Well, in the morning a deputation arrives from Jerusalem, and trudging through the mud come two military policemen and an interpreter, a certain Roger Owen, a graduate of Oxford, one of those orientalists our universities train, experts in the nuances of the Koran but completely tongue-tied when they have to ask for a cup of coffee in Arabic because their professors who themselves have never been further east than Madgalen Bridge teach them Arabic as if there were no Arabs in the world, in the same way that their colleagues teach Latin and Sanskrit, and he is irritable and angry after the uncomfortable journey on a cold night, resenting all this trouble on account of a crazy shepherd, now sitting in the corner wrapped in his cloak, head down.

– At once, sir. He sits there hunched in the corner while the little Irishman apologizes to them nervously and the interpreter mumbles away in his faltering Oxford Arabic and the other answers briefly and unwillingly and the military policemen make notes, a confused story about straying goats, about traces that the rain washed away, about a village behind the enemy lines, all of them angry at the stubborn Ulsterman who caused so much commotion over nothing and the interpreter already turning to go but the bowed head of the shepherd and his soft voice suddenly jolting his memory. He has described to us a thousand times already his feelings at the moment his memory was ignited and on his behalf too I would like to forward a recommendation for promotion or mention in dispatches; as you see, sir, this episode has already advanced the careers of several people. At all events, he asked them to bring another light and they ordered the Arab to stand and stripped off his head-dress and waved the lantern aloft and he looked him straight in the eye and ordered him to take off the cloak and he refused and struggled but the soldiers pulled it off and were amazed to see before them a man in a black suit and striped tie with a book and papers stuffed into the pocket of his jacket and the interpreter recognized him with a hoot of laughter and called him by name. Mister Mani, is it you?

– Mani, sir, is his name.

– Yosef Mani, it sounds a little like money but it doesn't mean that and it sounds a little like maniac but it doesn't mean that either.

– It has no meaning at all as far as I am aware, just a common Jewish name in the Orient, since the shepherd is neither a shepherd nor an Arab but simply a Jew who suddenly changes his tune and replies in fluent English with a genuine Inverness accent, but all this was not a game. He greets his fellow interpreter warmly and draws him aside as if to address him in confidence, he himself being an interpreter in the service of His Majesty.

– Yes, sir, an authentic Scottish accent. You'll hear it tomorrow when he stands before you and answers the questions of identification and this accent he acquired in his youth at the school of Saint Joseph's Monastery in Jerusalem, where, at the end of the last century, a Scottish priest implanted it in him so deeply that he has never been able to get rid of it. His father and mother are British citizens, sir, even though he's never set foot in England. This is why the prosecution will be obliged to demand his execution as a citizen who betrayed his homeland and this is why I have come to talk with you, colonel, before the trial begins tomorrow.

– Of course, sir, please excuse me.

– Of course, I realise I'm making the mistake of putting last things first, I was afraid I might tire you with the small details that intrigue me.

– Very interesting, sir, also strange and ironical. Anyway there he stands in the room stripped of his cloak, in his crumpled black suit, papers sticking out of his pocket, inventing some silly story about a mistress behind the enemy lines, a story told hesitantly and reluctantly, but our stubborn Irishman is excited to find his suspicions justified and he pulls out the papers and sees maps of Palestine and things that look like manifestos written in Arabic and, though he doesn't understand what's written there, he knows for a fact that these aren't love-letters a man takes to his mistress. So he goes and finds a rope and binds "his" prisoner and, having no confidence either in interpreters or policemen, he decides to escort him in person, leaving the command post with two of his soldiers. He goes down with the whole party to headquarters in Ramallah, whence they are immediately transported to Jerusalem. And I well remember the night they brought him in, a cold winter night with the light snow already melting in the alley and a few of us officers sitting in the Club, warming ourselves by the stove, when the Military Police duty officer comes in and announces that a spy has been discovered near Ramallah and is now under preliminary interrogation. A great commotion arose. It has always been my experience, sir, that we British are particularly scandalized by spies, no doubt because of the principles of good faith and trust ingrained in us from childhood.

– Yes indeed, sir, I suppose there isn't a single one of us who doesn't dream of catching a spy. And here stands this officer in the middle of the room, rain dripping from his cape, surrounded by all of us, imparting the information carefully, piece by piece. I remember pressing toward him and asking him, But who is this? An Arab surely, for I had no doubt that only Arabs could be capable of spying against the United Kingdom but he smiles at me and says, Not at all, one of our own people. You can imagine, sir, the sensational effect of these words and he looks straight into my eyes, unable to disguise his satisfaction as he corrects himself; one of our people, that is to say one of the Jews who's joined our service. Naturally he knows what I am and he smiles at me, taunting, half seriously and half in jest and I remember, sir, if I may be allowed to describe my own feelings, that at that moment I was dreadfully afraid. It was not the hint of antisemitism that alarmed me, this is something I consider harmless and learned to disregard, but the strange combination of circumstances: a Jewish spy here in Jerusalem, Major Clark leaving tomorrow night and this is my great opportunity to serve as prosecutor in an important trial, and maybe just because of my Jewishness, out of misplaced delicacy, they will disqualify me...

    — Precisely, sir...

    — Precisely, sir...

    — To spare my feelings...

    — Indeed, sir, and you are well aware of what our department deals with. Cases of absence without leave, disorderly conduct, drunkenness, disobedience, offences meriting thirty or sixty days detention and fines of one guinea and here is an investigation in depth, a trial possibly leading to the gallows. In my agitation, I left the Club and went directly to the divisional detention centre near Jaffa Gate where I supposed he was held. I was still unaware of his name and identity, but I knew for sure that I must not be removed from the case, so I stood for a while in the cold of the night looking up at the place called David's Tower, a kind of miniature Tower of London. Maybe I'm wrong, having been deep in thought at the time, but I believe I saw beside me in the empty street and then disappearing into the alley a Jew dressed in black, watching me. Suddenly I knew that he was somehow connected with the spy who had been caught and that he wanted to see what had become of him, that the rumour had reached that other Jerusalem and that was the first messenger to discover his whereabouts. They chose the most secretive, most persistent and most metaphysical of creatures, the black-clad Jew. Only later did I realize that the messengers and those who send them are one and the same...

    — Forgive me, sir, I am anticipating events, my tongue is running ahead of me, sorry.

    — The 28th of February, sir, and the next day a tense silence prevailed in our department. We all knew of the police interrogation in

David's Tower and from the General's office men were being sent to look for Major Clark who had already been absent several days with his packing and his presents, buying oriental jewelry, silk shawls and small rugs for the entire British aristocracy awaiting him impatiently and angrily at Blenheim Palace. Now a spy has fallen into his lap, and he's afraid they'll order him to stay and take care of the investigation while the forces of nature are taking their course in England and the British Army for all its might is powerless to arrest this process. So all day he runs from the tailor to the silversmith to the interrogation cell and from there to the brigadier's office and he arrives in a fever of agitation in the Provost's Department to glance at the law manuals but doesn't say a word to me, doesn't say take over, although he knows how eager I am and I observe how he's never without a bottle and the look in his eyes is that of a sad and hunted dog.

– He doesn't appear, sir, to favour any particular brand, he drinks whatever is available. At night an order is delivered by the staff sergeant to the four officers of the Provost's Department to stay behind in the office and Major Clark arrives, no longer appearing the worse for drink and the hunted look gone from his eyes, in full dress, his insignia polished and medals gleaming. We can tell he's convinced the Brigadier has obtained for him a permission to sail for his wedding and we all know he'll never return to the Middle East because his future father-in-law has already obtained a post for him on the General Staff, so that, once caught, the bird will never again flee the nest. He calls the four of us together, the Manual of Punishments and the secret file open before him, and talks to all of us but looks only at me, knowing my feelings and knowing that for the past twenty-four hours I've been preparing myself to take over the case. He recounts the events of his day, his confrontation with the Brigadier and finally he says to me: You, Jewboy, will take the case into your hands and have only one loyalty and conduct a thorough investigation and prepare a full indictment and you'll demand the death sentence because the law requires it and the entire Division insists on it, since because of this man men and material have been lost in Transjordan, and you'll give them this penalty quickly and efficiently, since no one will refuse a Jew who demands another Jew's death. I'm sure you appreciate the delicious irony of the situation...

– Yes, that was his expression, sir, delicious irony.

– Such is his manner, sir, but I have never taken offence at his words. For a whole year I have accompanied Major Clark, first in France and then in the Middle East and there is no man more decent and agreeable but his tongue is instinctive and sharp as a razor and he is a natural antisemite. For him antisemitism is a habit of mind, like his attitude toward women and horses, a set of inherited prejudices quite impervious to the facts but he means no personal harm to anyone, at heart he's always a perfect gentleman. So we finish our drinks and say our goodbyes and the file is clasped firmly in my hands, like a miraculous book that one is destined to read and to write at the same time and my thoughts fly to the prisoner I can now call mine! I know he's still being defiant and hasn't admitted anything and as soon as Major Clark leaves the room, I go out into the night, almost midnight by now, alone and wet to the tower, the melting snow crackling beneath my feet and a gigantic moon falling onto the wall, as if someone were pulling it with a thread and I cross the Old City from Shechem Gate to Jaffa Gate in utter silence and suddenly I hear bleating and bells ringing and a flock of goats without a shepherd suddenly emerges from one of the openings, pushing and brooding and scared, like a flock of demons seeking Satan, it sweeps down the alley and disappears as if under the paving stones. The Church bells ring out clearly and I smell the bread baking and tremble in my eagerness for this investigation and even at this hour of night I'm aware of the importance of the mission that has descended on my shoulders, a mission that has accompanied me day and night these past three weeks. This is why I'm here, boring you Colonel, and I still can't explain it fully because the story is a barrier between us and I wonder if I haven't already exhausted your patience entirely...

– Thank you, sir, I am obliged to you. I climbed the steps to the tower of Jerusalem, the one the Jews call David's Tower and the Arabs El Kalaa, and I woke the sergeants and the duty officer and showed them the file and the orders and presented the document giving me authority to conduct the investigation which henceforward was to be in my hands and I gave the order that no one was to approach the prisoner except through me and they took me down to the interrogation cells and all around were traces of four hundred years of Turkish rule and there in the cellar in a kind of round well surrounded by a railing was our prisoner, the accused, like a tiger or a dangerous snake, although he really looked more like an eagle in his black suit, sitting on a cot, reading a book by the light of a candle, his face lean and hard and wrinkled, reading as if he didn't want to, holding the book at arm's length. It was a Christian Bible given to him by the officer of the watch, an elderly Evangelical who sees him as already doomed and pities his soul. He was immersed in his stubborn and resentful reading and didn't feel that someone was standing and watching him and suddenly, with a theatrical gesture, he drops the book, blows out the candle and falls on the bed curling up like a foetus and closing his eyes. I thought of leaving and returning in the morning, studying the file and preparing my line of attack but a prophetic spirit descended on me, telling me that I would extract a confession only if I made my interrogation this very night, that the longer I delayed the more tightly he would draw the strings of his lie around himself. I asked them to put a room at my disposal and to make me a pot of coffee and I sat and read the file from beginning to end and thought my thoughts and at two o'clock in the morning I went down to him. It was very cold in the cellar and I touched him and pulled the blanket off him and he opened his eyes and they were young and big and pure, as if whoever had given him his other features had not given him those eyes and I began speaking to him quickly and softly, breaking into his dreams, casting a delicate net to draw up the fish of truth from the ugly morass of lies. He was confused and tired and depressed but made every effort to resist, replying in that pure Scottish accent we shall hear tomorrow in the courthouse, prattling on about a mistress in some village, as if behind the line in the hills of Samaria there are no impoverished communities of ignorant and fanatical Moslem peasants and their veiled and barefoot women; listening to him, you'd have thought it was the Loire flowing through French hamlets, the kind Maupassant describes with pretty girls in embroidered aprons waiting for love and he persists in talking of his mistress, although I understand now that he's not a man of women but of words and as soon as he's invented his beloved he has already forgotten her and if I were to ask him the colour of her eyes he'd be surprised at the idea that there is a colour to her eyes he's supposed to remember. I reject and dismiss this fabrication with all my might but he persists for a long time, claiming that there is a woman he has visited in secret for a whole month, continuing to cherish this foolish and strange lie he himself doesn't believe, as if the lie has forced itself upon him and he is the servant of the lie and not its master until at last he falls silent and shivers from cold, returning his beloved to his brain and erasing her there and then I brought him up to the office and sat him down beside the stove and gave him some hot tea and introduced myself and asked if he needed anything so that he would trust me and he told me of his little son he hadn't seen for three days and whom he sorely missed. I woke three soldiers of the guard and at three in the morning we went to the new settlement of Kerem Abraham outside the walls and knocked on the door. It was opened by a middle-aged woman in a clean gown, smiling pleasantly as if she had been expecting us and when she saw him in handcuffs she wept and he touched her lightly, muttered something in Hebrew, ran upstairs and returned with a little boy of about four in his arms, a pretty, fresh-faced lad with golden hair, who looked sickly and perhaps a little feeble. You will have the opportunity to judge for yourself tomorrow in court, sir, as I have given permission for him to attend the opening session, knowing that if the accused had a defending counsel he would no doubt use the child to rouse sympathy...

– At once, sir.

– Yes, sir.

– No, sir.

– Correct, sir.

– To the point, Colonel, because while he was embracing his son I ordered the soldiers to search the house, turn out the drawers and collect every scrap of paper and we sat silently in the kitchen, he and I and the child in his arms, until the men finished and brought me the papers they found. I told them to wait in the other room and the woman made them tea and they too were silent and the night was turning grey and a few lights came on in the settlement because the rumour had spread that the guard had come but no one came. The silence was deep, the stillness before dawn. The woman put the child back to bed and went to bed herself and the two of us sat alone and I said to him: Tell the story from the beginning or if you like from before the beginning. Who are you? We were both exhausted and weak, only the truth could make us awake, he talked and I listened and thus the breach was opened from which I extracted his story, the essential confession; everything that followed was simply the clarification of minor points.

– Thank you, sir, gladly.

– Indeed. He himself is a native of Jerusalem and so was his father and his grandfather came from Greece as a boy and there aren't many Jews like that for it's not as natural for Jews to be born in Palestine as it is for Englishmen to be born in England or Welshmen in Wales or Scots in Scotland and most of them you see about came here only recently while those who were born here tend to leave the country. Only a few are permanent residents and they are more highly esteemed in the eyes of others than in their own eyes and, while the admiration of others does encourage them a little, but only a little...

– Correct, sir, one would indeed suppose that Jerusalem for the Jews is like London for the British, and yet you find more Jews in the East End of London than in the whole of this country. London is too heavy for the

Englishman to carry in his heart and is getting heavier all the time. But the Jew can carry Jerusalem in his heart and wander around the world, and the more who carry it, the lighter it grows.

– In a certain sense, in a certain sense. This applies to me too, sir, I don't deny it. But my home is in Manchester and I long for London and a small corner of my heart is reserved for this city, as a concept only and not as reality, and though I have roamed around here for a few months, the concept doesn't have anything to do with reality, and that's marvellous.

– Thank you, sir. So who is he and who were his ancestors and how shall we sketch his biography? From Thessaloniki, which was then in Turkey, came his grandmother and grandfather, childless, in the middle of the last century, believing that in Jerusalem their prayers would be answered. Thus the father of the accused was born. An only child, his father died even before he was born and they called him Moses Hayyim and he was brought up by his mother who doted on him and because he was a pretty and charming youth the British Consul in Jerusalem, John Stone, who lived in their neighbourhood, decided to adopt him, and because the Consul was devoted to the Bible he saw the boy as a little reincarnation of the first Moses and resolved to make Moses a British citizen. As a present for his thirteenth birthday he gave the boy personal British citizenship. The passport of the accused's father has come into our possession and is included here in the file before you, Colonel, and a remarkable document it is, written in an old-fashioned and elaborate hand of yore. The picture shows a charming youth with clear and trusting eyes. The passport has a serial number and a telegram has already been dispatched to London to discover where it was issued and to which category it belongs, for it is highly unconventional for British consuls on their own authority to confer British citizenship on children simply because they are charming and fair of face. Anyway the boy was proud of his citizenship and would flourish his passport everywhere wrapped in coloured paper and amid the squalor and poverty of Jerusalem he would recite the poems of Byron and Shelley and retell the Canterbury Tales, since at his mother's insistence he attended the Mission School to learn English. When he finished school they sent him to study medicine at the American University in Beirut but he stayed there only a year because he missed his mother and his home in Jerusalem. They persuaded him to return, but his progress was slow owing to his tendency to come back to Jerusalem every few months. He took his mother with him to Beirut and continued his studies but reluctantly and only out of loyalty to his patron the Consul. So it went until he qualified as a doctor at the age of twenty-seven and they decided it was time he should be married, although he was a confirmed bachelor. But the Consul insisted that a British wife must be found to reinforce his Britishness. A woman was accordingly discovered, an orphan like himself, the daughter of a British Jew who joined Napoleon's army at the end of the eighteenth century. The Turks captured him, and the French forgot to ransom him and take him back so he stayed in Thessaloniki until he ransomed himself. They were married in 1880 and had a daughter who died and another daugher who died and then a son who died, because their blood was incompatible, and this Mani of ours was born in 1887 and he too wanted to die, but this was denied him and they fought for his life day and night and forced him to live and two years later his sister was born and she also lived. Out of the experience the doctor acquired in the struggles of childbirth he got the idea of opening a small maternity clinic. So he bought a house in Kerem Abraham in the early nineties when many Jews were moving outside the walls of the Old City and he found a skilled Swedish midwife, a nun from Malmö who came to the Holy Land on a pilgrimage and, failing to find God, abandoned her vocation and turned her talents to midwifery and he installed a few beds and imported the most modern equipment available from France and put a big mirror in the delivery room so the mother might see the birth for herself and invited the women of Jerusalem to come for their confinements. His first patients were women of dubious character, prostitutes, girls in trouble, fallen nuns and pilgrims. The Swedish midwife nursed them all with skill and determination and they suffered the minimum of pain, as if she absorbed part of their pain in her own flesh. The clinic's fame spread and respectable women began to come and soon his father became a public figure in Jerusalem, a man of charm and enthusiasm, trusted by women and accepted in society, a popular guest and host. At the first Zionist Congresses he became a fervent Zionist, an admirer of Doctor Herzl and an energetic campaigner on his behalf, and in the maternity clinic the loyal Swede did most of the work and he would arrive when the pains of labor were almost over to give the distraught father an encouraging pat on the shoulder and exchange pleasantries with the mother, cutting the cord and removing the placenta and advising in the choice of a name. His mother was at his side and he respected her more and more and his wife stood to the side. Mani and his little sister played hide-and-seek among the beds. At the end of the summer of 1899 the father went to Europe and brought a group of young Jews from Eastern Europe to see Jerusalem and his clinic and Mani remembers them well although they spoke in a language he didn't understand. Later his father accompanied them to the north and thence to Beirut and didn't come back. Several weeks later, they found out that he had been killed there in a terrible railway accident, at the age of forty-eight, and by the time they identified him and brought his body to be buried in Jerusalem it was autumn.

– Yes, sir, I gathered this information from the mouth of the accused himself but have verified it to the best of my ability from other sources, and I apologize for the length but I have a purpose... believe me, I have a purpose...

– Thank you, sir. Many years have passed since then, almost twenty years, sir. But I would suggest that time knows no barriers when we try to penetrate its innermost recesses to find the roots of treason and espionage, to nip them in the bud and stop the contagion. The family was stunned by the disaster that befell it and the Consul their benefactor had long since left and the clinic suffered a mortal blow. The Swedish midwife still tried to carry on the work, at first openly and later in secret since the authorities revoked the medical license after the doctor's death; there were debts; they were forced to sell most of the equipment and rent some of the rooms to pilgrims and gradually the place emptied out and the patients became fewer. At Christmastime Jerusalem was full of pilgrims coming to welcome the new century and the loyal Swede suddenly rediscovered her faith, left them and returned to her homeland. This was in December of 1899, our accused was now an orphan twelve years old. When his father had been alive he had possessed an independent mind; after his death this trait became even more marked. And if you will bear with me, sir, and observe this youth in your imagination for a moment, as I have tried to do, we see a thin, swarthy, bespectacled lad with his mother's dark features and a most melancholy temperament, a kind of visionary given to talking to himself. This was the end of December 1899, sir, and winter came at last to Jerusalem, with church bells ringing and great processions of Russian pilgrims in the street, all of them excited by the century that had passed and the new century beginning. He describes how one afternoon he went down to the basement of the empty clinic and found to his surprise a young woman on one of the beds writhing in the pains of childbirth, one of those Jewish adventurous immigrants who used to come from Europe to Palestine all by themselves to settle in one of the villages, out of ideology or just to escape from their parents' home. With her last remaining strength she came to Jerusalem after having been

given the address of the clinic. She didn't know it was closed so she came
and lay down alone on one of the beds. It was afternoon and his mother
and sister and grandmother had gone out to watch the processions, so he
was alone with the woman, whose time had come. She began to call him,
crying and whimpering, tearing the blanket off and the boy stood next to
her and watched her in the big mirror before him. She called him in the
cold room asking for help and he stands petrified at first, then tries to
take off her clothes and can't and she pleads with him and he goes and
gets a knife and rips her clothes, watches how her womb swells and
contracts, how she moans and her blood flows and the skull appears
slowly amid the terrible pain and weeping and he stands helpless in the
cold room and she makes him swear he won't leave her or put down the
knife before cutting the umbilical cord and he doesn't close his eyes but
looks sometimes at her and sometimes at the mirror and the birth takes
place on both sides of him and so, he says, in those moments in the cold
room with the knife in his hand his political consciousness was firmly
determined...

— Yes, political consciousness, sir, these are his words, his way of
thought, determined with an intensity beyond measure, more powerful
than anything else in the world, arranging and ordering the world, so this
thin, bespectacled boy of twelve, at the cold grim hour of *la fin de siècle*,
turned into what he terms a political animal, a *homo politicus*. Maybe
this is where it was planted, the tiny and negligible seed of this strange
and repulsive act of treachery committed nineteen years later for which
you, sir, were brought here from Egypt and you'll sit on the Bench with
your colleagues and I'll conduct a rigorous prosecution before you, and
look, the sky is clearing, as I told you before Jerusalem isn't Glasgow and
even the heaviest rain has its limit and I only wonder, sir, if I haven't
exhausted you. My mother gave me good advice when she told me never
forget yourself, meaning I should never forget those who listen to my
flood of words, of the kind which this excellent whisky has set loose.

— Certainly, sir, there is a clear purpose.
— It will come together in the end, with God's help.
— I shall make every effort, Colonel, every effort.
— Thank you, sir, it is most generous of you. Now where were we, oh
yes, at the beginning of this century dawning in Jerusalem for our
accused. I beg your pardon?
— Baby? What baby?
— Oh, that baby... excuse me, what was the question?
— Oh, sir.

– Yes, sir.

– Ah, sir. I confess, of course, I was forgetting the baby. Well... as I explained the baby was born in the end but regrettably I did not dwell on this aspect of the story, which I saw rather in the nature of a metaphor. I assume he cut the umbilical cord and set the baby free but did the baby live or not? We must hope for the best.

– Absolutely, sir. And so, the twentieth century dawns for us all, including the Mani family which is still stunned and confused by the disaster that has befallen it. The grandmother is extremely old, about eighty-five, but still youthful in spirit and greatly respected by her grandson. The mother is melancholy and aging fast, the sister no more than ten years old but already knowing she's destined for an early marriage and they eke out a precarious living by renting out rooms in the abandoned clinic. Our young Yosef Mani is already assuming a considerable degree of freedom and as a political animal by his own definition, sir, as a *homo politicus*, he determines his goals accordingly, choosing the groups and the means that will assist him. His first thought was to change the direction of his education and to make learning languages his priority, for he still remembered the pain of ignorance he felt when his father would chat with his young European guests, so he decided to study languages like an army storming across a river. With scant regard for the authority of his mother and grandmother, he secretly absented himself from the Hebrew school in which his father had enrolled him and wandered around Jerusalem until he came across *Terra Sancta*, the Biblical seminary run by the Scottish Mission. It was not the teaching of the Christian Scriptures that interested the boy but the English language he began to acquire with thoroughness and with an Inverness accent. But English was only the beginning and in the afternoons he would go down to the village of Silwan where an old Arab lived, a sheikh, a friend of his father's, who would chat with him in Arabic and correct his grammar. At night he sometimes visited an Algerian family to mind the children, listen to French being spoken and accustom himself to its accents. So he already reveals his talent for passing easily from one community to another even before he has had his Bar Mitzvah, the initiation ceremony for Jews, like confirmation for Christians or *tuhur* for Arabs. It consists mainly of reading extracts in Hebrew from the Old Testament in the synagogue and the stress and intonation are very difficult, believe me, Colonel, I have experienced it in my own throat in the main synagogue of Manchester. When the time did come for his Bar Mitzvah he relented and went to one of the small religious sects in Jerusalem, whose origins are in the distant mountains of Hungary. Jews in black with fur hats and sidelocks which you may have chanced to see in the East End of London, Colonel.

— Yes, precisely there... there you will see them dressed in these clothes and he came to them and said, I am an orphan, for that, sir, is how he used to introduce himself everywhere, as if he had no mother either, Let me be Bar Mitzvah here. And they taught him the chant and the cantillations and prepared delicacies and drinks and thus began the strange links with them that have continued to this day. I questioned these people thoroughly to clarify the nature of these links, for he does not belong to them and could not belong to them even if he wanted to, being an Oriental, a free-thinker and even a Zionist and he always will be a stranger in their midst. In spite of this, links of a kind were forged based on the principle of mutual benefit and reserved friendship, for even the most enclosed and esoteric sect needs some special and invisible outlet to the world, a person appointed to fetch and carry; and it is better that this person not be one of their own, lest they open an unstoppable breach. Better by far is a rare bird, and a dubious orphan whom they can get rid of at any moment and who performs tasks like writing letters in English to wealthy Americans, negotiating with Arabs for apartments and summarizing the newspapers they are forbidden to read, all this in exchange for money or the money's worth. They expect no religious observance of him, they don't even make him wear a hat and, though he's only a boy, he goes to visit the most venerable of them bare-headed and speaks to them with respect but as an equal. It's not that he sees himself as an unbeliever since he is in the habit of visiting the synagogue, not theirs but that of the Sephardi, his own people, where he is used to the chanting and the prayers are livelier, and there he prays with the red *tarboosh* on his head but absolutely refuses to be called a religious person, for he needs infinite freedom.

— In God Himself, so I understand, sir, but he doesn't admit this explicitly. In any case he refused to answer the question although I put it to him with the greatest of tact. The question was too intimate, he claimed.

— No, sir, the Jew is not compelled to believe in God although it is desirable because his choice of beliefs is limited.

— With your permission, Colonel, I'd rather not go into the question of this identity, it's like quicksand in which Jews themselves are frequently trapped however confidently they approach it. I fear I have already tired you beyond the limits of endurance.

– I am most keen, sir.

– With great pleasure, sir, and I too have a version of my own and hypotheses of my own. But meanwhile let us follow the course of the story as the light in Jerusalem grows stronger and the skies turn blue in the exquisite winter light. I should like to say a word about this sect, since from the day he was arrested, they have been quietly following him and everyone concerned with him, like a flock of birds, like the ravens in the tower of London, which all look alike although each one has a function and a place and a clear destiny and that very first night, that snowy night when I hurried to David's Tower, I saw the first of these black birds perched on the steps and from the way he was perched I knew he had been sent and had even been given the umbrella which is passed from one to another like a rifle in an honor guard. Since that night one of them always accompanies me, in the alley where I walk, in the shop I enter, on the steps I climb but when I approach them they avoid me and all they want is to read in my face if the prisoner has said anything that could incriminate them.

– Yes, sir, a thorough and vigorous investigation has been made with the assistance of an interpreter who speaks their language.

– Yiddish, sir. It seems they had no idea of his activities and are indeed incapable of comprehending his conspiracies. Britain, Turkey – to them these are meaningless concepts, yet they fear lest something of his guilt may be attached to them and they cannot withdraw their support from him, it may be that the chanting of the Bar Mitzvah ceremony still binds them to him but it is his story which concerns us, this adolescent boy, the dark-haired, bespectacled and ugly youth growing up independent and a little remote, this *homo politicus* who roams among the different sects and identities of Jerusalem and develops his political awareness, intent on learning languages as if preparing a bunch of keys to a house of many doors and still a bachelor, the gaping womb he saw and the scream he heard that day still troubling his spirit. In 1905, when he is eighteen years old, his grandmother passes away at a ripe old age, the only one he really loved. His younger sister, who since the age of ten has imagined herself a bride, finally marries the son of a wealthy Moroccan Jew who came here to buy a burial plot and died suddenly and the son took her and her mother to Marseilles and invited the brother, who by now was working as a clerk in the courthouse, to join them. But he refused absolutely, as he was still waiting for news from the North which came in 1907 with the revolt of the Young Turks and the proclamation of Turkey as a multinational and multiethnic State. The proclamation stirred his heart and he resolved to study law and enter the Turkish Parliament. So he rented out the two rooms he lived in in that clinic which had become a pilgrims' hotel, packed his own clothes in a suitcase, gave his father's old clothes to charity except for a large and warm overcoat his father left him and went to the printing-house and printed himself a journalist's visiting card, even though he did not yet have a newspaper to write for.

At the end of the summer of 1907 he takes the train to Jaffa and, while this is the first time in his life that he has left Jerusalem, he does not raise his head to look at the hills and mountains that pass beside him but sits with head bowed, the suitcase between his legs and his father's coat next to him, wanting to leave Jerusalem and not to pass through Palestine, refusing to acknowledge the route by which his father abandoned him and his family. From the Jaffa railway station he took a cab directly to the port and boarded a ship for Constantinople. After three days the ship anchored in Beirut which as I am sure you are aware, sir, is a pleasant city, developing fast and renowned for its gaming houses. All the passengers hurried ashore except him, so he says, for he decided not to move, and he stayed on the ship pacing the deck and looking at the bright lights of the city where his father had perished, hearing the sounds of laughter and song rising from the shore and toward midnight the first of the passengers return to their cabins but he is still wandering on the deck seeing how the lights go dim and the sounds of laughter and song die away and a late moon rises and then he hears a kind of wailing, that's what he says, sir, wailing, as if a great and powerful baby is crying in the city, so he says, and his hands tremble and he packs his suitcase and goes down to the shore passing through the checkpoint and walking down the little streets meeting groups of revellers returning homeward, passengers returning to their ships, and still he hears this wailing as he enters the twisting alleys leading to the old city, reaching the railway station, crossing the tracks hurriedly, plunging into an alley that climbs up and up and there he sees a hotel, a little hostelry for wayfarers seeking a room for the night and he hears voices and sees lamp light flickering in the lobby and asks if there is a room for him and they tell him yes and he goes up and puts his suitcase on the bed and goes out to the balcony and looks down at the railway station below him bathed in moonlight, the railway lines extending north and returning south and he opens the creaking closet and hangs up his father's old overcoat and it remains hanging there for seven years.

– Yes, sir, for seven whole years he stayed in this city until the outbreak of the war, in the same hotel and in the very same room and if the war hadn't broken out I doubt he would ever have been released from it. As if this railway station to which his father came held him in a steel vise. I've often wondered if the treachery and espionage which emerged ten years later were not born there in Beirut but all my efforts to discover if the Turks recruited him then and planted him as a mole have come to naught.

– Yes, Colonel, a rigorous interrogation, day and night, back and forth. I have left no stone unturned. If there were Turks concealed there I would have found them in the end. But no, sir, no Turks, nothing, not even Germans. All his activity springs from within himself, from the agitation of his mind and the confusion of his spirit. This has become clear to me the closer I've come to the end of the story and if we cherished hopes of drawing a lesson from this case, I mean ways of catching potential spies and traitors in the future, in point of fact we have learned nothing, since every man is interpreted through a single and unique story and so it is with this Mani, living by himself in Beirut for seven years, for the sake of study, he claims, who does indeed enroll at the American University where his British passport is respected. Money from the rent of the house in Jerusalem covers the cost of the room in the hotel and breakfast. For the rest of his needs he supports himself by working as a guide and occasional interpreter and hotel agent, since in these years many people pass through the city and foreigners are drawn to this burgeoning metropolis, this gateway to the Orient, Germans, Frenchmen, Britons, as well as Americans, Russians and Austrians, parties of pilgrims, archaeologists, missionaries and journalists exploring the East. Naturally Jews too, of various denominations. There is even a Zionist labour union office to cater to the needs of the young people arriving from Eastern Europe and the steppes of Russia. Destitute youths with no entry permit to the Ottoman Empire in general and Palestine in particular, they have no money for the boat trip and wander about the continent trying to steal into this land. He picks them out at the railway station where he loiters in the evening, seeing them alight from carriages, pale-faced young Russian men and women, still fleeing from the unsuccessful revolution of 1905, dirty, standing there with their bundles tied with string and toes peeping out of their sandals and they come on this dark, bespectacled Palestinian Jew, wearing a little tie, who makes them feel at home by addressing them first in Hebrew and then in French or Russian of which he also knows a few words and he directs them to cheap hostels in the hills from which he receives small agency fees, helping them to find cheap soup-kitchens, telling them about Palestine and showing them the way to the Zionist office but beyond this he has no social contact with them. At this stage he is still ascetic where women are concerned, as if haunted by the childhood memory of that winter day in the empty house when the womb opened up before him like a crater and rather than giving birth it seemed intent on swallowing him utterly. Furthermore, as a student...

– Yes, sir, a dedicated student who attends lectures at the American University every morning and throughout these seven years never ceases to see himself as a student but a leisurely student, one who enjoys special status because of his fluent English. He prolongs his studies and postpones his examinations from year to year and performs his obligations piecemeal, spending much of his time reading newspapers and magazines in the library. Since the age of ten he has regarded education and teachers as tools to be manipulated for his own purposes, an attitude which is reinforced in this cosmopolitan university, with its mixture of students from all classes and communities. He plans to graduate in political science and to this end he studies the laws of the Madjlis and the American constitution and the philosophy of the Koran but also attends courses in English poetry and the archeology of the Sumerians and the art of Byzantine icon-painting, organizing his curriculum calmly and thoroughly and if there is a course he has not fully understood he waits two or three years until it comes round again and attends the lectures a second time. In the afternoons he sets about deepening his practical education, going to meetings of Druses and Shiites and Christian social democrats, Maronites and Catholics and ordained priests, drifting from identity to identity, all of them mingling, to pass from one to another all he has to do is walk along the main avenue of Beirut and of course he does not forget the Sephardi synagogue and he attends it every Friday evening, even though he is not too meticulous about religious observance, he eats forbidden food but takes care not to light a fire on the Sabbath. He still sees his destiny in politics and treats it reverently as a calling with a deep inner logic, as cause and effect for everything, while the storm-clouds gathering over Europe and the Balkans stir powerful echoes in his mind and the approaching war disturbs him deeply.

His mother and sister beg him to join them in Marseilles but he refuses and meanwhile the Turkish Sultan hardens his position, Germans appear everywhere, aliens are deported and he is afraid to leave the Ottoman Empire lest he not be allowed to return and his British passport becomes like a burning coal in his mouth. Moreover, at the beginning of winter 1914 he's got a baby on his hands, Colonel, a baby without a mother.

— A real baby, sir, whose mother died soon after birth in that same room where his father's grey overcoat still hung where he had left it seven years earlier. A baby that had to be registered in the police department which was already swarming with German officers. In the tense and hostile atmosphere of the approaching war some people were beginning to wonder about this lean and bespectacled Jewish student, this "journalist" without a newspaper, who used to bring the baby every morning to a Druse wet-nurse, a trader in the Beirut market, sitting next to her waiting until the child finished nursing and meanwhile reading an old newspaper he picked up from the pavement. But the newspaper was not so old that he didn't know that in Europe the fire had already broken out and it wouldn't be long before Turkey joined the fray. Just as abruptly as he had come to this city at the end of the summer of 1907, so he left it at the end of the summer of 1914, took down his father's overcoat, wrapped the baby in it and began moving south toward his native city which seemed wretched after Beirut, gloomy with dry, harsh light. He came to the house in Kerem Abraham and found it full of lodgers, for every lodger brought another with him and there was no space left for the landlord. He hurried to the Hassids, his adopted sect, and knocked on their door with the infant in his arms wrapped in his father's overcoat and told them find me a wife and they were not surprised at his sudden appearance because they're not surprised at anything, so that their minds can be free to think about heavenly doings, and they ask him, A wife to take care of your son or a wife to bear you children? And he replies let me think, and he stands and ponders and finally decides and says, You must find me a wife to take care of the child and me too. Though they have unattached women among them, young widows and divorcees who will marry whoever they are told, they don't bring him one of their own women, as if they are saying silently: keep away from us, for they find him a woman about forty years old — thirteen years older than he — a pleasant, childless woman who came from Mesopotamia at the end of the last century and has already been married twice, one husband died and the other left her and she has a little property and a shop to sell souvenirs to tourists in the Old City between the Jewish and Armenian quarters. She immediately adopted the baby with infinite affection and devotion and admitted the father into her house and he was swallowed up there among the pillows and quilts left by her two husbands and he hid his British passport under the mattress and fell asleep for the whole winter of 1915 while the great armies massed and spilled their blood in the rivers of Europe. His new wife prepares Iraqi dishes for him and brings him food in bed as if he has been gravely ill and needs to convalesce and the child too eats with him, surrounded by love, fattening on delicacies, but even there in the depths of his bed he still sees himself as a political person and at his urgent request she goes around Jerusalem collecting newspapers for him and among the pillows and quilts he reads everything that comes to hand, even newspapers that are out of date, reading of the dead as if they are alive, looking at the printed maps and diligently studying positions that have been captured in the meantime, lines that have been broken. Gradually he emerges from his hiding place into this Jerusalem drained dry by the war across the sea and again wearing the Turkish *tarboosh*, he drifts among identities, sitting in the morning in the Arab coffee-houses in the Old City, mediating in minor disputes, writing appeals to the courts on people's behalf, introducing himself as a lawyer although he brought no certificate with him from Beirut and at noon he returns home and sleeps for a long time and rises in the same clothes he wore in the morning but now with a white hat and goes to the New City to teach a pious German-Jewish professor Arabic grammar and for the afternoon prayer goes to the Sephardi synagogue and prays, then goes to those Hassids and translates letters from English and returns home bareheaded in the evening to eat supper with his son and his wife, and goes to the Zionist club where he sits in the back row next to a fat Turkish secret policeman, listening to the speeches and debates and from time to time rising and asking a question in the name of the old-time local population and at night he returns late, silencing in his own mind all the speakers he has heard and telling them what he thinks, and he doesn't yet think anything against Britain because it never entered his mind that Britons intended to come here and if treachery sneaked into his heart it was a hidden, barely visible seed, barren as gravel, a pip falling on dry ground and still seen as the residue of fruit and not as the progenitor of a new tree. So the long years passed and 1917 dawned and the Expeditionary Force arrived in Egypt and crossed the desert and Britain touched the fringes of Palestine and on the 9th of January as you know, sir, Rafa was taken.

– Major-General Philip Chetwood, sir, with mounted troops from Australia and New Zealand. It was a short and easy battle and when the news reached Jerusalem at the beginning of February there was tumult and his mind was stunned, by his own account he was nervous and agitated and I wonder what was the effect of this shock. Was this the jolt that moved the dry seed that looked dead in a dark, warm crack in the ground.

— Yes, sir, please forgive my eagerness to talk and my literary tongue, is it hidden here, the beginning of the treachery that was later to erupt in all its intensity, for how are we to understand this agitation on the part of a man who calls himself a political person, a *homo politicus* who stands fixed in Jerusalem with his face according to his testimony set to the north and blind to what's happening behind him, what does he expect? Isn't this the boy still waiting for his father to return home and now suddenly when Britain is touching the South, he is shaken as if his father has secretly circled Palestine and is coming back from the South.

— His father as a parable, sir, his father as a parable only...

— Forgive me, sir, I was attempting to draw an interpretation...

— As you wish, Colonel... certainly...

— Absolutely, sir, such a synthesis is precisely what I am striving for, begging your indulgence, sir.

— I shall indeed be brief, I assure you, sir, seeing that events themselves are now moving quickly as the armies rush toward confrontation and although in March we suffer an embarrassing setback at Gaza it is clear to all that this is by no means the end of the battle. In summer, news begins to trickle in, piecemeal and unclear. It isn't that the Turks don't want to repel the invader but they just don't know where he'll turn up, the "Bull" from England, our much-admired Sir Edmund who in the last days of summer advanced his foot soldiers and cavalry to the Holy Land. Now it's autumn, sir, the Holy Days of the Jews, and there's no difference between this season and summer except that a light westerly breeze is blowing and this is when they begin their year and they get up at night to sound a strange trumpet and he feels the currents of southern wind and one day he gets up and sets out taking his British passport from under the pillow and sewing it into his old overcoat, goes to Bethlehem and sees a world going about its business as usual, the Turks moving lazily and the Arabs dozing and only in the eyes of the Jews does he see a soft gleam and their heads are tilted slightly as if listening for the strange voices. On the second day of the festival a party of Jews goes to pray in Hebron and he goes down with them and then a Turkish army column heading towards Gaza blocks the road and he leaves the road and climbs aboard a cart descending into the Judean Desert, in late afternoon with the sun setting and a platoon of Turkish cavalry and infantry passes him with a cheerful Turkish song as if they were going home and an officer roughly orders them off the road and tells them not to move and he doesn't know that even as the last Turkish soldiers pass by him Turkish rule has been uprooted from the earth and has vanished like the wind, a rule that has lasted four hundred years and the only rule he has known since his birth. So they were left in this no-man's-land south of Hebron on the road to Beersheba and there was a camp of nomads there. They approached them and were received hospitably. This was the 31st of October and he did not know that Sir Edmund had already taken Beersheba that day and the night descended and they lit a fire to warm themselves and stayed there.

— Not gladly, sir, but impatiently, he wanted contact even though he didn't know what it meant and this contact wasn't long in coming and he knew that if he stayed here he wouldn't be able to return. Sure enough, the next morning they were surrounded by a platoon of soldiers led by Captain William Dagout of the Quartermaster's branch of Chetwood's 67th Cavalry Regiment. His testimony is included here in the file, sir, and he will be the first witness for the prosecution tomorrow. He is a brave officer and highly esteemed by Chetwood, an elderly Scot with pride and a fiery temper who refused at first to be questioned. In fact we had to place him under arrest for two days to draw the story out of him.

— Precisely, sir, this officer is seventy years old and his passion is horses, as if he himself were sired by a stallion and in the region of Edinburgh he breeds and trains racehorses and is renowned as a master in this field. The whole purpose of his life is to improve the breed, make them run faster and win races for him and so his whole life is spent searching for one horse, the unique horse that is worthy of him. Then the war broke out and he immediately joined the army, although because of his age he didn't have to enlist and he was immediately appointed officer of the 67th Cavalry Regiment and sent to France to inspect horses and stables and he sees the whole war as one gigantic steeplechase and he can't understand why the riders have to shoot one another. Then in Europe the horses fell and the riders died and tanks came to replace them, and he grew depressed and turned his sights eastward, being in the West, but his heart in the East; he joined Allenby's staff with the sole purpose of travelling overseas in the hope of finding the lost horse here, the finest Arab steed of all to ship back to Edinburgh, and impress all his friends. His only desire is to find this horse, as if this whole great war, the Archduke murdered in Serbia and the millions dying in Flanders, had no other purpose than to bring him to the deserts of Arabia in search of the lost horse. He goes from place to place and commandeers horses and camels for the regiment and before the conquest of Beersheba is completed, while smoke is rising from the burning buildings and the dead and wounded are carried from the battlefield, he dons his kilt and takes his acolytes and two interpreters and goes riding into the wastes of the Judaean Desert to seek out the horse that is his heart's desire.

– Thank you, sir, another small glass would be most agreeable. It's raining again and I'm sorry I'm wearying you so but our Dean at Cambridge taught us that perfection consists of details and I believe this applies to perfection not only in the aesthetic but also in the legal sense. Here every detail is important since this is the link that joins our accused to the British Army and were it not for the enthusiasm of Captain Dagout he would not have penetrated so easily to the very heart of our headquarters.

– Quite, sir, no proper check of his identity was made and to account for this we must understand Captain Dagout and his passion for horses. He rides from one camp to another and orders them to bring out the horses and stand them quietly in front of him and examines their teeth and legs and blows a whistle, a special high-pitched whistle he brought with him all the way from Scotland, a sound every horse in the world finds pleasant and responds with a special movement of the ears which only Dagout can interpret and then he waits for the horse to shed its droppings so he can sniff them and find out what the beast has been eating.

– Indeed, sir. I've seen it with my own eyes. There's no telling where expertise ends and madness begins. Then they bring him the owner of the horse so he can ask about its pedigree, and to assist him he has two interpreters roasted by the sun of Cairo and recruited from some of our colleges in Oxford, taught by professors of Eastern languages who themselves never travelled further east than Magdalen Bridge and they're so scared of him they forget even the little Arabic they know and when he asks the Bedouin a question the interpreters confer and leaf through a dictionary searching for a word which they can't always make out in English, and in a whisper they debate the final version, while the Bedouin waits there patiently and the grey-haired Captain gets red with anger and finally the wondrous word is cautiously uttered with a limping pronunciation born of their imagination and the face of the Bedouin turns white with fury, he spits on the ground, folds his tent, takes his horse and all his belongings and disappears over the horizon leaving nothing behind but a plume of dust and the embarrassed interpreters can't imagine how they went wrong.

— Of course, sir, this may be an exaggeration, a caricature, but its clear purpose is to account for the excitement that gripped our Captain that morning of November 1, when he encountered Mister Mani for the first time wearing a dark suit crumpled after a sleepless night, his face unshaven, watching our Captain as he paces around the horse, blows his whistle and waits for the droppings to fall and the anxious interpreters are conferring feverishly and the Bedouin are already gloomy because they know he intends to take their horses and he approaches quietly, staring intently at the soldiers and their weapons and uniforms and the harness of their horses, because until this moment he has only seen Britons in civilian clothes and suddenly he opens his mouth and in the pure Scottish accent of the Bible School of Terra Sancta he translates for the Captain with fluency and eagerness a veritable treatise on equine lore and it is no wonder that by evening Mister Mani was surrounded by riders and horses and treated with great respect by the Captain who saw his saviour descending from Heaven and they tied him to the horse that was commandeered because the horse and the interpreter had become inseparable in the mind of the Scotsman and in the evening in Beersheba they brought him to the former residence of the Turkish governor where the Union Jack was already flying and I myself, sir, if I may be permitted a personal note, was in the very same building with the administrative staff of the Brigade, gathering documents into boxes, identifying the dead and moving the wounded into the open so they could die quietly in the desert sunset, stabling the horses and then I saw him for the first time when he was untied from the horse, tired, pale, his face old, climbing the steps, treading on broken glass and empty Turkish ammunition-pouches still burning in the evening sun and he didn't look English or Jewish or Arab or Turkish or anything although he had more right to belong here than any of them and I wonder if he was already contemplating treachery.

— This was the 1st of November, sir, the eve of the 2nd of November 1917, sir.

— Yes, Colonel.

— Yes, Colonel.

— Of course, sir.

— Not yet, sir, and from that time on he became the chief interpreter of the Division and because he also spoke Turkish his services were indispensable but according to him the idea of treason had not yet sprouted in him and the cold exposed seed that rolled into the dark and dry crevice didn't yet know whence would come the moisture to awaken it.

– Yes, sir, that's how he explained himself on one of the nights of interrogation and for this reason he did not draw out the British passport sewn into his overcoat but said to himself bitterly: Behold, again strangers are coming to us to take the place of other strangers, but still he hesitated, watching from the side in silence to observe how things were going. Gaza falls into our hands and the breakthrough is successful and our raging bull Sir Edmund urges his army north along the coastal plain through the fields of Philistia and the sand dunes and the marshes, intent on reaching Jerusalem and taking it before Christmas to present it as a gift to Lloyd George and the British people, since in London there is longing for some victory as consolation for the endless slaughter in Flanders, since this is the fourth winter with nothing achieved. Was this the moisture that invigorated the treachery?

– No, sir, initially he was like a prisoner in the custody of the elderly Scot, who kept him hidden among his own staff and wandered with him between Beersheba and Gaza in quest of that horse he longed for. But news of him soon spread through the Intelligence and Military Administration departments and they wrested him forcibly from the Scot and set him to work for them and British interpreters followed him around to learn from him and be amazed by him, since he is an interpreter of remarkable accuracy and speed, as if the words don't have to enter his brain for him to translate them but while they're still in the air they change species, grammar and sound so that it seems to the one whose words are translated that a miracle has taken place and the unknown language is flowing from his own lips. The army streams like a mighty river up the coastal plain, picking off the Turkish positions that are weaker than the sand piled up around them and one after another the little villages surrender and officers of the Military Administration take him along to translate the decree of occupation to the locals, and he walks among us, a thin civilian, bespectacled, taciturn, eyes blazing, wrapped in his father's overcoat which is rapidly growing shabby, still bewildered by the sudden change, uprooted from his city and his family and unable to tell them where he is but meanwhile he is becoming acquainted with his homeland, tied to the horse because still liable to fall off, brought into small, remote Arab villages, clusters of cottages, groves and tents, standing there a diminutive civilian among the political officers with swaggersticks under their arms, facing an ignorant crowd of swarthy peasants in robes and Arab headdresses and translating the decree of

occupation and the curfew regulations of the new administration and
before the British officer has opened his mouth to make his statement, the
translation is already being delivered and this is not a translation but a
little independent sermon of his own, composed by himself and no one
knows what he's saying. He no longer looks like an interpreter but rather
like a stern commissar sprung up from the ground with his escort of
officers roaming the countryside to give tidings of the war and he sees
before him the faces of the Arabs brimming over with curiosity at the
spectacle of the Jewish youth in an old overcoat.

He comes surrounded by British officers. If the *mukhtar* asks a question
he answers him at once on his own and with absolute authority and the
officer asks what they said and he replies nothing important and the
officer says but tell them this and that and he says I've already said it
and then he dismisses them, signals to the officers accompanying him and
moves on.

   – Yes, sir, his style is so authoritative that sometimes it seems the
officers themselves are afraid of him and this continues until the 20th of
November when Allenby turns to the east and marches on Jerusalem and
then one night he goes into divisional headquarters and finds the
telegram from London, the Balfour Declaration which he reads with
astonishment.

   – So I understand, sir. It's a short document, like a personal letter
signed by Lord Balfour and I have included a copy in the file as an
aide-mémoire.

   – It comes as a considerable shock, sir, for he wasn't expecting such
news at such a time and it was three weeks since he left his home and
especially his son to whom he is deeply attached and here he is held
prisoner in the British war machine which is thrusting deep into the Holy
Land and suddenly there is a marvellous and generous declaration of
intent which he never expected and in fairness to him it should be said
that others didn't expect it either and he can't sleep and the return to
Jerusalem excites him and he wanders about at night among the horses
and the guns and the sentries and now there's rain and a cold wind and
the army is gradually climbing the hills of Judea and by now his father's
old overcoat is worn out and they give him a cape and big boots and so
he finds himself in the vanguard of the army, in a mixture of civilian and
military clothing, looking from forward positions through binoculars,
amazed that a month ago he left his city and crept away to the south and
now he's returning to it with a mighty imperial army to conquer it again.
On the 6th of December, Colonel, he is sent with the infantry to Nebi

Samuel where another fierce battle takes place and from there he sees Jerusalem, the city of his ancestors, which looks very small and stubborn and hostile and on December 9th, as you know, sir, Jerusalem was taken and two days later Sir Edmund entered on foot with his troops behind him and the church bells rang and the dignitaries greeted him with bread and salt and our accused at first also walked in the ranks of the conquerors, feeling alone and out of place among the bagpipes and the bush hats, looking with burning eyes at the crowd but near Jaffa Gate he veered off to the right and turned toward his home as if simply returning from a day's work, sank into the pillows and quilts, his son beside him in bed, and for a whole week he doesn't leave his house. He has no friends to tell his adventures to and even to his wife he says little, only staring out at the distant artillery barrage of Colonel Chetwood's force repelling the Turkish counter-attack and pushing the front line forward to Ramallah.

– Indeed, sir, a very vigorous counter-attack but I am sure the Brigadier is looking forward to taking you on a tour of the battle zone and explaining the details of the action to you himself and it is not my wish to deny him this right, furthermore in matters of military strategy I am an amateur, not a professional, and at the moment my main concern is our accused and his story. Toward Christmas the skies cleared and he left his house; and went out into the streets to find a new atmosphere of great tumult, buildings had already been requisitioned for command and administrative functions; barbed wire was everywhere and policemen, clerks, political officers and busybodies of all kinds were running to and fro amid the rejoicing Jews and the dazed Arabs, and the rain and the fog came back as if our army dragged the London fog along with it and he said to himself again, behold, strangers are replacing other strangers.

– Correct, sir, this is a question which I put to him repeatedly, what did he expect, this *homo politicus*, did he imagine that having conquered the city we would hand over the keys of power to the local populace, bow and take our leave?

– A good question, Colonel, if I may say so. This was indeed the decisive and possibly the fateful moment when the seed of treachery which had long lain neglected in the darkness came to rest in moist soil and began to suck the moisture dripping beside it, suddenly sprouting and multiplying as if fed on yeast, dissolving into thousands of tiny tendrils, minute fibers invisible among the clods of earth. But the skilled observer sees that the seed is split into two parts, root and stalk; from now on each independently exerts inexorable pressure on the other and so he returns to headquarters and everyone is glad to see him, since in the turmoil of the conquest the loyal interpreter was quite forgotten and he goes, sir, to the Adjutant of the Division, Major Stanford, and shows him his British passport. The Major recruits him into the army then and there, issuing him a uniform, a cap and even an old revolver, messtins and kitbag. He is appointed to the rank of corporal and given a salary of five shillings a week and our Major Clark signs the document on behalf of the legal department and from this moment on he is an officially accredited interpreter in the service of His Majesty.

– Indeed, sir, all the documents are signed and deposited in the file before you and they certainly add to the weight of his guilt.

– I agree, sir, the manner of his recruitment was somewhat lax, with no security checks or testimonials of loyalty but then they had all become acquainted with him during the autumn march to Jerusalem and it will come as no surprise to you, Colonel, to learn that the officers who signed the documents are now the ones most anxious to destroy him. In any case, from now on he is accepted at Command Headquarters like one of the family and even has a desk assigned to him in one of the offices. He translates the directives issued by the military administration and at night returns home, lies in his big bed with his son and his quiet wife beside him, dreaming of the days when he walked and preached in the Arab villages in the plains of Philistia and suddenly his heart melts with pity for the Arabs, sir...

– Yes, for the Arabs, sir, but only as a concept, not as individuals, since the root sucks at whatever nourishment is available in the darkness of the ground to feed its growth.

– Yes, sir, I assure you I'm coming to the point. I'm trying to comprehend his disillusionment. The days go by and he walks around in his British uniform and everyone treats him with respect but at night he takes off the uniform and puts on his dark suit and takes his son and crosses the Old City, passing the Wall of the Temple and the great mosques and going out by the eastern gate which they call the Dung Gate and climbs the Mount of Olives where his father and grandfather are buried and comes to the hospital of Augusta Victoria and the monastery of Tur Malka, yes, all these places are on the map, and from there he goes to a little Arab café and listens to the conversations at the brass tables and goes to meetings of his own people to listen to speeches and sees deputations of Jewish dignitaries arriving hastily from overseas to bear witness and go back again, while on the northern horizon from time to time there are echoes of artillery, occasional shells idly exchanged by the armies, but still the creeping root of treachery doesn't know what will bloom from it until one day he goes to the headquarters to throw a rough draft in the wastepaper basket. The room is empty and he hears a distant laugh from the courtyard where the officers are playing soccer with tennis ball and in the wastepaper basket he sees a rolled map, picks it up and hides it in his shirt. At home, that night he sees he has taken the 22nd Regiment's campaign-plan for the assault on Transjordan. He folded the map into his phylactery-case and went as usual on the Sabbath to the Sephardi synagogue in Rabbi Isaac Street and when prayers were over he took his son home but didn't go in himself. Instead he went to the Old City where he bought an Arab cloak, wrapped himself in it and went out by Damascus Gate and walked for three hours, the line is drawn here on the map, sir, so if you wish you can follow the route of his treachery. He came to the small town of Ramallah and passed through it as if in a trance and came out into the fields and saw the British sentries camped there, sitting comfortably in shallow trenches, quite unlike the battered dugouts of Flanders. He descended one hill and climbed the next and rain began to fall and before long he smelled the Turkish campfires and the coffee and saw them in their crumpled uniforms and faded ribbons, just as he always remembered them, from his earliest days he has seen them patrolling the alleys of Jerusalem and here they sit, a defeated army, warming themselves by the fire and laughing softly, hungry as ever, chewing their moustaches and he approached them, called the sergeant, gave him the plans and told him to find an officer and an officer came and stared at the paper and didn't understand and said this has to be shown to the German, assuming he too must be a German and they went to call the German as he stood, waiting near the fire while the soldiers stared at him open-mouthed. In the distance were the houses of an Arab village whose name he did not know, which is El-Bira on the map. He swallows his spittle and waits, unaware of the rain drenching his cloak. Three horsemen arrive and the German dismounts in great excitement, this is Werner von Karian, an agent we've heard of before, a cunning fox who knows immediately that the plans are genuine and extremely important and can't wait to get his hands on the treasure. But now the interpreter himself needs an interpreter, a Turk in a *tarboosh* and spectacles, his dark twin from the other side of the hill, and gold coins sparkle but the accused rejects the offer at once, in fact he never took money from them. Instead he demands that they gather all the villagers because he intends to make a speech and they ask him what speech and he doesn't answer, doesn't even look at them but insists on speaking. They bring the people together quickly and roughly with their whips and call the shepherds and the farmers in from the field, grim peasants who arrive with hoes and halters and pitchforks still in their hands, leading their sheep and donkeys and here and there is an intellectual, a teacher in a dirty red *tarboosh*. Twilight is approaching but the skies are clearing and the rain stops and bright red rays of a fierce winter sun are reflected in the muddy pools. He asked for a table but there was none in the village so they brought him a bed and laid a plank across it and he stripped off his cloak and stood before them in a suit and tie, looking suddenly shrivelled like a black tongue of fire, and he climbed up on the bed with the plank, sir. Silence reigned and he began to sway a bit as if continuing the morning prayers and speaking Arabic. Who are you? Wake up before it's too late and the world has turned. Develop an identity and be quick about it. He takes from his pocket Lord Balfour's declaration which he has translated into Arabic and reads it to them without a word of explanation and goes on, this is your land and our land, half for you and half for us and he points to Jerusalem which they see dimly in the mist of the hills and says, there are the English and here are the Turks but they will all go and we will be left alone. Wake up, don't go to sleep.

    — Yes, sir.

    — Precisely, sir, 'wake up and don't go to sleep' is the gist of his speech which lasts only a few minutes and he holds out his arms to the Turkish officers standing around, their gleaming boots sunk deep in the mud and they lift him off the bed and carry him in their arms so he won't sink in the mud and the great crowd is still silent. They haven't understood anything and can't comprehend the new reality and political declarations imposed upon them, for they have no sense of nation and are barely aware of the borders of their own village. He dons his cloak, darkness falls and the German pays special attention to him, they escort him to no-man's-land and he promises to come the next Sabbath with new documents.

    — Yes, sir, this is all the reward he got and we've had confirmation from our agents on the other side, but he went to them every Saturday in January and February, eight times in all, and they provided him with a small flock of goats so he could lead them like a shepherd and by the time he reached the slope of the first hill he would lose most of them and only two or three remained and every time they varied slightly the route of his treachery but the German organized a unit of expert trackers who would pick him up and keep him from losing his way and first he would derisively give them the documents he brought and say you are not entitled to these and they would escort him respectfully to the designated village, where the crowd had been waiting on its feet since dawn and the Arab population between Ramallah and Nablus sees him as a punishment inflicted on them by the Turkish authorities to avenge their defeat and see this strange and ignoble punishment as a sign of disintegration and weakness. He stands surrounded by Turkish officers and begins by reading Lord Balfour's declaration and then he shows them a map of Palestine he has drawn for them, coloured with crayons, with the blue sea in the middle. They look at it in astonishment, for this is the first time they've seen their homeland reduced to a small piece of paper. He shows them the blue sea and the Jordan and Jerusalem and tells them to wake up and they look at one another to see if anyone will dare sleep and he goes on: find an identity, all over the world nations are taking identities and afterwards it will be too late, afterwards there will be disaster, behold we are coming and he takes a pair of scissors from his pocket and says half is yours and half is ours and he cuts the map down the middle and gives them the half with the mountains and the Jordan and keeps the shore and the sea and they're sad he has cut the map and they come to him and some of them want to touch him but the Turkish soldiers around him with their legs deep in the mud, hungry, bleary-eyed, fix their bayonets and wave their rifles, for the German has given strict orders that not a hair is to fall from his head and the more he rages at them insulting and challenging them, the more compassion they feel for him and like children they say, we want the sea too, and at first he's stunned and speechless with anger and then furiously he takes another map out of his satchel and cuts it cross-wise.

– About eight Saturdays, sir.

– In many villages, sir, and he went as far as Nablus and Jenin and they even took him into the houses of the dignitaries but he was proud and obstinate, refusing to drink the coffee offered him and still his audience doesn't understand and grins indulgently but there are always one or two who listen to him intently and with no laughter on their faces, an intellectual for example who has studied in Beirut or Haifa or Jerusalem and wanders around the countryside in a suit and tie and white shoes like a poet or philosopher, Virgil or Plato, and they listen to him in amazement when he speaks of the Jews who will come and they don't know what he's talking about when he says that a swarm of locusts has settled in the desert and is poised to attack them. Not once, Colonel, did our sentries observe anything. He would cross the lines at midday smooth as butter and would return in the dark walking quietly and quickly the six miles or so and reaching Jerusalem at midnight, tired and wet and dirty, arriving by the northern road, entering Damascus Gate and slipping into the desolate rain-swept alleys with the moon rising from Jericho walking with him. He'd climb the stone steps and the big woman would open the door before he even touched the handle and she had no idea where he had been but she would trip off his clothes, bathe him, dry him, feed him and lift the quilt on the bed and only then would he start trembling, sinking and the moon would sink into bed with him...

 – Oh, I do beg your pardon, sir.

 – Yes, forgive me, sir, I was a little carried away, I know

 – Horovitz, sir, I do apologize.

 – Ivor Stephen, sir, Ivor Stephen Horovitz, excuse me, I let my tongue run away with me.

 – Yes, Colonel.

 – Yes, sir.

 – I am indeed a little tired since I've been engrossed in this case for three weeks now, day and night, and my desire to recognize the truth won't let up, every possible detail has been investigated. I've been in and out of his house a hundred times and I've personally walked over the route of his treachery there and back and where facts are missing I've conjured them up in my imagination for I'm bound to plumb the depths of this treachery.

 – No, Colonel, absolutely not, most assuredly not, if this were an Arab or an Indian or a Nepalese I would conduct myself in the same way, wherever the Empire exists it is my desire to understand and to know. But I fear this trial will run like a swift river towards an inevitable end since Mister Mani essentially admits the charge and doesn't deny it and the prosecution, don't misunderstand me, sir, will be sharp as a razor and Lieutenant Colonel Cooper and Major Jahawallah have already come to a verdict in their hearts and when you see the quantity and nature of the documents he smuggled across the border you'll be enraged too, Colonel.

 – Certainly, sir, the list is here before you and he himself kept a precise list and got a receipt for every document and this information has been confirmed from the other side, where there is, and I tell you this, Colonel, in strictest confidence, a British citizen disguised as a German who has been performing small services for Great Britain for some years.

 – Here it is sir, but I'm not sure in what order the documents were turned over to the enemy. The campaign plan of the 22nd Regiment for the invasion of Transjordan, dated January 3, 1918. A list of the wounded and sick of the Brigade in the week between the December 30th 1917, and January 6th, 1918. A report on the state of discipline in the 3rd Battalion in the third week of January signed by Captain Smugg.

– Many complaints, sir. The contingent of officers in the Division and the number of those on leave from January 13, 1918. A draft of the campaign plan for the capture of Damascus, signed by Major Smith, January 26, 1918. A list of guests entertained by the Governor of Jerusalem at a gala on January 30, 1918. Two signed photographs of General Allenby, undated. A list of food supplies sent to the Australians of the 5th Batallion. A map of the artillery emplacements near Jericho as of February 1, 1918. Copies of personal letters from Lieutenant Colonel Cooper to his wife.

– Unfortunately, Colonel, there is indeed more.

–A description of the firing mechanism of the Mark F gun, undated and unsigned. A requisition for new shell stocks. A photograph of an unknown young woman in the Via Dolorosa, evidently a prostitute. A map of Jericho showing gun emplacements dated February 3, 1918 and these, sir, are the guns captured shortly after in the failed assault across the Jordan. The German counted the shells fired and when he knew we had run out, he ordered the attack and a hundred and fifty men were lost. However, the Australians were more upset by the loss of guns than by that of men, since guns are less easily replaced.

– Precisely, sir, all this was in the wastepaper baskets or on its way there.

– There already was a big scandal, sir, officers were held for questioning and indicted, new procedures were devised and a special officer was brought up urgently from Cairo and has been here for a week. When you visit the General at headquarters tomorrow you'll see that the wastepaper baskets are empty and spotless because a sergeant of the Military Police and two men burn the rubbish day and night, so every paper is destroyed even before it gets to the basket and there is a perpetual pillar of smoke rising beside the Russian church, which you can see from this window, sir, now that the sky has cleared and over there is another one of those black ravens who know, don't ask me how, that the presiding judge is here and that I'm with you.

– Yes, sir.

– Yes, sir.

– Over there, Colonel, if you make him out.

– A black smudge, just so, a black smudge and these black smudges,

Colonel, have accompanied me constantly these last three weeks, for they know that danger is approaching and the noose is tightening around the man's neck and I have already been visited by two emissaries, an elderly lawyer and a legal clerk who speaks a little halting English. They asked to see the Manual of Military Law which I gladly lent them, giving them a corner in my office. They sat there all day, reading and discussing abstruse technicalities as if they were debating some point of royal protocol and I brought them tea but they didn't touch it and at the end of the day, exhausted and pale, they returned the book, grasping it with their fingertips as if the gallows were already folded inside it. They shook their heads sadly, looked at one another and asked if I knew the Horovitz family in London and when I said I didn't, they went on searching for some Horovitz somewhere in the world I would agree to be related to so they could give me his regards and finally they gave up and sighed and said in a whisper, this Mani is crazy and it doesn't reflect credit on Great Britain to deal with a madman, after all his father was deranged, maybe you'll take pity on him. But I looked them straight in the eye, Colonel, and said: you know as well as I do that he's not crazy.

– No, sir, he doesn't even have the madness that hides behind superficial sanity which you smell all of a sudden like a sour odor in a warm room. No, under no circumstances, he simply cannot be regarded as unbalanced, he even lacks the slight barely perceptible mental flaw which ultimately makes a man go mad. He is rational, sir, and however complicated his personality may be he is in control of his tongue and his actions, saying what he wants to say and refusing to say anything else and I know he's preparing a long political diatribe directed not at us but at the public and the press, since he's the kind of man who's always trying to enlarge the audience that will be shocked by what he has to say. So he wants me first to say all I'm entitled to say, so he can rise after me and make a speech that will stun Jerusalem since we all know that afterward he'll go to the gallows, I feel this, in fact I know it and this was why his feet took him straight to the Ulsterman's command post, though he could easily have turned right or left and got away, because he's not satisfied with an audience of Arabs listening to him at the orders of the Turks, he wants all Jerusalem to hear him.

– That is indeed the case, sir, I know nothing definite but I sense that he's honing a poisoned dagger and despite all my efforts to discover his intentions I've gotten very little out of him, since he wrote the notes for the speech in Hebrew and when I tried to confiscate the papers he ate them, so now the whole speech is stored in his mind.

– You'll see him tomorrow, in the dock, Colonel, and if you see him listening to the evidence don't be misled, he's thinking only of the speech he'll make, about this land as a great eternal battlefield bearing the seeds of disaster and he'll talk about masses of people not yet here but who will swarm out of the desert like the locust and settle upon the land, although if you look around you, sir, you'll see only massive desolation and few people. So I said to him, give up this plan, hire a lawyer who will speak of your childhood, your dead father, in the end they'll hang you and if you talk a lot of political nonsense you'll only bind the noose tighter around your neck. But he smiles peacefully, a calm political animal sure that all his actions have a political purpose. And yet I know, sir, and this knowledge makes me most uneasy, that there's another story here and he wants to take revenge on somebody far away and all this political rot became an obsession with him.

– The same idea occurred to me, sir. One night I ordered a rope to be left in his cell and when he was out a hook was fixed to the ceiling and I told the guards to ignore it, hoping he would do away with himself, but at night he removed the hook and in the morning he handed me the rope neatly coiled without a word, which means that he has absolutely no intention of losing the chance to deliver the speech he's preparing, though I don't know what's in the speech. I'd be very happy to be spared such an oration which is surely aimed at us and bound to cause trouble.

– No, sir, of course the speech will not affect the verdict, his death is already certain, unless those ravens fly to Buckingham Palace and get a royal pardon. The prosecution's case is clear, airtight, well prepared. Don't misunderstand me, Colonel, if it seems I've come here to express my misgivings, tomorrow morning I shall stand firm as a rock in court and your two colleagues will be convinced of his guilt and Lieutenant Colonel Cooper is determined to hang him for the guns lost in Transjordan and he won't yield... he won't yield... but, sir... now I... speaking as a citizen... yes, as a citizen of Great Britain... if it's possible... once the trial begins it will all happen so fast, I mean so fast that... that none of us can control it... I think we should consider... here there is...

– I beg your pardon?

– Yes, sir, the matter has already been checked by those who are concerned... and a Turkish gallows has been found in the Citadel with enough ropes and hooks to hang us all, and if the Turks had taken as much trouble with shells for their guns as they did with nooses our victory might have been harder and there is an Arab who used to be the assistant hangman and he promises to have everything in order... that's

why I say... that... excuse my incessant talking... we have actually seen...
we have actually seen...

— Pardon me, sir?

— The child? Which child?

— Oh, the child, yes the child... but as I already explained, sir... it's
my impression... I mean... in what sense?

— Oh...

— Oh...

— Yes, yes, sir, at once, of course, this child...

— Ephraim's his name and he claims he's his son and there's no
reason not to believe him even though there's not much resemblance. The
youngster is fair and has blue eyes. His mother is dead and, according to
rumor, she was a young Jewess from Russia or some such place, a sick
girl with tuberculosis he found among the bundles and valises dumped
from the train at the Beirut railway station where he was waiting for
young Jews from the north. I don't know if she was a real revolutionary,
sometimes young people quarrel violently with their parents and think
they've revolted against the government itself and they flee the country.
Anyway, her name was Shapiro, he told me, and she clung to him and
though he was an expert in the whims of vagrants and knew how to get
rid of them, he couldn't get rid of her, maybe her political consciousness
was as strong as his. Anyway something in her touched the heart of this
stubborn confirmed bachelor, maybe she only wanted a child from him
because she was afraid to enter Palestine or didn't think she could, and
she wanted something from this land that she could call hers, it is hard to
know for sure, and he didn't talk much about it, sir. Anyway they were
poor and they lived together for a year or two in the hotel near the station
I have described to you, in West Beirut, sir, in the Moslem quarter which
he says is wretched, near the ancient Sephardi synagogue he used to
attend on Fridays and, with God's help, we'll be there soon and see it
with our own eyes. When the time of the birth approached they were
afraid to go to the hospital lest they be forced to identify themselves; and
the Turks were already beginning to expel foreign citizens. Anyway he
believed he could deliver the baby himself. After all at the beginning of
the century he saw a birth in his own house and cut the umbilical cord
with a knife and they brought a Muslim midwife to help them and the
mother was weak, lost a lot of blood and died the day after the birth, and
he was left with the baby who looked a little slow and perhaps retarded
but sweet-tempered, and from day to day he grew more beautiful for he
inherited his looks from his mother's wild beauty. When Mani found her

she was weak and sick and only now, as the petals of the son unfold like the blossom of a flower, it was revealed to him how beautiful his wife was, and this beauty came back to him, and you'll see his son tomorrow, Colonel, in the front row, a four-year-old boy, for I've given permission for him to attend the opening session so he can enjoy seeing the hall and the officers and the uniforms and remember later on that his father had a proper trial and didn't simply perish...

— Yes, sir, in short, the sky really has cleared now and the dryness of the desert makes Jerusalem afternoons sweet and golden and I'm embarrassed and confused that I've tried your patience...

— In brief, sir, my instructions are clear and, in accordance with the Manual of Military Law section 10 sub-section 3 regarding a state of war and occupied territory and a British citizen and espionage leading to loss of life, the prosecution is obliged to demand the death sentence and the court is prepared to deliver this sentence and there can be no appeal... but...

— I understand... yes, sir...

— Yes, sir.

— The one I mentioned, sir...

— Correct.

— I see, sir... one thing leads to another...

— This is indeed a surprise, sir...

— Colonel...

— Certainly, sir... another question...

— This was my feeling... sir... this is the system...

— With pleasure, sir... we shall consider this at once...

— Thank you...

— So I've succeeded after all in drawing the threads together...

— I am grateful...

— I am overwhelmed, sir, I'm grateful that you've been so patient with me and have listened so attentively. When they told us you were coming from Egypt to preside over the court I was terrified, and when I came into this room two hours ago I trembled because I knew whom I was about to meet. Your name has been on the lips of all our officers for days, the hero of the battle of the Marne! But when I saw you sitting here in this dark room with black sunglasses and the empty sleeve on the arm of the chair and those scars, my spirits sank and I was greatly alarmed, I hadn't realized your wounds were so serious and I thought, tomorrow the tiger and the viper will be joined on the bench by the wounded lion and who knows what desire for vengeance is in his heart and this is a serious case of espionage in time of war which has caused damage and loss of life and here's a stubborn Jew who refuses legal counsel and is willing to be hanged just so he can make a strong political speech which will sow discord among the communities, and if the trial begins it will have to go on to the bitter end, since that's my duty as prosecutor. But is this how the history of Britain in the Holy Land should begin, with a Jew hanged in Jerusalem? But I said to myself, can I be understood and if I speak plainly will he understand me without suspecting me of divided loyalty for I can't conceal my Jewishness like some of the Jewish officers in our Division and I don't want to, not just because of my name and the way I look, my build and my spectacles, the flow of poetic and literary speech not yet blunted by the inarticulate mumble favoured by the aristocracy at Cambridge. All this creates revulsion and prejudice from the outset, for I had to suppose that you too, sir, might be a little influenced by antisemitism, if only on the social level, because of your status and the circles you move in, and I came prepared for instant rebuttal, perhaps even a stern reprimand, but I remembered my mother's advice: Don't hesitate, son, don't be afraid, as long as you're sure your motives are pure. So I stand and appeal to you, sir, not only as a soldier obeying orders but also as a citizen of Great Britain and the Empire who sees victory near and complete, the end of the war and the glorious era that awaits us and all the peoples under our rule...

    – Sir.

    – Sir.

    – Sir.

    – Sir.

    – I am extremely happy that I have succeeded in gaining your trust.

    – You really think so, sir?

    – Certainly, sir, if he weren't a British citizen the prosecution wouldn't have to demand the death sentence and he would be treated as an indigenous subject in occupied territory.

    – Exceedingly dubious citizenship, sir, and granted illegally in spite of the official document.

    – If we examine it closely and wish to be pedantic.

    – His grandfather, sir, came from Thessaloniki which was then in Turkey but is now in Greece.

    – Certainly, sir, if we like, it shall be Greece but since his mother was deported can we force them to accept him?

    – The islands, did you say, Colonel?

    – Certainly, sir, every ship leaving Jaffa for the west passes by them, Rhodes, Crete, whichever is most convenient...

Biographical Epilogue:

Lieutenant Ivor Stephen Horovitz continued his military service until the end of the war as an officer on General Allenby's staff and accompanied the British forces to Beirut, Aleppo and Damascus, He was involved in an administrative capacity in the final offensive against Mosul before the cease-fire was signed with Turkey in October 1918. After Germany's surrender, in early December, Horovitz was discharged from the army to complete his studies at Cambridge, where he graduated with honours in 1920. After qualifying as a barrister in 1921 he began his professional career in the Crown Prosecutor's office in Manchester but soon joined the legal firm of a well-known Jewish solicitor who also gave him his daughter's hand in marriage. During this period he completed his doctoral thesis on the subject of espionage trials in time of war, which was very well received. He was appointed Lecturer in Law at Manchester University and in 1930 moved to London with his wife and two young sons to take up a professorial appointment at the London University Law School. In London he became associated with local committees of the Zionist Federation and even served as honorary legal adviser to them. His academic career flourished and he was considered an outstanding lecturer. In 1957 he celebrated his sixtieth birthday by travelling to Israel with his children and grandchildren and subsequently visited the country several times. One of his grandsons emigrated to Israel and settled in Kibbutz Revivim. In 1973, in London, he suffered a stroke and died shortly afterward at the age of seventy-seven.

Colonel Michael Woodhouse continued his military service after the war, presiding over courts-martial throughout the Empire. Because his sight progressively deteriorated until he became almost totally blind, the army assigned him an assistant of Armenian origin who accompanied him in his travels as military circuit judge to Malaya, Burma, India and Ceylon. In the mid-1930s he was knighted by King George V. He became a famous imperial judge, his blindness only adding to his renown. He presided over many cases concerning British officers serving with colonial units and gained a reputation for originality of approach and depth of understanding. At the outbreak of the Second World War he was in Kenya, but insisted on returning to Britain to share in the defence of his homeland. He was killed in an air raid in London in June 1941 at the age of sixty-four and was buried in his native village with full military honours.

Translated from the Hebrew by Philip Simpson and Barbara Harshav.

Dennis Silk

On the Situation

Prose Poems

Neologism

I'm in my friend's garden in Abu Tor, numbering the streaks in a tulip,
when the new species draws up. Straight from the Gehenna nursery.
We spot a man with an Assyrian beard and competent movements.
Field-glasses to his eyes, through the car-window, a tactician appraises
Mount Zion's arid slope. Then off, in mufti, with the despatch of a
temple-plotter. It's a hybrid in motion, it's a militarabbi.

Amateur

We walked with the Old Man of the Mountain through his secret rooms
– teasing a shadow with a scimitar he said *This is for you, baybars*.
To-day, in the capital, we offer our back to a provincial without a least
knowledge of anatomy. He must be driving from Jenin with the kitchen
knife he's too stingy to get sharpened beforehand.

Vanishing trick

Demographer's defeat: invisibility powder. Rubbed into the skin of a
million Ahmeds bussed in from the Territories. Into the skin, the hair,
the *kefiya*, the shirt. For Arabs should be worked but not seen.
And not too thrifty with the powder, please. Do you want an Arab
button or shirtsleeve molesting a Jewish street? *Not a sleeve not a sleeve
not a sleeve* – that's the new song of the irredentists.

At the building site, a hundred unheld spatulas point the wall.
Pails of gravel fill of their own accord.

"The invisibility quotient" (Ministry of Interior) vexes Security but
they cope. Mursted the kitchen hand's told to carry a dishcloth,
it identifies him, Farrij the plasterer a trowel. Ahmed's awarded the
replica of a dustbin lid.

It's eerie to meet these detached functions filling arteries between Old
and New Cities quite early in a working day. Here's a pair of waders
asking to be tried on, a thimble works back and forth back and forth,
a butcher's cleaver is making its way toward you.

Hospital cake and vaporizer
Independence Day 1987

Their national flag made its point. Chauvinism bit into the cherry.
It was their flagship on my cake.

Clandestine, all night, the vaporizer. It sends a kindly search party
of steam and eucalyptus to look down my throat, and tells my inflamed
vocal cords to calm down.

I light out on the only unintercepted boat in the Mediterranean.
It runs blockades of phlegm.

Public transport

"There are today in Aleppo twenty prophets, among them Rabbi Galante and
Master Aaron Isaiah ha-Kohen, and four prophetesses."

Letter quoted in Gershom Scholem's *Sabbatai Sevi*.

Number Sixty Two bus-stop outside Tzavta, for instance. *Sixty Two*,
a thick number, transports you to the morose town of Hebron.

Zeal-of-the-Land Busy and Win-the-Fight Littlewit stand here with
briefcases of important documents. Vague though powerful waves thud
about them. You sniff the smoke of the third temple.

Someone mad as they drives up to rescue them from mere town.
He retrieves them for Hebron. Zeal-of-the-Land Busy and Win-the-
Fight Littlewit descend into the bus of a school of prophets, an artillery
spotter, several sacrificial doves and a deranged map-reader.

On the housetops of Balata

The three-day curfew's blanked out a lot but they're up here.
Sky's legal, reached by a staircase. Up here, at least a floor higher
than the troops.

In this fable by Aesop, men manage to become birds. They salute
each other across little parcels of air. *Space be about you, Raja.*
Double space be about you, Marwan.

Wreckers

A nightshift of sneaks crowbar out the cornerstone, and slick down a something quarried and cut in the Territories. A hundred grinning men in green berets shore the building up, till the new something is talked into place.

To conclude this event, the untidy sibyl of redemption prophesies in hysterical hexameters.

On the way to the Territories

We're passing a suburb of redemption on the left, the saved like these barrack affairs. They have broody rectangular dreams above which they hang the flag of their disposition.

The more romantic plant Swiss chalets guarded by a bemused militia. Here they yodel a psalm, there they mensurate it in a barrack.

From her twilight hilltop, Brunnhilde mopes at a palisade. A mawkish cement mixer woos a Siegfried moon.

Behind all this hides a great happiness. Gun-happiness in holster or from sling or hip. Cowboy.

Under the film-lot moon I ride a horse-laugh: it's not a war-horse unless a laugh is an act of war.

Odd man

This smoke observer at the dry run for the temple sacrifice phones HQ.
Coordinates working out. The bribing smoke goes up, godhead inhales
it through a hookah of good will, temple elevation OK, moon dandy.
Felicity of doves.

An odd man to belong to a conventicle. Back-slapping and broody.
Somewhere between a second-sighted man and a riding master you
wouldn't trust with your daughter. This womaniser could bottle
a homunculus.

What he phones they note on the smoke-map. Till now, they've justified
three hamsters, a budgie confiscated from an atheist's cager, a gecko
that might have been the good luck of their house. Now it's doves,
the real thing.

Undifferentiated heads bob down there. He could phone anything from
his chancy ledge. Prophesy over a dormouse or write a tract. What do
they gaping hope for down there? Not to be caught unawares by their
temple. Priests, and servants of priests, to be dressed nicely. The temple
laid.

What if it doesn't, this observer asks himself, the temple doesn't arrive?
All that botched linen. Must the shop close down? There's still that
matter of Solomon's gold mines. Everyone knows they're located in
Mali. By a certain secret correspondence in his gold tooth, he knows
where. It whispers him the latitude and longitude of those mines in
Mali.

Stingy dunams

I lose my beret down at the farm. I hope the soppy man doesn't
pick it up.

After an absence of some years, here he is, mapping not sowing.
The owner.

I bend to listen to the land. Is he right I ask. No one owns me,
she says. A grin corrugates her at the doctrine of this poor rustic.
A painful horse-laugh leans over the half-door of the stable.

So much for the rustic of this place. Dunces pitchfork me out of this
settlement, I run fast as my no doctrine takes me. Foulard de luxe,
goodbye.

Couturier

The clay model of a temple pouts at the side of a sewing machine.

'Can I be intense about my sewing and not about *that*?' says Hanoch.
'I snip back to the First, and forward to the Third, Temple. My cutting
is not only religious but chic. My *dernier cri* is heard in the Territories,
where young men define themselves. From Ariel to Shilo, they wash out
their ears and listen. Yet will they shed their rig-outs? The entire sewing
circle of Inner Jerusalem is asking. When will they sink into the archaic
mind-set induced by my Josephus tunics?'

'Hanoch,' I say, 'you cannot stop at the chic blessing of a biblical
ensemble. We must sink, after all our scurry, into monarchical postures
only you can prescribe.' He ponders. He flips through his pattern books.
'A kind of parting of the Red Sea eurythmics, perhaps?' 'Nothing so
harum scarum, Hanoch.' A captain of thousands, poised by a dummy,
turns his deliberate head. 'We're relying on you.'

Hanoch takes out of a drawer his sterner designs. Hilltop kings pass out
the order of battle. The putting away of magicians. Agag's First Samuel
haircut. 'Will these do?' I nod. I see fifty thousand, bony and absolute,
under the sun of the Lord of Battles. Ponchos cover their simplicity, and
in Sanhedria sandals designed by Hanoch they put down their biblical
foot where it hurts.

"The moonlight Prophet felt the madding hour"

Why, that must be Rabbi L***. In a mucksweat under the east wall of Jerusalem. This temple-plotter looks up at much more than a finger of moon over town. A local infection spreads. He howls because he's moon-mad. With the shove he gets from up there he lopes back to Hebron.

Generosity shrinks as he lopes. The fig trees of Silwan say: *Stingy kid*.

His midwife helpmeet waits with cold wet towels for a steamy forehead. She says, It's all right, all right. Madam Mandrake yanks out his howls. The ungenerous litter of his thoughts bark all night, and wake up anyone needing a decent night's sleep in the town of Hebron.

On the situation

How they wept because they hadn't carried out God's will, which was (according to the Joshua scribe) to be nasty. They called the place *Bechi* – that is, Weeping. I need the dangerous banter of Voltaire or Etheredge to save me in the *Book of Joshua*.

When they blew up the mayors' cars, and Bassam Shak'a lost his legs, I was writing a comedy. (About a girl who wouldn't sew the buttons on her husband's jacket.) I hope to maintain myself in comedy. If they blow up any more cars, I'll apprentice myself to a horse-laugh.

After the war

All those young men the billiard table
unites, and the poet Saba retrieved in Trieste,
and then there was Schweik and his Magyar friend
at six after the war

Italian, Slav, Sudeten German,
men from the Alpine countries,

Arab landowner or ex-soldier,
slave, ex-slave, Armenian, Jew, Greek,

from baize or war,
stranded unstingy ones,
generous crossers,
wave at us.

The relief

In the alternative suburb of the army camp, a young soldier funnels petrol into a command-car that will take it 800 kilometres in any direction except up or down.

But a beast is advancing on the Levant in tentacular silence, baffling the simplifiers with the squid-like inkiness of its speculations in the literalist noon.

Raft

Travelling considerable. Huck and Jim – this runaway nigger has handbills printed against him in lynch offices – Schweik and his Magyar. River holds all: it's the townships are so ratty.

Schweik snitches for us in the townships. Prague dogcatcher, Mississippi chickens. He's the batman of the big river now.

Arkansas Cairo Sidon Tyre. Twenty miles to the free states, as if we knew where they were.

From the bank a great dark figure on a horse points with his lance our new direction.

Watering-place

Sauntering down Prophets Street – here chunks of thought have
solidified and mouldered – I arrive at the street of Antara.

Antara Ibn Shadad. Black knight of the Banu Abs. Mothered by an
Abyssinian. Child, therefore, of the Blue Nile.

Sauntering down a received idea – I won't let it conduct me as it has
many – I listening bend to Ezekiel's once subversive waters. His sea,
from under the temple, sniffs the Blue Nile of Antara. It asks to be let
out.

Antara tires of uncompromising battle. He sheathes a sword white as
his girl's teeth. Dismounts from Abjer his horse. He says he likes this
notion of a sea in Ezekiel. He salaams the obdurate man. He says he'll
water his horse here.
A sea revives at the words of the great dark figure. It refreshes itself in
Nile blue as the eyelids of Abla. Antara ponders. Abjer dips its crescent
– "weapon of its brow" – in these waters.

On The Situation began as notes for a longer poem: *A Year among the Simplifiers*.
The notes have become terse prose poems, outriders, I hope, of the poem still to be
written.
The simplifiers are the enthusiasts, the wreckers, self-sufficiency fed by their morose
and inturned culture. Their posture is a stingy one: hands pushing away, averted
head and heart.
    Anger does not recommend. Then perhaps the banter of the old English poets
and wits can help. They met their times – persecution, civil war, entire suburbs of
dunces – with "intellectual gaiety". So I enlist George Etheredge, nonchalant
Restoration playwright, to dawdle with me through the *Book of Joshua*. Alexander
Pope provides the coordinates to pinpoint Rabbi L★★★, "the moonlight Prophet", in
the Vale of Kidron.

D.S.

Alan Montefiore

The Jewish Religion – Universal Truth and Particular Tradition

According to the customs governing the delivery of memorial lectures, the lecturer should commence his performance by some properly memorial remarks in honour of whoever is being commemorated; that done, he may proceed to discourse on any topic that may more or less plausibly be supposed to fall within the range of interests or concerns of the commemoratee. I have to confess to some uncertainty as to just how these rules should apply to a lecturer embarked on a lecture in memory of his own direct ancestor. Claude Montefiore was, among many other certainly much more important things, my own grandfather. If I were to speak of him personally, as I actually remember him, I should have to speak of things that could be of no general interest whatsoever. I should have to try to describe the peculiar smell and taste of the particular type of chocolates that he kept in a particular drawer of his desk in his study in the house in Portman Square, and which he would unfailingly produce whenever we, my brother and myself, were taken to visit him there; I should have to try to conjure up the curiously worn shininess of the cuffs of his jacket, which he used to encourage us to try and restore by the repeated application of black water colour paint when he came to visit us in my father's study in Weymouth Street, and the pleasure which he took in our pleasure both in the privileged nature of such repair work and in the all too evidently perplexed balance of feelings of outrage and indulgence with which our mother struggled to contain her reactions to his encouragement of it; I should have to report on how he used to make use of his deafness to exhort us to repeat ever more loudly and distinctly things which we should not have said (and he should not have heard) in the first place; and on many other matters as well, of equal importance or unimportance. He was, as I remember him, a perfectly splendid grandfather. But that alone would scarcely entitle him to a series of lectures dedicated to his memory – nor me, his grandson, to the self-indulgence of a lecture constructed entirely out of such personal childhood reminiscence.

As well as being my grandfather, however, C.G.M. was, of course, the founding father of the movement for Liberal and Progressive Judaism in this country. He was also, as is – or at any rate used to be – very well known, prominent among those Jews who were on principle opposed to Zionism (though it should also be remembered that among his closest and most revered friends and allies in all sorts of other causes were some whom he respected as being wholly committed to it). Since he died in 1938, it is evidently impossible to say with conclusive authority just what his reactions would have been to the creation of the State of Israel or to all the varieties and complexities of Zionism as they are to be found to-day. My own guess is that his views would have been closely and appropriately similar to those expressed by Rabbi John Rayner in his four talks on *Progressive Judaism, Zionism and the State of Israel* given last year in this very synagogue and subsequently published, together with a short postscript, in brochure form: "The State of Israel is a fact, and the sort of anti-Zionism which consisted in a principled opposition to its very establishment as a Jewish state has no continuing relevance to-day. Not to establish it might have been one thing, now to dismantle it would be very much another." Israel, the Jewish State of Israel, exists. It has become a major centre, arguably the major centre, of Jewish life in all its diverse – often mutually contradictory but also inextricably interconnected – forms, and all Jews conscious of themselves as Jews must inevitably feel themselves, for better or for worse, to be somehow involved in its virtues, its failings and its fate. Must it not be, then, a now natural objective of Progressive Judaism to establish itself and to flourish in this Jewish State? As Rabbi Rayner put it, when in 1976 the World Union for Progressive Judaism founded its first Kibbutz, "the metamorphosis was complete. Progressive Judaism, which had at first been diametrically opposed to Zionism, had become totally identified with it." (p.17) But not, as he went on to stress, with any and every form of Zionism. "Is Progressive Judaism compatible with Revisionism? My answer is an emphatic 'No!'... Is Progressive Judaism compatible with traditional, mainstream, liberal Zionism? I believe it is. Not indeed with every version of it... For instance, in so far as it depreciates the Diaspora, we must continue to dissent from it. But in so far as it seeks to build a society which shall be both a refuge for the homeless and a fulfilment of the highest ideals of our heritage, and therefore, among other things, endeavours to do justice to the other inhabitants of the land, and to make peace with its neighbour,we must surely endorse it." (p.24)

But issues of Zionism, anti-Zionism or modified pro-Zionism constituted, of course, neither the heart, the foundation nor the source of C.G.M.'s deepest concerns with religion and with Judaism. Nor, in fact, did they constitute the starting-point of my own reflections as I was wondering what I might possibly have to say of appropriate interest on the occasion of a lecture such as this. My starting-point presented itself to me rather in what, on re-reading, I am now inclined to think I may, on first reading, have tended to read into some remarks by Rabbi Michael Williams in a short piece called 'La recherche de la Justice', which he wrote for the seventh number of the review *Combat pour la Diaspora* – a number given over to the theme of Education and published in 1982. Michael Williams is, of course, the British rabbi of the Liberal Jewish congregation whose synagogue is in the Rue Copernic in Paris. The time and place of his teaching is thus very different from any which my grandfather occupied at any time of his life. Be that as it may, let me just quote – quite admittedly out of all context – the two remarks which on that first reading struck me most forcibly:

First then: "Une assistance française risque simplement d'ignorer que le but du judaisme non-orthodoxe, libéral si vous voulez, est un but strictement pratique – comment garder nos juifs, juifs – et que nous nous intéressons beaucoup moins au genre de débat polémique théorique que bon nombre de juifs français... trouvent tellement fascinant... En un mot, nous ne sommes pas concernés par le fait de définir et de redéfinir le mot 'juif' sans cesse... mais simplement par le fait de prendre *pour acquis* notre point de départ, notre appartenance à un peuple et à une communauté religieuse, et de poser, la seule question qui compte – une question pratique: 'et maintenant?'" ("A French audience runs the risk of simply failing to see that the purpose of non-orthodox Judaism, Liberal Judaism if one prefers, is a strictly practical one – how to keep our Jews Jewish – and that we are much less interested in the kind of polemical theoretical debate which so many French Jews find so fascinating... In a word, we are not concerned endlessly to define and to redefine the term 'Jew' ... but simply that we should take our starting-point *for granted*, that is to say our belonging to a people and to a religious community, and to ask the only question which counts – a practical question: 'And what now?'")

And secondly: "Que cela plaise ou non, la ligne de démarcation... entre le marxisme, n'importe quel système materialiste et le judaisme réside en ceci: nous tenons que la raison *n'a pas* toujours raison..." ("Whether one likes it or not, the line of demarcation... between Marxism, or whatever materialist system, and Judaism lies in the fact that we maintain that reason *is not* always right...")

Reading these passages again, and reading again some of my own grandfather's writings, I have to acknowledge that it would be hard to establish any determinate contradiction between them. Nevertheless, they certainly seem to convey a certain notable difference of spirit, or, at the very least, a notable difference of emphasis. The spirit in which I had thought myself to have been brought up, and which I had supposed to derive from my grandfather, was, as I had always conceived of it, of a much more rationalistic and universalistic nature. Let me cite just a few illustrative passages from the volume of sermons delivered at the services of the Jewish Religious Union, which were collected together and published in 1906 under the title of *Truth in Religion and other Sermons*. Such as: "There can be no opposition between Science and Religion, for Science must be a part of Religion... If any doctrine of religion is in conflict with an ascertained law of science, that doctrine cannot be true; therefore it cannot be religious." (p.3)

Or: "Articles of religion which happen to deal with matters that primarily belong to science, history, and criticism to decide, may need recasting, or even revoking, in the light of history, criticism and science." (p.7)

Or again: "Jews are a righteous people *because* of their religion. But is truth not universal and catholic?... Should not the truth which Israel possesses be carried afar?" (pp.24/25)

Or: "the question of making the truth known... is independent of the question whether the Jews are not merely a religious community, but also a nation... If the Jews are a nation, then it must be possible for the members of that nation to include believers in many creeds, and if Judaism is more than a tribal religion, then it must be possible for the believers in that religion to include members of many nations." (pp. 32/33)

And, most significantly perhaps: "...what is most important in Judaism is not its ceremonial, but its teaching, not its rites but its doctrines. If the doctrine, so far as it is true and pure, prevails, we shall mind less about the embodiment; nor shall we, in the last resort, mind about the *name*. If

Judaism triumphs under another name, if we can even help in and further such a triumph, we shall be content. 'Not unto us, O Lord, not unto us be the glory.'" (pp. 35/36)

So far as *these* passages are concerned the emphasis is evidently not so much on the importance of being (or remaining) a Jew as on that of holding to the truths enshrined in the Jewish religion; and these truths seem to be represented as esentially a matter of doctrine. "What is most important in Judaism... is its doctrines." This certainly was what I, as my grandfather's grandson, grew up learning to believe. No doubt, I had, as I grew up, far too uncomplicated and unquestioning a view as to what is involved in the acceptance of a doctrine, as to what is the relationship between purely intellectual assent and practical enactment, or even as to the sense in which there *can* be no ultimately sharp distinction between them. At any rate, so far as I can now remember, I took the doctrines of Judaism to be its attempted statements of the nature of God, of His relationship to man, of man's place in God's universe and of man's proper relationship to God and to his fellow men; and while I may not have been altogether sure of their truth, I certainly took them to be closer to the truth than those of any other religion. I also took them to be of unambiguously universal import; in claiming to be true, they laid claim to universal assent, and the truths that they claimed to assert must hold, if true, for all men. In view of the especial claims to purity and truth of their historically given religion, it was no doubt proper for Jews to regard themselves as bearing peculiar responsibility for the maintenance and transmission of its doctrines from one generation to another until such time as it might come to be recognised and accepted by all the nations of the world. But it was no part of the doctrines themselves that the Jews, as a historically determined community, were to be regarded or to regard themselves as being alone capable of receiving and practising the true religion of God; to understand doctrines in this way would be to treat them as constituting, in my grandfather's words, no "more than a tribal religion".

This, then, is a first main theme to be found running as a central thread through the pages of my grandfather's writings. It is a theme of the nature and paramount importance of Judaism as a religion, that is as a body of knowledge about the nature of God and of moral teaching as to the nature and proper behaviour of man. These two, incidentally, seemed in my grandfather's view to come fairly close to being the same thing. Not *quite* the same thing, of course: "Religion is a wider term than morality" (p. 105), and "the *highest* religion must contain a touch of rapture, of poetry, of mysticism" (p.106). All the same, "If we say that God is good, this means that the test of divineness, like the essence of the divine nature, is goodness" (p. 48); and "those who think the ceremonial laws good – good for us to observe here and now – need not worry themselves about their authority. The very fact that for them the laws are good is itself their authority and an adequate authority." (p. 50/51). (It is interesting to note that the view that C.G.M. here expresses is strikingly close to that put forward by G.E.Moore in his widely influential *Principia Ethica* published only a very few years before.)

Judaism as a religion, then, was first and foremost a body of doctrine, of true, or very nearly true, moral and religious belief; as such it laid claim to acceptance and defence not only by Jews as a 'peculiar people' but indeed by all mankind. But it was also – of course, and of course my grandfather fully recognised it to be so – a practical way of life of a peculiar people, derived from and hallowed by tradition, passed on from one generation to another and serving as a badge of recognition for all those who, by virtue of their fidelity, accounted themselves and each other to be recognisable as Jews. But, however large such practices might loom in the life of this Jew or that, their properly religious significance was to be understood as stemming from the doctrines that they embodied. Practice as 'mere' observance of ritual, however ancient, had no religious significance as such; while the vagaries of history might very well lead to different observances being taken to embody the same basic doctrines or beliefs for men or women of different congregations or communities, or of different 'national' commitment. No matter; "what is most important in Judaism... is its doctrines".

There is, however, a second main theme to be found even in this same volume of sermons, a theme that is in part complementary to this first one and in part in tension with it. It is a theme of deep pride in and loyalty to... but now what term *is* one to use? 'The Jewish people', 'the Jewish nation', 'the Jewish race', 'the community of Jews *qua* Jews'...? All of these expressions have, as is almost comically well known, their own different difficulties and disadvantages. "If the Jews are a nation, then it must be possible for the members of that nation to include believers in many creeds..." "If the Jews are a nation..."; well, this was not really, of course, a supposition that my grandfather would have liked to take very seriously. More often, in fact, he seems to have used the expression 'The Jewish race', at any rate around the time of the Sermons; but this is evidently not an expression that anyone could use very confidently or comfortably to-day. He also talked of 'born Jews', meaning presumably by that what anyone else would mean, that is simply those who were born of Jewish mothers – who themselves to be accountable as Jewish must either have been born Jewesses in their turn or have been accepted as converts to the Jewish religion. This – traditional – line of argument would seem to point to the indispensability at some point in the regress of a recognisable religious commitment on the part of some recognisably Jewish mother, grandmother or great-grandmother. But – it is worth pushing the question – in what must such a commitment or conversion consist for it to carry the relevant weight? Not, so Sermon No.19 of this collection would seem to maintain, in the mere intellectual or even moral-practical acceptance of "precisely the same beliefs as to the nature of God and man and their relations to each other which are held by the Jew" (p.271), for such beliefs – or so C.G.M. seems to have been ready to accept – may also be accepted and held by Unitarians and Theists. But, he insists, the fact that Jews may share "precisely the same beliefs" with others "is no reason whatever why we should falter in our allegiance to Judaism, or let the flame of our Jewish consciousness grow dim and flicker out. It is not for me", he goes on, "to explain or defend the separate identity and the justified separate consciousness of those who hold the essence of the Jewish faith, but not the Jewish name; but it *is* for me to defend the retention of the Jewish name and the Jewish consciousness among those who hold, though even feebly and falteringly, the *essence* of the Jewish faith." (p.271) The exact bearing of these remarks on the nature of conversion to Judaism is not, certainly, explicit. But they do seem to imply that to become a Jew or a Jewess even the appropriate doctrinal assent or conviction cannot after all be enough, but that the Jewish name and a Jewish consciousness must be embraced as well; and if this cannot be taken to consist in the acquisition of doctrinal conviction alone, it must presumably further involve some deliberate self-commitment to the practices of what may be publicly recognisable as a Jewish way of life. And if this is the case, reference to the particularisms of Jewish tradition also turns out to be in the last resort indispensable; and the second theme leads back to Rabbi Williams' concern with the basic value and first importance of Jews being and remaining Jews.

If this sounds somewhat circular or even confused, that is – so it seems to me – because it is so. Let me quote another couple of passages from this same Sermon No.19. First, then: "We shall all, I hope, agree that some measure of religious belief is necessary to constitute the Jew. Birth is adequate as a test of race; it does not suffice for religion." (p.259) And secondly: "I too glory in the fact that Judaism is an ancient and historical religion... This ethical Theism in which we find the essence of Judaism... Is it not ours by right of origin and history? Is it not ours by heritage and descent?" (p.267) What all this seems to amount to is (i) that appropriate religious belief is to be taken as being a necessary condition of being a Jew; (ii) that it is nevertheless not a sufficient condition; (iii) that a further necessary condition lies in one's recognised belonging or adherence to a certain historical tradition, descent or heritage; (iv) that this further necessary condition is not to be taken as constituting a sufficient condition in itself – for if it *is* further to condition no.(i), it cannot be taken as if already including that condition as one of the sub-conditions of recognisability; but (v) that, notwithstanding what has just been said, condition no.(iii) may have to be taken as a sufficient condition nonetheless – for although my grandfather may indeed have hoped for general agreement "that some measure of religious belief (was) necessary to constitute the Jew", the fact is that if one way of achieving recognition as a Jew is simply to be born to a Jewish mother, the possession of "some measure of religious belief" cannot be counted as a strictly necessary condition after all. (Unless, perhaps, one was to move in the direction of arguing that the possession of "some measure of religious belief" is a necessarily constituent condition of the being of 'Jews in general', but not necessarily so of any individual Jew in particular.)

We may seem at this point to be slipping back into just that sort of "polemical theoretical debate" which Rabbi Williams seemed to find so tiresome. Like it or not, however, the questions of who is or is not to be counted as a Jew, by whom, and why, may evidently take on at times the very greatest urgency and importance. This is not to say, of course, that they may not at other times, in other contexts, be treated as little more than occasions for essentially idle disputation, or that Michael Williams may not have had very good tactical or strategic reason for his impatience. Be that as it may, for a man of C.G.M.'s convictions and commitments, the importance of these apparently definitional questions becomes in the end inescapable. It was, after all, the complexities and tensions of his vision of what it is for a man to be a Jew that lay at the heart of his life, his faith, his teaching and his works, and that explains his involvement in most of the major controversies into which he found himself drawn.

I have already mentioned my grandfather's anti-Zionism and I shall return briefly to this topic later on. But let us consider first for a moment what was for him another quite fundamental problem, that of assimilation. Assimilation was something to which C.G.M. was, in fact, in general deeply opposed; when Rabbi Williams refers to the purpose of Liberal Judaism as being the practical one of "keeping our Jews Jewish", he remains wholly within the line of my grandfather's own concerns. This, as he – my grandfather – saw it, was a main reason for and justification of his repeated insistence on the absurdity, the wrongheadedness, of religion seeking to oppose or to reject anything that science or reason might be able to establish as true. Like Kant in this, he sought to make and to preserve room for faith by ensuring that it should never commit itself to anything that might be shown to be scientifically untrue or irrational. Modern men, modern Jews, would not, he was convinced, continue to go along with any such evident obscurantism, and would simply abandon a faith that appeared to instruct them to confine themselves within it. It was not, of course, that he thought it actually wrong to continue to respect the traditional observances as such. But nor, as we have seen, did he think that to do so was of any religious value in itself; a mere "soulless observance... may be useful as an external bond, but as an outpouring, an uplifting, even a safeguarding, of the religious life and of religion, it is surely of no spiritual worth whatever." (p.69) Not only is it degrading in itself; it is in practice bound – or so my grandfather thought – to end up by turning away from religion Jews of the contemporary Enlightenment – away from that very Judaism which he thought, in one dimension of his thinking at any rate, was a necessary element in their very constitution as Jews.

It is not surprising, then, that one of the attacks which C.G.M. felt most acutely was the accusation, repeated by many of the orthodox, that it was on the contrary precisely his teaching that provided the most powerful encouragement towards assimilation. For people like himself, perhaps, the arguments from rationality and reasonableness might always prevail; but for the majority such arguments, even when supported by a touch of mysticism (though never, one presumes, of the militantly *anti*-rational variety), provided absolutely no long-term security to compare with that offered by the bulwarks of law and tradition. On the contrary, if one maintains *both* that "what is most important in Judaism is not its ceremonial but its teaching, not its rites but its doctrines", *and* that similar religious assent and commitment, similarly high ethical character, may perfectly well exist in members of other nations and even other religious communities, what after all *can* the argument be for the overwhelming importance of remaining a Jew as such? (And this quite independently of the fact that rationality and reasonableness have no very good record in maintaining the structures of ancient traditional religions, or even of religious beliefs; and that indeed it may be neither rational nor reasonable to expect them to do so.) Certainly, one may continue to affirm the overwhelming importance of doing everything possible to bring about, to deepen, to spread and to sustain the type of religious conviction and ethical character in question. But if it is this and not traditional community identity that is really so important, why should it matter so much that any particular individual remained a member of any one such community rather than another, provided only that his religious beliefs and his ethical character continued to be of the right kind? Why should the on-going balance of numbers between such communities be of any serious concern? Why, to be more precise, should one care so much about Jews marrying out, if, to take my grandfather's own examples, the Gentile marriage partner to be was an ethically admirable Unitarian or Theist? Certainly, he insisted, as we have seen, that it *was* for him "to defend the retention of the Jewish name and the Jewish consciousness among those who hold, however feebly and falteringly, the *essence* of the Jewish faith"; and this insistence sprang no doubt from a most deeply felt loyalty to both and from his own profound sense of identity. But if the essence of the Jewish faith can also be held by those who do *not* bear the Jewish name, how can his insistence on the importance of the latter be justified purely on the sort of religious grounds which he presented as constituting that essence? It might be safer, if that is how one sees one's priorities, to agree with Michael Williams that "La raison n'a pas toujours raison", and to stick with the immediately practical business of somehow keeping one's Jews Jewish.

In fact, as is shown by the somewhat strained arguments which go to make up the last three sermons in the collection, my grandfather did not really attempt any such justification. On the contrary, in the very last of them – that on 'Religious Differences and Religious Agreements' – he speaks of "the circle composed of all those who accept and cherish our simple but sublime Unitarian doctrine, the pure Fatherhood of God", and goes on: "Jews, Unitarians and Theists compose this circle, but there are thousands more who are sincerely with us to-day, though officially they may not call themselves by one of these three names." (p. 279). But to speak like this is in effect to acknowledge that what he called "the Jewish segment of this circle" is Jewish not in virtue of its doctrinal commitment as such, for this it shares with others, but rather in virtue of its own special history. As he says only two pages further on, "We are united by a common and striking past, by partnership in the martyrdoms of the past and in the martyrdoms of the present, by a common aspiration, and above all by a common mission, a common charge." (p.281)

It is C.G.M.'s passionate attachment to this history, to this traditional community identity, that constitutes the second of the two themes to which I earlier referred. It is, in effect, in the name of fidelity to this tradition that he asserts the fundamental value of Jews refusing all temptations to assimilation in order to remain distinct as Jews. And yet... if the value of the tradition and of its continuation lies in that of the universal religion to which it bears witness, and if the same religious faith can also find embodiment and witness in other forms and in other traditions, how, to parody one of his own expressions, can loyalty to the particularisms of Jewish tradition be anything other than a form of tribal loyalty at best? Certainly, there is nothing wrong with tribal loyalty in its proper place; but for one such as my grandfather this place must surely be always subordinate to the universal imperatives of ethics and religion. It is all very well to insist, as he did on page 257, that "the Jew who, through his faith in God, is a good man, must also be a good Jew"; but he was also, of course, the first to insist that there are very many good men who are not Jews al all. We may seem to be moving back once again to a certain state of confusion.

The same sort of tension, a tension between the universalism of religious and ethical truth and the particularism of a given historical tradition, was also involved in his attitudes towards Zionism and in the controversies to which they gave rise. There were, no doubt, many factors which went into the making of his anti-Zionism. He was deeply concerned for the full emancipation and equality of status of Jews in all the countries of their settlement, and was fearful lest Zionism be seen as evidence of their primary allegiance to another country and so, once again, of their obstinate 'foreignness' and even untrustworthiness. He himself, by virtue of his social position and his culture, was in very many ways a typical upper-class product of late Victorian Britain; he *felt* himself to be both an Englishman *and* a Jew, and with his characteristic belief in the fundamental power of reason he was bound to seek a standpoint from which he could consistently and without reservation affirm himself to be both at once. The anti-Zionism in which I was, almost without noticing it, brought up seemed to rest on what now seems to me to be the impossibly over-simple, but then apparently obvious idea that to be a Jew was essentially to believe in Judaïsm, that is, the Jewish religion; and that this religion, being a matter of universal truth, accessible to and in principle acceptable by all, could not possibly figure as the particular property of one nation or people alone.

From this it seemed to follow, of course, that there must be some fundamental incoherence in the idea of a Jewish State as such – or at the very least in the idea of a Jewish State that by virtue of its particularity must necessarily also be *the* Jewish State. (How could the potential universality of all mankind constitute the membership of one particular state?) It might, naturally, have happened, for whatever historical or Divine reason, that one particular people had been the first to come to possession of the truth of the One and Universal God. But if so, then their mission could only be to preserve and to bear witness to this truth until such time as *all* came to acknowledge and to live by it – that is to say, to bring an end to their own particularity through their reunification with all mankind in the universality of man's reunion with God. To reinforce one's own particularity within the structures of a nation-state was to move, so it seemed, in precisely the opposite direction. Zionism was thus, so I grew up to believe, a sort of betrayal from the inside of the peculiarly Jewish religious insight.

All this, as I said at the outset, belonged to a time before the establishment of the State of Israel, and most of it, indeed, to before the rise of the state anti-semitism in Germany of the 1930s – a development that cast a black cloud over the last years of my grandfather's life. Such anti-Zionism has, in the words of Rabbi Rayner, "no continuing relevance to-day"; or not, certainly, in the forms of the past. But if there is, undeniably as I would now think, some deep inner tension to be found within my grandfather's double commitment – to the universality of his faith and to the particularism of his tradition, similar tensions are surely to be found reproduced and embodied within the Israel of to-day, tensions that still find a focus, indeed, in the endless unanswerability but unavoidably recurrent urgency of the question of who is and who is not to be counted as Jewish, and by virtue of what criteria.

Let me not, however, get lost in some amateur attempt at a rehearsal of the complexities of the Law of the Return, of the problems of civil marriage or of any other of the entanglements of the diversely religious with the diversely secular in present-day Israel. Let us turn back rather to reflect again on the nature of that inner tension itself, that tension between the universal and the particular, which, while far from being peculiar to Judaism and the Jews, they have lived with a perhaps peculiar intensity, implicitly always but often explicitly too, throughout their very peculiar history.

There is, to start out with, no special difficulty in supposing that a given form of religion, claiming the status of universal truth and of validity for all mankind, should first appear and first be developed within the historical experience of a particular people. That such a people should seek – by whatever means, justifiable as they may now seem to us or not – to bring others to an understanding and embracing of what they thus see as the truth is equally easy to understand. So too is the fact that many of these others should reject such pretensions, reacting sometimes with violence and even by persecutions; and that, in the face of such hostility, the people of 'The Truth' should eventually retreat to within themselves, and that their own self-preservation across history, and with it the preservation of their Truth, should become their prior, perhaps even their exclusive concern.

Such a people, living, enduring, such a history, is bound to collect and to reinforce, in the course of their own self-transmission across the generations, a whole tangled web of traditions, practices, customs, loyalties, rules of social cohesion and codes of mutual recognition of all sorts. And to the degree that all that happens to them is bound up with the practice of their religion, with their perception of Truth and of their own special responsibilities towards it and to the God who has revealed it to them, it is also easy to understand how it may have become hard to distinguish, within all those traditions, practices and beliefs which go to make up and to sustain their identity as a people through time and in the face of adversity, between what is and what is not social custom, religious ritual and religious doctrine concerning the nature of God and the proper conduct of man. For in the course of such a history all of these strands will have entered into the thread of their identity as a people – across and throughout the scattered diversity of what, through the accidents of history, may have come to be their dispersion.

How, however, once they are thus scattered and dispersed, is it to be known of anyone whether he or she properly belongs to such a people or not? It is again not difficult to understand that in the course of such an evolution, the evolution of a people centrally preoccupied with the observance of its 'own' religion, two different kinds of answer may have come to be acceptable, one in terms of one's birth to someone indisputably recognisable as being already a member of the community and the other in terms of one's adherence to its religion. Nor, of course, need it be surprising that in the cases of those claiming membership by virtue of their religious conversion, controversies should arise as to the criteria on the basis of which such conversions may be accepted as genuine and as to whom may be authorised to make such judgements on behalf of the community as a whole.

The fact that all this may be historically understandable does nothing, however, to lessen the always potential tension between the universalism of the religious and ethical message and the particularism involved in the maintenance of the traditional identity of a given people, especially when those traditions and that identity have become bound up with the particular embodiments and practices of their religion. Moreover, the identity here in question is identity in the very strong sense of that which makes for identifiability. There is a sense in which for very many Irishmen, for instance, Catholicism and Republicanism on the one hand and Protestantism and Loyalism on the other hand go almost automatically together as part of their identities, that is to say as part of who they feel themselves and each other to be. But there is here no confusion between the actual criteria of religious identification and those of political commitment. A Republican *might* turn out to be a Catholic, a Protestant or, for that matter a Jew, while there may well be Catholics indifferent or even opposed to the reunification of Ireland – and more to the point, there would be in principle no problem about how to recognise the existence of any of these cases. The peculiar problem in the case of Jews and Judaism, however, is that the criteria of particular loyalty and belonging and those of commitment and adherence to doctrines and practices of universal import are not clearly distinct in the same way.

Is there any new way of looking at these matters, any new variation of standpoint from which it might be possible to resolve these tensions? I am now more inclined to think that the right, perhaps the only honest thing to do, for us in our time and place, is to recognise them as being for the immediately foreseeable future at any rate not fully resolvable and to accept them for that future as being what they are. By this I do not mean that we should simply sit comfortably with them, and relax in the pretence that there is no reason why anyone need ever be tense even in situations of objective tension. I mean rather that we should accept as irreducibly messy fact that, history having been what it has been, there is for the present no one overall, self-consistent account to be given of what it is to be a Jew, no account which would apply in some univocal way to everyone who thought of himself or herself as Jewish, or who was thought to be Jewish by others. We should accept this fact in the sense of not striving to pretend that it is not so: in the sense of recognising that the extraordinary and extraordinarily competitive diversity of Jewish institutional commitment and religious conviction that exists to-day is not going to give way to any sort of non-problematic unity to-morrow, however powerful the reasoning or blinding the sincerity of this or that representative of one section or another of it: and in the further sense of recognising that such tensions need not necessarily be experienced as merely confusing or even destructive, but that they may also serve as sources of creativity and fresh development.

The trouble with very general formulations of this sort is, of course, not so much that they may not be valid as that already they may seem to strike too comfortable or too comforting a note. In fact, no mere formulation, however rotund, can remove the real discomfort from a situation of built-in tension; at most it may serve as disguise or as temporary tranquilliser. However 'simple and sublime' the doctrines of one's religion, if its actual rites and observances take essentially social form, the universality of its message must inevitably risk entanglement in the particularity of its medium. If the very role of religion (acceptance of its doctrines and respect for its observances) in the constitution of Jewish identity be itself a matter of deep dispute between the diversity of those who, on one count or another, presume themselves or each other to be Jews; and if, in addition, all these problems of identity become caught up in those of one's involvements as a Jew with a State which – somehow – defines itself as Jewish, then certainly the mere diagnosis and recognition of the associated tensions will not suffice to remove them.

Where, then, are we to look for the sources of creativity in this situation of tension? There are all too obvious risks in trying to provide any too abstractly theoretical answers to this sort of question. Abstract and theoretical though it may seem at first sight, however, one answer may be found to have its roots in the sense in which the tensions involved in the impossible but unavoidable attempt to live at the levels of both the universal and the particular 'at the same time' constitute themselves an inescapable and universal feature of the human condition. In this sense the position of the Jew is perhaps not so much peculiar as exemplary; and the challenge that Jews have to meet is to create ways of living that position in such a manner as to provide a proper example to themselves.

Not only humans, but every describable individual entity is, of course, to be situated at one or more of the intersections of universality and particularity. By this I mean nothing more mysterious than the fact that to be an individual is necessarily to be that particular one and no other, and that to be describable is to be of a kind of which there may be other instances. Of what sort or kind are human beings *qua* human beings? There is an old theological doctrine according to which the soul is to the human body as a form is to matter. The particular piece of matter of which any particular thing consists is its principle of individuation; our principle of individuation lies in our bodies, our spatially and temporally determinate but perishable bodies, which provide us with our numerical identities as the particular persons we are. God, Who has no body and Who is immaterial, is truly universal; our soul, the divine spark within us, is that by virtue of which we participate in God's universality – we are, as it is said, all one in God. Animals, who have no soul, simply are and remain at the level of being the kinds of entity that they are. Men, however, are called upon not merely to exist each as an individual instance of his kind, but, knowing themselves for what they are, to seek always to transcend their particularity and to live at the level of the Universal itself.

Not everyone, of course, will share the theology of this doctrine or be ready to speak its language. Its main point, however, may also be expressed in a variety of more secular forms. For example: – Man is the kind of creature that he is by virtue of his peculiar capacity for self-conscious reflection; and this capacity is in effect the same as that for the elaboration of common forms of discourse with others. (At this stage I can only present this assertion as some sort of philosophical dogma; but those familiar with such things will know of the widely ramifying arguments which have been built up by Wittgenstein and others to underpin such claims.) But this capacity, this potentiality for self-awareness, for thought and for language, this Faculty of Reason as some have conceived it, cannot serve to individuate. We are, we may say, so many embodiments of Reason, but not so many Reasons – Reason itself, being a true Universal, has no plural. What differentiates us as so many distinct individuals are our different bodies with their different genetic inheritance and their different personal and social histories – their different space-time paths through the world. Moreover, and here we are close to the heart of the argument, our bodily, spatio-temporal particularity is as essential to our peculiarly human Being as is our universal capacity for language, reflection and Reason. This is not just for the evident reason that we could not constitute the plurality that we do, were we not indeed plural, but for the very much less immediately obvious reason that the very possibilities of conceptualisation and of reflective self-awareness, in any terms in which we can understand them, are only available to beings who can distinguish between themselves and others, other possible users of the same concepts or language – in other words, beings capable of recognising themselves as particular individuals among others.

It follows from this that even as we aspire to the very highest exercises of reason, as we reach, as it is our nature to reach, for the universality of true doctrine or for the selflessness of a truly universal ethic, we remain tied and committed to the maintenance and onward development of our equally constitutive particularity, whatever it may happen to consist in; for our particularity remains for us an untranscendably necessary condition for the exercise of our reason as theoretical and moral beings. The phrase 'whatever it may happen to consist in' is, moreover, peculiarly appropriate to the situation. For the exact nature and circumstances of particularity are always contingent; we may say indeed that both the contingency and the particularity of our condition are universally necessary features of it. If in its flight towards the heights our reason fails to keep one foot at least on the ground of its own embodied particularity, it must end up with a discourse from which all content will have been lost – which is to say that it must end up by losing itself.

All this is exceedingly condensed, abstract and, no doubt, exceedingly abstruse. Moreover, it cannot even pretend as yet to amount to an outline of what could be filled in as an argument of rigorous detail. It may be read, rather, as an outline of some sort of philosophical parable, a parable of the human situation that may cast such light upon it as the reader may choose. And my thesis, my tentative thesis, is that Jews may, in the historical particularities of their situations to-day, choose to read those situations as parables of similar sense.

They *may* choose so to read them. To this it may be replied that anyone may choose to read anything as anything, but that this banality is in itself of no interest or importance whatsoever; what one needs to know is whether there is reason to go for any one reading rather than another. It has to be admitted that it is no doubt impossible, impossible in principle, to impose such a reading through any sort of argument of logically constraining force. We are surely constrained to accept that our present situation is one of great muddle and tension – historically determined, historically intelligible no doubt, but not for that reason any the less inextricable, at any rate for the moment. Different people – both Jews and non-Jews – have different ideas as to what is essential to the identity of Jews *qua* Jews, different views as to the role within that identity of the Jewish religion, different views as to the exact or proper nature of that religion and different views, therefore, as to how it may be determined whether anyone is to be accounted a full member of the community or not. To hope within the diversity of such a spectrum to be able to impose by rational and universally compelling argument just one view of what precisely its diversity consists in, would be to show – however paradoxically – that one had not properly understood it oneself. But *that* there is some such diversity, and that it is part of its nature that its nature be essentially problematic, does seem to demand recognition and acceptance.

Honesty and lucidity may demand that we recognise such facts and that we accept that neither this diversity nor its associated tensions are going to disappear, as it were, overnight. But neither honesty nor lucidity are sufficient to commit us to the acceptance of these tensions as sources of creativity and further development. *This* sort of acceptance, the sort of acceptance that transforms itself as if into a welcome, is rather a matter of resolution, attitude or choice – or, one might say, of a certain sort of faith.

In fact, faith must always, no doubt, include a certain crucial element of resolution or choice – all the more so if it is to be sustained over any length of time or variety of circumstance. It is not for me to try and assess the degree to which my grandfather was explicitly aware at the different stages of his life of the tensions implicit not only in the nature of twentieth century Jewish identity in general, but, more specifically, in his *own* dual allegiance to the universality of his religion and to the particularism of his community. He would, almost certainly, have been far less ready than I am to accept the possibility that some such tensions may be ultimately ineliminable, and that the human condition may have in the end to be characterised as rooted in humanly unresolvable paradox. We are of different generations and belong to different times. But certainly I see him as committed – indeed, quite explicitly committed – by the universality of his faith to look towards the day when all mankind would have come to embrace "the essence of Judaism" as their religion, and so committed to look towards the day when, all men being alike to the Jews in virtue of their religion, Jews bearing the name as such and continuing to live in their particular communities need for all religious purposes exist no more. Of course, to the extent that one may be able to separate questions of religious adherence and commitment from those concerning the membership in given cultural communities or nation-states, one might look towards the day when the Jews would cease to exist as one religious group among others while *continuing* to exist as a group or family of groups with certain recognisable social forms or traditions. But then it is hard to make consistent overall sense, from what seems to have been my grandfather's point of view, of a continuing passionate allegiance to the particularity of a distinctively Jewish identity were that identity no longer to be based on *any* particularity of religion.

I think that, faced with such a challenge, my grandfather must have accepted that a religious and ethical commitment such as his, being both universal and over-riding, must in the end be regarded as independent of membership of any particular historically determined community, however that membership be acquired. But he may well have balanced this acceptance with the argument that pending the ultimate (and still all too uncertain) acceptance of "the essence of the Jewish faith" by all mankind, its preservation and onward transmission could only be assured through its preservation by those historically particular communities for whom adherence to it had always traditionally functioned as a crucial criterion of their own very identity; and across the centuries, what other community than the Jews? (He was also undoubtedly tempted to appeal to the argument from the value of a sheer richness of cultural diversity. But this could only count as a *religious* argument, if one felt it possible to show that the maintenance of cultural diversity was itself a religious – or ethical – duty. This would seem a bit difficult, however. It is one thing to exhort someone not to marry the Gentile whom they love, in the name of fidelity to the command of God – but not so easy to press the exhortation in the name of the preservation of a given culture, or of cultural diversity.)

Naturally enough, however, where adherence to a given religion, even if its message is a universal one, functions also as criterion of the historical identity of a particular people, it is bound to take determinate form as the observance of certain distinctive and publicly recognisable norms. In turn the more socially determinate the criteria of adherence to the religion in question, the more difficult it will become in practice to discern the universalism of its message through the particularisms of its embodiment. "Why should we behave in this particular way?" is a question to which there may, of course, be a religiously universal answer: – "Because the Lord God has so commanded men to behave." But if the answer is rather of the form "Because our forefathers behaved in this way", or even "Because the Lord our God commanded our forefathers so to behave", we are back with the particularisms of history and those particular communities to which we happen to belong. And if this is, *pro tem.*, the best we can do by way of securing the survival of the message of universality, then – we must recognise once again – the tensions must inevitably remain.

What, then, is the positive moral that we may decide to draw from a recognition of these tensions? From a perspective such as that of my grandfather, it seems that we must commit ourselves always to seek both the openness of our own culture, including most notably its religion, to the universality of mankind, and yet also its age-old distinctiveness at one and the same time – and even to seek always this openness as a mark of its very distinctiveness. In as much as this commitment may be formally contradictory, it can provide no universal formula for action in every particular circumstance; it can only remain a matter for judgement, a judgement ever to be renewed, as to how reconciliation between the universal and the particular is best to be pursued in the ever changing particular circumstances of to-day, tomorrow and the next day. But it is here precisely that a recognition of the nature of the contradiction, tension or paradox may provide a principle of continuing creativity and renewal. For if consolidation and preservation may ever and again demand reinforcement of whatever currently goes to constitute a particular identity, we must find ourselves ever and again called upon also to discover fresh ways of recovering the universalism of what we distinctively stand for even in the very reinforcement of our own particularity.

Thus I think that it is, if not mandatory, at least permissible to read the renewal of my grandfather's message of dual allegiance as being one of a continuing fidelity to a Jewish identity that must always strive to transcend itself in the direction of a merging with all mankind even in the very moment of its own self-reaffirmation. And just as the reaffirmation of a particular identity can only take place in particular circumstances, so its transcending must always pass in the first place by way of a movement towards whoever happens to be one's own closest partners at the time – partners in struggle, partners in conflict and tension, maybe, but partners certainly in inextricable mutual involvement. The Jews of Israel and the Jews of the Diaspora: have they not *now* both to recognise each other as the very other of themselves, each a presently indispensable reminder to the other of the values by which, if he is to remain true to his special identity, he must strive always to live? Jews wherever they may live and the there surrounding Gentile world; Jews and Arabs; Israeli Jews and Palestinians. The harder the struggle for survival in one's own particular identity, in one's given historical particularity, the more difficult, but also the more urgent, the task of ensuring that the sense of one's survival always be that of a renewal of the movement towards openness and self-transcendence. The way onwards, so one might say, can be no other than one of a never-ending zigzag.

It is in this sense, then, that I believe C.G.M., if he were still alive to-day, might, like Rabbi John Rayner, find the contemporary meaning of his once upon a time anti-Zionism in what might now seem rather more like an equally passionate support for one kind of 'Zionism' against others.

As for assimilation, he would no doubt have continued to oppose it as vigorously as ever for the still foreseeable future. At the same time, and even if it might have gone very much against some emotional grain, he would surely have seen the problem as one that must lose all religious substance if and whenever the day should come when indeed the whole world should be brought to the unity of a Judaic or Unitarian faith. In the meantime, I like to believe, he might have accepted the existence of some special if modest middleman or 'matchmaker' role for those 'marginal' Jews who, while uncertain of their position in relation to the faith, or even perhaps certain of their own inability to sustain it (Jews whom not even Rabbi Williams may be able to keep in his sense Jewish), nevertheless cannot, in the particularity of their particular circumstances, do other than recognise themselves as indissolubly committed to that paradoxical status of 'Jew' which they have somehow inherited.

A Jew, as I see my grandfather to have seen it, must always remember and bear witness to the fact that neither in the eyes of God nor in ethical principle is he to think of himself as more important than anyone else. But he may, even must, be proud to belong to a people whose traditional mission it has been – as we may choose to see it – to bear witness to this fact.

The text of this essay was originally delivered in 1984 as a Claude G. Montefiore memorial lecture at Jewish Liberal Synagogue, St. John's Wood, London.

Gabriel Moked

Four Domains of Israeli Existence

I would like to speak here about the four domains of Israeli existence as related to writing in Hebrew. Our existence, of course, also includes experience, and I hope that some part of the Israeli experience is also Jewish and not just Israeli. It seems to me that the real spiritual existence of most Israeli writers and intellectuals is related not just to one but to four domains of national culture and history. This de facto quadruple allegiance is, first, in sharp contrast to monolithic descriptions and prescriptions of more single-minded ideologists and controversialists in Israel as well as in the Diaspora (for example, an ultra-orthodox Agudat Israel approach, or the conventional anti-Diaspora *Halutzi*-socialist Zionism, or the ultra-Hebrew, so-called Canaanite and completely un-Jewish tendency. However, by 'single-minded' I do not mean 'wrong from a dignified – e.g., religious or national – point of view', but just 'single-minded' or 'non-pluralistic').

Although such examination and analysis of the relevant spiritual frames of reference are pertinent first and foremost to intellectuals and writers, they also pertain to the ideas and beliefs of the vast majority of ordinary Jewish people, in Israel and the Diaspora, who do not live solely on a physical or economic plane but also have social, national and religious feelings and opinions. All those levels of Jewish religious and non-religious experience and of the unique Israeli experience are, of course, connected with more general and universal beliefs, which do not deal specifically with Jewish or Israeli issues. But I shall refer here to the more general principles and experiences only as they apply to the main subject of our discussion.

According to my view, the four domains of our national experience are these

1) Judaism as a religion and a religious civilization.
2) The Jewish people in the Diaspora – meaning by 'people' a rather less closely knit entity than 'nation'. People welded together mainly by the past but partly also by some present experience.
3) The Israeli-Jewish or the Jewish-Israeli nation.
4) The Hebrew universe of discourse; the universe of the Hebrew language, its semantics, and so forth.

This last domain of experience is much more ancient than the other three. It dates back to the beginning of the 3rd millennium B.C., to the background of proto-Semitic Antiquity (the 'Well of the Past' as Thomas Mann termed it), with its Akkadian, Ebla, Ugaritic forerunners. Perhaps the first allegiance of Hebrew writers should be to the Hebrew language as one of the few classical languages of West and East alike and perhaps the only classical language that remained alive, or, in any event, was successfully resuscitated.

Judaism as a religion and religious civilization is, of course, the most important of all four domains, at least from a spiritual point of view. After a certain period in history, the Hebrew universe of discourse became completely imbued with Judaism. As for the Jewish People, this national entity has suffered more than any community in the world; but despite enormous losses has always been obstinate whenever the continuity of its existence was in question. The Israeli-Jewish nation is a relatively young organism which has become – perhaps undeservedly – the sole guardian of domain (4), and it has highly complex and dialectical relations with both (1) and (2). In their relations with the first domain, both (2) and (3) resemble small secular duchies against the background of the gigantic ruins of the past. Nevertheless, some religious people claim that area (1) exists almost exactly as it did in the past, although we, secular writers, simply cannot see it. In fact, most of area (3) and also area (2) were to a large extent detached from area (1) even before the Holocaust. My parents, for example, spoke mostly Polish and supported the left-wing Polish socialist party, and my uncle and aunt were leading members of the Yiddish-oriented and completely anti-religious Bund in Warsaw. When my father, Dr. Jacob Munvez, fell in the Warsaw Ghetto uprising, he did not fight under a religious banner. Even before the Holocaust, those members of my family would have objected to any identification of the Jewish people with religion. But they were not Zionists either. In fact, the Zionist approach has been justified on only one count: it is fair and just that those Jewish people who wish it should have their own country. In every other respect Zionism is, in a sense, a misinterpretation of the real, complex situation in which all four areas of our experience are intermingled. Thus, the left-wing Zionist attempt to provide a secular substitute for area (1) was doomed to failure, and not only because of the crisis of socialism on a worldwide scale. Moreover, Zionism did not manage to save most of the Jewish masses in Eastern and Central Europe. But if someone – conservative officers or a socialist political party, – had managed to prevent Hitler's rise to power, my whole family would perhaps have been saved. In any event, all these domains of our historical and spiritual existence can survive and carry on a useful and friendly dialogue among themselves without leadership of or supervision by Zionist headquarters; the combination of such supervision with religious-*cum*-chauvinist zealotry and populist Pieds-Noirs leanings in Israel may well be dangerous. What we need both in Israel as well as in the Diaspora is a recognition of the mutual *independence,* and not only the interdependence, of those four spheres of Jewish and Israeli experience. Although these domains overlap and coalesce in part, each is unique and cannot be reduced to another experience.

It also seems to me that the Israeli intelligentsia need such an honest dialogue more than their Jewish brethren in the West. Situated far away from the West in the midst of the Third World in a predominantly Moslem region, enclosed in the shell of a dignified and classical, but still isolated, Hebrew language and literature, the Israeli intelligentsia should be very interested in such a dialogue, based upon a patriotic but pluralistic conception of the multi-layered Hebrew and Jewish universe.

Remarks made at a symposium of the *Jewish Quarterly*, London, December 1986.

Raphael Loewe

Abraham Ibn Ezra, Peter Abelard, and John Donne

Anyone who ventures to translate poetry gives a hostage to fortune; but I am often puzzled by the view of those who maintain that if poetry is to be translated at all, it ought to be translated into prose, since in this way the translator's own aesthetic interpretation is reduced to the minimum and the reader is left to supply his own without having to discount any intrusive veils. The same principle, if applied to the translation of a prose original, would obviously be self-defeating, and its *reductio ad absurdum* is the occasional word-for-word translation technique applied – since antiquity – to holy writ, on the assumption that since the words themselves are divinely inspired, they can afford to let syntax and mood go hang. Normally when we are confronted by prose and are persuaded that circumstances demand translation, we do not shy away from the necessity of making some aesthetic judgment, but where poetry is at issue we often take fright; and probably it is trivialities – nursery rhymes, lampoons, etc – which alone, if rendered into verse, get away scot free.

An excuse that is frequently advanced is the arbitrariness involved in deciding what is an appropriate medium in which to parallel the original form. Where both the original and the receiver language fall within a single major cultural tradition, e.g., that of Europe, such a pretext is often specious: Racine can be rendered reasonably enough into English couplets. I suggest that the real reason is the recoil of the present age from the disciplines of classicism. The problem of finding a receptor-medium for those romantics who have been in revolt against traditions of form leads to an understandable despair, which is then quite illogically appealed to as licence for abandoning formal, disciplined schemes even where the original itself obeys the canons of its domestic tradition: on the grounds that any rendering that resorts to such alleged artificiality will not be "meaningful" to a generation in revolt against such things, but which ought nevertheless not be denied access to the aesthetic power of Aeschylus, Virgil or Dante. That argument appears to me to answer itself. A reader who has a sufficiently substantial knowledge of the general background of culture ought, if he is seriously interested in any poem written in a vernacular not his own, be encouraged to learn the language and study it in the original. If he feels unable to undertake that, or if he lacks the necessary background, he must rely upon the translator's capacity to provide him, as a substitute, with a framework of aesthetic reference drawn from his own experience, no less than he relies upon him for accuracy in rendering. A half-way house, in which the translator accepts the latter responsibility but, in abdicating the former one, insists on providing as clinically sterile a rendering as he possibly can, seems to me to be erecting barriers that will inevitably detract from his reader's capacity to appreciate the original as seen in the mirror that he provides. If I translate a poem I am aware that my version may not seem satisfactory to others as rendered by me into poetic form, and it may well seem even less so to myself. But I am no less aware that were I to abandon all attempt at paralleling the form of the original and to translate it into straight prose, what I produced would be – in my own judgment – worse still.

Where Hebrew is concerned the problem is complicated, at least so far as concerns the Bible, by the status which the scriptures have been accorded beyond Jewry, as being a classic in their various vernacular forms in Europe. Thus in English, the familiar cadences of the prose version of the psalms, both in the Prayer-Book version and in that of the King James' Bible, have been affected by a mystique. The churchgoing public, itself ignorant of the Hebrew original but prepared to accept on trust that it is possessed of great poetic beauty, tacitly credits the translation with the same quality, virtually treating the prose version as poetry, and, as such, sacrosanct. It has also done the same thing in the case of a few verse translations, for example Isaac Watts' rendering of Ps. 90, *O God our help in ages past* – a translation which does happen to have literary merit in its own right, even though sentiment has invested it with more. But where a familiar prose version has become, so to speak, "transfigured", discretion is probably the better part of valour; it is doubtful whether most of the rhymed versions of Ps. 23 would escape ridicule, were they not protected by the simple hymn-tunes which have secured them a place in the affection of a church-going public. With less well known parts of the Bible, some of them virtually unknown in translation save to specialists, it might be a different story; for whilst a translator might well be nonplussed in his search for a suitable English poetic form in which to render the dithyrambic outpourings of a cultic prophet (e.g. Nahum) or the rapturousness of the Song of Songs, it is not too difficult to suggest appropriate models for the relatively measured elegiac mode of the book of Lamentations.

When it comes to post-biblical Hebrew poetry the translator at least has the advantage of starting with a *tabula rasa,* since, except for a few familiar liturgical pieces translated into various European vernaculars in the nineteenth century, those who know it at all know it (for the most part superficially) in the original. But the translator also has another advantage, which is generally lost sight of. However magisterial the command of the language displayed by post-biblical Hebrew poets prior to the emergence of modern Hebrew within the last hundred years, not one of them had Hebrew as his vernacular. It might be surmised that the anonymous authors of such early pieces as *Nishmath kol hai* spoke Hebrew, but the form of these is exalted, rhythmical prose rather than formal poetry. The earliest Palestinian and Babylonian *payetanim*, such as the shadowy Eleazar Ha-qalir, presumably spoke Aramaic and, in Palestine, Greek (the world *payetan* is, of course, itself a borrowing of the Greek *poietes*), or Pehlevi in Babylonia; Solomon ibn Gabirol and Judah Hallevi in Spain spoke Arabic. That does not mean that they were in any way constricted in their use of Hebrew – its bold, indeed arbitrary treatment in the hands of the early *payetanim* proves quite the contrary. But it does mean that they all approached Hebrew with a built-in self-consciousness – and one which they knew how to turn to good account, as, for example, Milton did with Latin. (It might be also noted, in passing, that although Latin was indeed the vernacular of Virgil and Horace, they obviously did not speak as they wrote). It should follow that no one is fully ready to translate post-biblical Hebrew poetry (excluding here modern Hebrew poetry) until he has appreciated this circumstance, and has allowed it to dictate his approach to the original and his choice of form in which to render it into his own vernacular. Conceivably his decision may automatically preclude any "popular" acclamation for his version, but that ought to be a secondary matter. And he might well ponder on the fact that insofar as the original authors met with an immediate response (and they did not all succeed in so doing, nor was it in every case truly "popular"), their success was due to the high standard of Jewish education amongst the readership – probably always a limited readership of fairly scholarly worshippers, or fellow-members of a literary *coterie* – that they had in mind.

For an English translator concerned with the Hebrew poets of the so-called "golden age" of mediaeval Spain a solution seems to me to lie quite readily to hand. Their diction is characterised by a biblicising classicism which, whilst admitting occasional rabbinic coinages of vocabulary but eschewing post-biblical particles and syntax, is in no way stunted in expression. Their metres are basically Arabic schemes which, in adaptation to suit the sonorous vocalisation of massoretically pointed Hebrew, have been made more rigid; in the same way that the Roman poets of the Augustan age tightened up their Greek models and, in so doing, subjected themselves to a metrical discipline that subsequent European culture came to admire, and sometimes to echo. As for their themes, their understanding of the theological challenges and the philosophical implications of a belief in revelation through Torah saw to it that, for them, many of the conventional topics and occasions for Hebrew poetry had to be handled in such a way as to make them vehicles of the poet's own metaphysical thinking: for example, Solomon ibn Gabirol's correlation of sin, penitence and atonement with Ptolemaic cosmology and Aristotelian psychology in his great *Kether Malkhuth*, or the central significance of Zion in Judah Hallevi's love of God.

All three of these aspects of what we might term the Hispano-Jewish school of metaphysical poets are paralleled, *mutatis mutandis*, in the work of English poets of the sixteenth and seventeenth centuries, some of whom evolved their own formal disciplines for the handling of themes that needed extended treatment, such as Spenser's *Prothalamion* or , as an example of a shorter type, Milton's *Hymn on the Morning of Christ's Nativity*, and, for tightly compressed thought, the Miltonic sonnet with its rhyme-scheme more rigorous than that of its Shakespearean counterpart. Moreover, the diction that they adopted will often have sounded slightly archaic to their own contemporaries, as was the diction of King James' Bible when it appeared in 1611. The Jewish and the English metaphysicals were, it seems to me, of a kindred spirit, despite their avowal of reciprocally dismissive faiths; and it has been my own experience that the works of each group furnish appropriate models for the translation of the work of the other, be it from Hebrew to English or *vice versa*. Of the effectiveness or otherwise of the result, others must be left to judge.

Let us take, as an example, a poem by Abraham ibn Ezra, who was born in Tudela, and who died in 1164 – mathematician, astronomer, bible-commentator and traveller, as well as a poet who produced, in addition to some well-loved religious pieces, items of humour and self-mocking irony, and also two most moving poems relating to the conversion of his son Isaac to Islam. Abraham ibn Ezra's wide travels brought him to England, and he also visited certain places in France. He is likely to have found himself at some time in or near Nogent-sur-Seine or Sens, where he could conceivably have rubbed shoulders with Peter Abelard, his senior by ten years. They were, indeed, cast in the same mould. The rationalism in ibn Ezra's biblical scholarship finds its counterpart in Abelard's *Sic et Non* – and it was a rationalism which in the case of neither of them eroded the capacity for emotional response to the transcendent. Abelard's hymn composed for Saturday vespers,

O quanta qualia sunt ista sabbata
Quae semper celebrat superna curia

of course presupposes Christian theological categories, even though its imagery is drawn almost exclusively from the Old Testament and its beginning recalls a well known rabbinic trope: one may, indeed, wonder whether he possibly learned it from some Jew, familiar from the post-prandial grace for the sabbath with the prayer that God may bring us to "a day that shall be one long sabbath and life everlasting" (based on the closing words of Mishnah *Tamid*). But in Judaism, despite the vigour of the notion that the sabbath is a foretaste of the world to come (Babylonian Talmud, *Berakhoth* 57b), it is the spiritual and aesthetic experience of the atmosphere and institutions of the weekly day of rest that give body to that conceit; and it is the impact of these that finds such happy expression in ibn Ezra's poem, composed to be sung over the sabbath meal, *ki eshmerah shabbath el yishmereni:*

If I keep Sabbath day, God safe will keep me,
From Him to me 'twas given, a sign for aye to be.

(Herbert Loewe's translation)

I like to think that had Abelard and Abraham ibn Ezra ever met, they would have understood one another.

Ibn Ezra's penitential poems include a long piece of 90 lines, the formal cohesiveness of which is cemented by the convention that the same end-rhyme must be maintained throughout. It is not now widely known except amongst the eastern Sephardi communities, who have it as an introductory hymn for the service that begins the Day of Atonement; but it is a powerful poem, once its form and structure have been appreciated, and it deserves to be brought to the attention of the larger Jewish community most of whom, insofar as they are still familiar with the traditional prayers, know the Ashkenazi liturgy. Indeed, it merits the notice of all those who may lie outside Jewry and be innocent of Hebrew, but are able to respond to metaphysical poetry. But how to translate it into English? As it happens, John Donne comes to the rescue with his *Holy Sonnets,* which include (c. 1608–9) the linked series of seven that he aptly christened *La Corona* – La Corona, Annunciation, Nativity, Temple, Crucifying, Resurrection, Ascension. Since readers might have difficulty in locating the text I reproduce it here, from Herbert Grierson's edition of 1933, which retained the original spelling. I have adopted Donne's scheme in my own rendering of ibn Ezra's penitential *Lekha 'eli teshuqathi,* and set it out in parallel with the original below.

John Donne / *La Corona*

La Corona.

1. Deigne at my hands this crown of prayer and praise,
Weav'd in my low devout melancholie,
Thou which of good, hast, yea art treasury,
All changing unchang'd Antient of dayes;
But doe not, with a vile crowne of fraile bayes,
Reward my muses white sincerity,
But what thy thorny crowne gain'd, that give mee,
A crowne of Glory, which doth flower alwayes;
The ends crowne our workes, but thou crown'st our ends,
For, at our end begins our endlesse rest;
The first last end, now zealously possest,
With a strong sober thirst, my soule attends.
'Tis time that heart and voice be lifted high,
Salvation to all that will is nigh.

Annvnciation.

2. Salvation to all that will is nigh;
That All, which alwayes is All every where,
Which cannot sinne, and yet all sinnes must beare,
Which cannot die, yet cannot chuse but die,
Loe, faithfull Virgin, yeelds himselfe to lye
In prison, in thy wombe; and though he there
Can take no sinne, nor thou give, yet he will weare
Taken from thence, flesh, which deaths force may trie.
Ere by the spheares time was created, thou
Wast in his minde, who is thy Sonne, and Brother;
Whom thou conceiv'st, conceiv'd; yea thou art now
Thy Makers maker, and thy Fathers mother;
Thou'hast light in darke; and shutst in little roome,
Immensitie cloysterd in thy deare wombe.

Nativitie.

3. Immensitie cloysterd in thy deare wombe,
Now leaves his welbelov'd imprisonment,
There he hath made himselfe to his intent
Weake enough, now into our world to come;
But Oh, for thee, for him, hath th'Inne no roome?
Yet lay him in this stall, and from the Orient,
Starres, and wisemen will travell to prevent
The effect of *Herods* jealous generall doome.
Seest thou, my Soule, with thy faiths eyes, how he
Which fils all place, yet none holds him, doth lye?
Was not his pity towards thee wondrous high,
That would have need to be pittied by thee?
Kisse him, and with him into Egypt goe,
With his kinde mother, who partakes thy woe.

Temple.

4. With his kinde mother who partakes thy woe,
Joseph turne backe; see where your child doth sit,
Blowing, yea blowing out those sparks of wit,
Which himselfe on the Doctors did bestow;
The Word but lately could not speake, and loe,
It sodenly speakes wonders, whence comes it,
That all which was, and all which should be writ,
A shallow seeming child, should deeply know?
His Godhead was not soule to his manhood,
Nor had time mellowed him to this ripenesse,
But as for one which hath a long taske, 'tis good,
With the Sunne to beginne his businesse,
He in his ages morning thus began
By miracles exceeding power of man.

Crvcifying.

5. By miracles exceeding power of man,
Hee faith in some, envie in some begat,
For, what weake spirits admire, ambitious, hate;
In both affections many to him ran,
But Oh! the worst are most, they will and can,
Alas, and do, unto the immaculate,
Whose creature Fate is, now prescribe a Fate,
Measuring selfe-lifes infinity to'a span,
Nay to an inch. Loe, where condemned hee
Beares his owne crosse, with paine, yet by and by
When it beares him, he must beare more and die.
Now thou art lifted up, draw mee to thee,
And at thy death giving such liberall dole,
Moyst, with one drop of thy blood, my dry soule.

Resvrrection.

6. Moyst with one drop of thy blood, my dry soule
Shall (though she now be in extreme degree
Too stony hard, and too fleshly,) bee
Freed by that drop, from being starv'd, hard, or foule,
And life, by this death abled, shall controule
Death, whom thy death slue; nor shall to mee
Feare of first or last death, bring miserie,
If in thy little booke my name thou enroule,
Flesh in that long sleep is not putrified,
But made that there, of which, and for which 'twas;
Nor can by other meanes be glorified.
May then sinnes sleep, and deaths soone from me passe,
That wak't from both, I againe risen may
Salute the last and everlasting day.

Ascention.

7. Salute the last and everlasting day,
Joy at the uprising of this Sunne, and Sonne,
Yee whose just teares, or tribulation
Have purely washt, or burnt your drossie clay;
Behold the Highest, parting hence away,
Lightens the darke clouds, which hee treads upon,
Nor doth hee by ascending, show alone,
But first hee, and hee first enters the way.
O strong Ramme, which hast batter'd heaven for mee,
Mild Lambe, which with thy blood, hast mark'd the path;
Bright Torch, which shin'st, that I the way may see,
Oh, with thy owne blood quench thy owne just wrath,
And if thy holy Spirit, my Muse did raise,
Deigne at my hands this crowne of prayer and praise.

Abraham Ibn Ezra / *Hymn in Penitence*

For Thee, Lord, yearn I; love in Thee I own,
My heart, my soul my parts, my breath are thine,
My hands, my limbs – all these are thy design,
My flesh and blood, my skin, my ev'ry bone,
Eye, thought, imagin'd forms are thine alone,
My faculties, and all hopes that are mine:
And so I bring my heart's blood to thy shrine,
The lamb wherein my sacrifice is shown.
Unique art Thou: my soul, unique to me,
Shall give Thee thanks, to whom there doth belong
All royal pomp, fit subject for my song;
Help is of Thee – my help in trouble be
When I, as if in childbed writhing, strain:
In Thee I hope, O Lord; heal Thou my pain.

בְּךָ חֶשְׁקִי וְאַהֲבָתִי.	לְךָ אֵלִי תְּשׁוּקָתִי.
לְךָ רוּחִי וְנִשְׁמָתִי	לְךָ לִבִּי וְכִלְיוֹתַי.
וּמִמְּךָ הִיא תְכוּנָתִי.	לְךָ יָדִי לְךָ רַגְלִי.
וְעוֹרִי עִם גְּוִיָּתִי.	לְךָ עַצְמִי לְךָ דָמִי.
וְצוּרָתִי וְתַבְנִיתִי.	לְךָ עֵינִי וְרַעְיוֹנַי.
וּמִבְטָחִי וְתִקְוָתִי	לְךָ רוּחִי לְךָ כֹחִי.
כְּשֶׁה אַקְרִיב וְעוֹלָתִי	לְךָ לִבִּי וְדַם חֶלְבִּי.
לְךָ תּוֹדָה יְחִידָתִי	לְךָ יָחִיד בְּלִי שֵׁנִי.
לְךָ תֵּאוֹת תְּהִלָּתִי.	לְךָ מַלְכוּת לְךָ גֵּאוּת.
הֱיֵה עֶזְרִי בְּצָרָתִי	לְךָ עֶזְרָה בְּעֵת צָרָה.
כְּיוֹלֵדָה בְּאַנְחָתִי.	לְךָ אוֹחִיל בְּעֵת אָחִיל.

In Thee I hope, O Lord; heal Thou my pain:
To Thee I cry, unsilenc'd in my plight
Until my darkness Thou shalt turn to light.
Thou, everlasting, wilt my trust remain,
I cling to Thee for succour till again
Earth turns to earth, knowing me thine by right
In life, still more in death: so I recite
Confession of my sin before Thee; deign
To grant me thy salvation, and forgive
My faults; to Thee I bow, my palms are rais'd.
Lord, hear my contrite heart's recitative,
My tears, my musings, sighs through grieving craz'd.
Pity my sorry state, my misdeeds spare:
My wayward sin is more than I can bear.

וְאֶת צִירִי וּמַכָּתִי	לְךָ שִׁבְרִי רְפָא שִׁבְרִי.
עֲדֵי תָאִיר אֲפֵלָתִי.	לְךָ אֶהֱמֶה וְלֹא אֶדְמֶה.
וְאַתָּה הוּא אֱיָלוּתִי	לְךָ נֶצַח בְּךָ אֶבְטָח.
עֲדֵי שׁוּבִי לְאַדְמָתִי.	לְךָ אֶזְעַק בְּךָ אֶדְבַּק.
וְאַף כִּי אַחֲרֵי מוֹתִי	לְךָ אֲנִי בְּעוֹדִי חַי.
עֲלֵי חֶטְאַי וְרִשְׁעָתִי.	לְךָ אוֹדֶה וְאֶתְוַדֶּה.
וְאֶת פִּשְׁעִי וְאַשְׁמָתִי	לְךָ יִשְׁעִי סְלַח רִשְׁעִי.
שְׁמַע נָא אֶת תְּחִנָּתִי.	לְךָ אַכַּף וְאֶפְרוֹשׂ כַּף.
בְּרוֹב שִׂיחִי וְתוּגָתִי	לְךָ אֶבְכֶּה בְּלֵב נִדְכֶּה
חֲמוֹל עַל כָּל תְּלָאוֹתִי.	לְךָ חֶסֶד לְךָ חֶמְלָה.
וְגָדְלָה יַד מְשׁוּבָתִי	וְגָדוֹל מִנְּשׂוֹא חֶטְאָי.

My wayward sin is more than I can bear,
And so my pangs increase, and what I sow'd
Must I now reap. Alack! Ill would it bode
Shouldst Thou judge my deserts. My passion e'er
Lays siege to me, mine Adversary's snare
Ill counsel offers in seductive mode;
On him, none else, anger'd reproach I load.
But when upon my couch my faults I dare
Survey, I shudder to recall, confus'd,
My twisted nature's acts, beneath thine eye
Naked I stand, nor can I make reply
To-day, by my deceitfulness accus'd.
Fruit must I eat of deeds my law had bann'd:
Requital looms: for doomsday is at hand.

וְלָכֵן גָּדְלוּ צִירַי.
וְאוֹי עָלַי וְהָה לִי. אִם
וְיִצְרִי צוֹרְרִי תָּמִיד.
יְעָצַנִי וּפִתָּנִי.
וְעָלָיו לֹא עֲלֵי בִלְתּוֹ.
וְעֵת יַעֲלוּ עֲלֵי לִבִּי.
מְאֹד אֶפְחַד וְגַם אֶרְעַד.
וְאֶרְגַּז עֵת אֱהִי זוֹכֵר.
וְאֶעֱמוֹד נֶגְדְּךָ עָרוֹם.
בְּיוֹם כִּי יַעֲנֶה כַחֲשִׁי.
וְיָבֹאוּ יְמֵי שָׁלוֹם.

וְקָצַרְתִּי זְרִיעָתִי.
תְּדִינֵנִי כְּרִשְׁעָתִי.
כְּמוֹ שָׂטָן לְעֻמָּתִי.
בְּמוֹעֲצוֹת לְרָעָתִי.
חֲמָסִי עִם תְּלוּנָתִי.
עֲוֹנוֹתַי בְּמִטָּתִי.
מְאֹד יִגְדַּל מְהוּמָתִי.
לְפָנֶיךָ מְעַנָּתִי.
וּמַה תִּהְיֶה תְּשׁוּבָתִי.
וְאֹכַל מִפְּרִי דָתִי.
וְתִקְרַב עֵת פְּקוּדָתִי.

Requital looms: for doomsday is at hand;
Lord, I have heard the tale of Thee, and quake,
For who shall stand before Thee? Who could take
My place, could I, with exculpation bland
Account to Thee with self-excuse expand?
Guilty am I, who all thy code did break,
I stole, corrupted; others did I make
To share my sin; I err'd, deceit I plann'd,
In youth I sinn'd, in age play'd false, contemn'd
Thy law in chosing mine; I gratified
My passion's will, nor thought I of mine end,
But, adding sin to sin, guilt multiplied.
So shame his veil about my face doth wind:
In Thee alone can I forgiveness find.

וּשְׁמַעֲךָ עֵת שְׁמַעְתִּיהוּ.
וּמִי יַעֲמוֹד לְפָנֶיךָ.
וְאֵיךְ חֶשְׁבּוֹן לְךָ אֶתֵּן.
וְאָשַׁמְתִּי וְאָרַכְתִּי.
וְגָזַלְתִּי וְגָנַבְתִּי.
וְגַם זַדְתִּי וְחָמַסְתִּי.
וְטָעִיתִי וְיָעַצְתִּי.
וְלוֹצַצְתִּי וְגַם לַצְתִּי.
וְנִאַצְתִּי וְנִאַפְתִּי.

מְאֹד זַעְתִּי וְיָרֵאתִי
וּמִי יִהְיֶה תְּמוּרָתִי.
וְאֵיךְ אֶצְדַּק בְּטַעֲנָתִי
וּבָגַדְתִּי וּבָזִיתִי.
הֲרֵיעוֹתִי וְהִרְשַׁעְתִּי:
וְחָטָאתִי וְהֶחֱטֵאתִי.
וְכִזַּבְתִּי וְכָפַרְתִּי
וּמָרַדְתִּי וּמָרִיתִי.
וְסָרַרְתִּי וְסָרַחְתִּי

וְעָוִיתִי וְהֶעֱוֵיתִי.
וְצָרַרְתִּי וְצִעַרְתִּי.
וְרָשַׁעְתִּי וְשִׁחַתִּי.
וְסַרְתִּי מִדְּרָכֶיךָ.
וְהִגְדַּלְתִּי עֲשׂוֹת רֶשַׁע.
וְכִחַשְׁתִּי וּמָעַלְתִּי.
וְחָטָאתִי בְּרֵאשִׁיתִי.
וְאָשַׁמְתִּי בְּיַלְדוּתִי.
וּבָחַלְתִּי בְּתוֹרָתָךְ.
וְעָזַבְתִּי רְצוֹנֶךָ.
וְהִשְׁלַמְתִּי רְצוֹן יִצְרִי.
וְהִרְבֵּתִי לְהוֹסִיף חֵטְא.
וְלָכֵן כִּסְּתָה פָנָי.
וְאֵין לִי בִּלְתָּךְ מָנוֹם.

וּפָשַׁעְתִּי וּפָגַמְתִּי.
וְקִלַּלְתִּי וְקִלְקַלְתִּי.
וְתִעַבְתִּי וְתָעִיתִי.
וְכִסַּתְנִי כְלִמָּתִי
וְהֶחֱזַקְתִּי בְּרִשְׁעָתִי.
וְעָשַׂקְתִּי וְרַצוֹתִי
וְרָשַׁעְתִּי בְּאַחֲרִיתִי.
וּבָגַדְתִּי בְּזִקְנָתִי
וּבָחַרְתִּי בְּתוֹרָתִי.
וְהָלַכְתִּי בְּתַאֲוָתִי
וְלֹא בַנְתִּי לְאַחֲרִיתִי.
עָלַי רִשְׁעִי וְחוֹבָתִי
כְּלִמָּתִי וְגַם בּוֹשְׁתִּי.
וּמִמְּךָ הִיא סְלִיחָתִי

In Thee alone can I forgiveness find,
No pardon save in Thee, my sole resort;
But shouldst Thou bring thy servant into court
What am I? What my strength, what pow'r of mind?
My life is nought but chaff, toss'd by the wind:
Why, then, of my backsliding reck'st Thou aught?
Dumb, swath'd in what mine own disgrace hath wrought,
I beg; to what I seek, pray be Thou kind:
Cleanse me of all my sins, O cleanse me well
From faults, look on me, wearied with dismay
In exile languishing: close not, I pray,
Thine ear to pleas when for release I yell;
Say to my troubles "'tis enough, no more",
So pledge thy servant good Thou hast in store.

וּמוֹחֵל בִּלְתְּךָ אָיִן.	וּמֵאִתְּךָ מְחִילָתִי.
וְאִם תָּבִיא בְמִשְׁפָּט עַבְ־	דָּךְ מַה הִיא גְבוּרָתִי
וּמָה אָנִי וּמַה חַיָּי.	וּמַה כֹּחִי וְעָצְמָתִי.
כְּקַשׁ נִדָּף מְאֹד נֶהְדַּף.	וְאֵיךְ תִּזְכֹּר מְשׁוּגָתִי
וְנֶאֱלַמְתִּי וְנִכְלַמְתִּי.	וְכִסַּתְנִי כְלִמָּתִי.
רְצוֹנָךְ אֶשְׁאֲלָה תָמִיד.	לְמַלֹּאות אֶת שְׁאֵלָתִי
וְהֶרֶב כַּבְּסֵנִי	עֲוֹנוֹתַי וְחַטֹּאתִי.
וְהַבֵּט רֹב תְּלָאוֹתַי.	וְדַלּוּתִי בְגָלוּתִי
וְאַל נָא תַעֲלֵם אָזְנָךְ	לְרַוְחָתִי לְשׁוּעָתִי.
עֲרוֹב עַבְדָּךְ לְטוֹבָה. גַּם	אֱמוֹר נָא דַי לְצָרָתִי.

So pledge thy servant good Thou hast in store;
Show me deliverance, ere death his snare
Snaps, and I fall – stay me from slipping there.
Gall sateth me, till I my life abhor;
Show me some sign for good; rise, I implore,
Help me, who art my portion, from despair,
Thou source of joy, light of mine eyes, Thou air
Of rest to ease that which in me is sore:
Teach me to know thy service, and I learn
To serve Thee only: do but mark the trail,
Then I do Thee in penitence return
Nor will thy favour my repentance fail.
Show me thy ways, and make my path run straight:
Hear me: O answer when I supplicate.

בְּטֶרֶם יוֹם תְּמוּתָתִי.   וְהַרְאֵנִי תְּשׁוּעָתֶךָ.

סְמוֹךְ נָא אֶת נְפִילָתִי   וְיוֹם נָפְלִי בְּפַח מוֹקְשִׁי.

עֲדֵי קַצְתִּי בְּחַיָּתִי.   וְלַעֲנָה שָׂבְעָה נַפְשִׁי.

וְקוּמָה נָא לְעֶזְרָתִי   עֲשֵׂה עִמִּי לְטוֹבָה אוֹת.

וְרַנָּתִי וְטוֹבָתִי.   הֲכִי אַתָּה מְנָת חֶלְקִי.

וְכָל גִּילִי וְשִׂמְחָתִי   וְגוֹרָלִי וּמַהְלָלִי.

וּמָעוּזִּי וְחֶמְדָּתִי.   שְׂשׂוֹן לִבִּי וְאוֹר עֵינִי.

מְנוּחָתִי וְשַׁלְוָתִי   וּמַרְגּוֹעִי וְשַׁעְשׁוּעִי.

וְלָךְ תִּהְיֶה עֲבוֹדָתִי.   הֲבִינֵנִי עֲבוֹדָתֶךָ.

וְתִרְצֶה אֶת תְּשׁוּבָתִי   הֲשִׁיבֵנוּ וְאָשׁוּבָה.

וְיַשֵּׁר אֶת נְתִיבָתִי.   וְהוֹרֵנִי דְּרָכֶךָ.

וְתַעֲנֶה אֶת עֲתִירָתִי   וְתִשְׁמַע אֶת תְּפִלָּתִי.

Hear me: O answer, when I suplicate:
In tears that I for my libation shed
Blot all my sins away; inherited
As my soul's portion, Thou that art my Fate,
Take, with my life, my sin: and on the date
That I for judgement am before Thee led
Look kindly on my coming: with the stead
Of those that did thy will, mine designate.
Send angels to conduct me, crying "peace!"
With one voice, to escort me to the field
Of Eden, and the light therein conceal'd,
In that light to find shade, glory, release,
Beneath thy wings – there stow my soul alone:
For Thee, Lord, yearn I: love in Thee I own.

בְּכָל לִבִּי דְרַשְׁתִּיךָ.   עֲנֵנִי יָהּ דְּרִישָׁתִי.

אַנַּסֵּךְ אֶת דְּמָעַי לָךְ.   מְחֵה חֶטְאִי בְּדִמְעָתִי

וְנַפְשִׁי אָמְרָה חֶלְקִי.   יְהֹנָה הִיא וְנַחֲלָתִי.

אֱסוֹף נָא אֶת עֲוֹנוֹתַי.   בְּחַסְדָּךְ יוֹם אֲסִיפָתִי

וְיוֹם לֶכְתִּי לְפָנֶיךָ   רְצֵה נָא אֶת הֲלִיכָתִי.

וְעִם עוֹשֵׂי רְצוֹנֶךָ.   תְּנָה שְׂכַר פְּעוּלָתִי

וְתִשְׁלַח מַלְאֲכֵי הַחֵן.   וְיֵצְאוּ נָא לְעֻמָּתִי.

וְשָׁלוֹם בּוֹאֲךָ יֹאמְרוּ.   בְּקוֹל אֶחָד בְּבִיאָתִי

יְבִיאוּנִי לְגַן עֶדְנֶךָ.   וְשָׁם תִּהְיֶה יְשִׁיבָתִי.

וְאֶתְעַדֵּן בְּאוֹרֶךָ.   וְשִׂים כָּבוֹד מְנוּחָתִי

וְאוֹר גָּנוּז לְפָנֶיךָ.   יְהִי סִתְרִי וְסֻכָּתִי.

וְתַחַת צֵל כְּנָפֶיךָ.   תְּנָה נָא אֶת מְחִיצָתִי

Abelard and Divine Sabbaths

Although as I mentioned above nearly all the imagery in Abelard's hymn for Saturday vespers is drawn from the Jewish Bible, its first and last stanzas contain specifically New Testament allusions to major Christian categories, and these cannot be retained in a Hebrew version without incongruity. Appropriate substitutes have to be found, and in place of the closing reference to the trinity there leaps to a Jewish translator's mind the apologetic expansion of Isaiah's *Holy, holy, holy* as elaborated in the Targum – a disavowal of trinitarian exegesis, felt to be important enough to embody as a quotation in the daily liturgy. Here, then, is the original text of Abelard's Latin hymn, its English rendering by Helen Waddell published in her *Mediaeval Latin Lyrics*, and alongside them my own Hebrew version which is modelled on the sabbath table-hymn by Abraham ibn Ezra.

O quanta qualia sunt illa sabbata,
quae semper celebrat superna curia,
quae fessis requies, quae merces fortibus,
cum erit omnia Deus in omnibus!

Vere Jerusalem est illa civitas,
cuius pax iugis est, summa iucunditas,
ubi non praeuenit rem desiderium,
nec desiderio minus est praemium.

לחן כי אשמרה שבת אל ישמרני

How mighty are the Sabbaths,
How mighty and how deep,
That the high courts of heaven
To everlasting keep.
What peace unto the weary
What pride unto the strong,
When God in whom is all things
Shall be all things to men.

יוֹם זֶה מְנוּחָה אוֹת לָנוּ חֲנַנְתּוֹ
לַיּוֹם אֲשֶׁר כֻּלּוֹ שַׁבָּת צְפַנְתּוֹ
הַנּוֹחֲלִים שַׁבַּת נֶצַח נְצָחִים
הֵם שׁוֹכְנֵי מָרוֹם לָעַד שְׂמֵחִים
גַּם שַׁאֲנָנִים שָׁם נוּגֵי טְרָחִים
חֵלֶק לְצַדִּיק מַשְׂכֻּרְתּוֹ גְּנַזְתּוֹ
לַיּוֹם אֲשֶׁר כֻּלּוֹ שַׁבָּת צְפַנְתּוֹ

Jerusalem is the city
Of everlasting peace,
A peace that is surpassing
And utter blessedness,
Where finds the dreamer waking
Truth beyond dreaming for,
Nor is the heart's possessing
Less than the heart's desire.

אָכֵן יְרוּשָׁלַיִם הִיא מְעוֹנִי
לָעַד נְוֵה שָׁלוֹם הִיא רֹאשׁ שְׂשׂוֹנִי
לִבִּי תְכַדֵּם עֵת תָּפִיק רְצוֹנִי
גַּם מֶרְצוֹנִי לֹא תִקְצַר בְּתִתּוֹ
לַיּוֹם אֲשֶׁר כֻּלּוֹ שַׁבָּת צְפַנְתּוֹ

Quis rex, qua curia, quale palatium,
Quae pax, quae requies, quod illum gaudium,
huius participes exponant gloriae
si, quantum sentiunt, possint exprimere.

Nostrum est interim mentem erigere
et totis patriam uotis appetere,
et ad Jerusalem a Babylonia
post longa regredi tandem exsilia.

Illic molestiis finitis omnibus
securi cantica Sion cantabimus,
et iuges gratias de donis gratiae
beata referet plebs tibi, domine.

But of the courts of heaven
  And Him who is the King,
The rest and the refreshing
  The joy that is therein,
Let those that know it answer
  Who in that bliss have part,
If any word can utter
  The fulness of the heart.

מָה רָב כְּבוֹד מֶלֶךְ עַל מַלְאָכָיו רָם
שָׁלוֹם בְּהֵיכָלוֹ שִׁירָם וְאָמְרָם
אַף כִּי לְמַלֵּל כָּל־הוֹדוֹ בְּזִמְרָם
לֹא יוּכְלוּ שְׁנָאָן לָהֶם חֲלָקְתּוֹ
לַיּוֹם אֲשֶׁר כֻּלּוֹ שַׁבָּת צְפַנְתּוֹ

But ours, with minds uplifted
  Unto the heights of God,
With our whole heart's desiring,
  To take the homeward road,
And the long exile over,
  Captive in Babylon,
Again unto Jerusalem,
  To win at last return.

עַד לֹא יְבִיאֵנוּ אֵלִי לְדִינוֹ
נָקוּם וְנִתְחַגֵּן תָּמִיד לְחַנּוֹ
לָשׁוּב לְאַרְצֵנוּ חָמַד לְשָׁכְנוֹ
עוֹלִים לְצִיּוֹן מִכָּבֵל לְבֵיתוֹ
לַיּוֹם אֲשֶׁר כֻּלּוֹ שַׁבָּת צְפַנְתּוֹ

There, all vexation ended,
  And from all grieving free,
We sing the song of Zion
  In deep security.
And everlasting praises
  For all thy gifts of grace
Rise from thy happy people,
  Lord of our blessedness.

שָׁם חָדְלוּ רוֹגֶז יָגוֹן וְצָרוֹת
מָלֵא לְבָבֵנוּ שַׁלְוָה וְשִׁירוֹת
תּוֹדַת שְׂפָתֵינוּ תַּתְמִיד זְמִירוֹת
יוֹדוּ לְךָ עַם זוּ חֶסֶד גְּמַלְתּוֹ
לַיּוֹם אֲשֶׁר כֻּלּוֹ שַׁבָּת צְפַנְתּוֹ

Illic ex sabbato succedet sabbatum,
perpes laetitia sabbatizantium,
nec ineffabiles cessabunt iubili
quos decantabimus et nos et angeli.

Perenni domino perpes sit gloria
ex quo sunt, per quem sunt, in quo sunt omnia:
ex quo sunt, pater est; per quem sunt, filius,
in quo sunt, patris et filii spiritus.

There Sabbath unto Sabbath
    Succeeds eternally,
The joy that has no ending
    Of souls in holiday.
And never shall the rapture
    Beyond all mortal ken
Cease from the eternal chorus
    That angels sing with men.

שַׁבָּת תְּכוּפַת שַׁבָּת שָׁם וְתָמִיד
כָּל־שׁוֹמְרֵי שַׁבָּת עוֹנֶג לְהַצְמִיד
לֹא יִשְׁבְּתוּ קוֹל הַמַּנְעִים וּמַחֲמִיד
אֶל־קוֹל שְׂרָפִים נִקְשׁוֹר קוֹל עֲדָתוֹ
לַיּוֹם אֲשֶׁר כֻּלּוֹ שַׁבָּת צְפַנְתּוֹ

Now to the King Eternal
    Be praise eternally,
From whom are all things, by whom
    And in whom all things be.
From Whom, as from the Father,
    By Whom, as from the Son,
In whom, as in the spirit,
    Father and Son in one.

קָדוֹשׁ בְּשָׁמַיִם כִּסֵּא כְּבוֹדוֹ
קָדוֹשׁ אֲשֶׁר אֶרֶץ הֲדוֹם לְהוֹדוֹ
קָדוֹשׁ לְעוֹלָם עַד נִשְׁאָר לְבַדּוֹ
נַקְדִּישָׁךְ עַם יִשְׂרָאֵל בְּחַרְתּוֹ
לַיּוֹם אֲשֶׁר כֻּלּוֹ שַׁבָּת צְפַנְתּוֹ

Dannie Abse

Under the Influence of...
(or David and Dafydd)

I

I am told by scholarly critics, some of whom are presently anchored not too far from here, that Anglo-Welsh poetry is imbued with certain characteristics. These, it would seem, are derived from the Welsh language literary tradition. No matter that the Anglo-Welsh poet cannot read the old language, that real thing strange; or that he does not even know translations of Welsh poetry despite the efforts of those like Gwyn Jones; the influence of it on his creativity, though he may deny it, is still active. 'Seepage' is the word our scholarly critics bandy about. The seepage 'on all cultural levels between the two language-groups of Wales' as Anthony Conran puts it.

Certainly it is a somewhat mystic notion that allows an Anglo-Welsh poet, ignorant of Welsh literature, to be most marvellously, most miraculously, affected by it. I do not mock. At least I do not mock with conviction because I know things can exist even when they cannot be invulnerably defined – like the concept of Welsh nationality itself.

In the introduction to the recently published *Anglo-Welsh Poetry 1480–1980* Raymond Garlick and Roland Mathias attempt to identify the idioplasm of the poetry they anthologise. The first ingredient they refer to is the 'inborn Welsh feeling... that praise is what poetry should be about.' They argue, for instance, that when Dylan Thomas declared his poems were written 'for the love of Man and in praise of God' he spoke as a Welshman; in the same way, centuries earlier, when George Herbert asserted that a poet should be 'secretary of thy praise,' he was defining the Welsh view of a poet's function.

What Garlick and Mathias do not do is ponder on the relationship of David and Dafydd. After all, the Old Testament poets, when not uttering the poetry of curses, were also secretaries of praise. They extolled the Lord. They heaped praise on praise, image after image. Theirs was a most wondrous and rhetorical propitiation. Almost one thousand and eight hundred years ago the illustrious Rabbi Judah said, 'In our days the harp had seven strings, as the Psalmist has written: "By seven daily did I praise thee."' Or consider the Talmudic blessing of the same century that is still sung over a goblet of wine at present day Jewish weddings: 'Blessed art thou our God, King of the Universe, who created joy and gladness, bridegroom and bride, mirth, song, delight and cheer, love and harmony, and peace and companionship. Soon the Lord our God, may be heard in the cities of Judah and in the streets of Jerusalem, the voice of joy and the voice of gladness, the voice of the bridegroom and the voice of the bride, the jubilant voices of the espoused from their wedding canopy and the young people from their feast of singing. Blessed art thou our Lord who rejoices the bridegroom with the bride.'

Wouldn't that blessing fit nicely in Welsh? Or even uttered in a broader Welsh accent than I own? Doesn't it, come to think of it, sound like Dylan Thomas larking about, setting it up, in one of his prose pieces? When my grandfather, in 1887, was invited to preach in the chapel at Ystalyfera, when he uttered translated Hebrew rhetoric of this kind, David spoke to Dafydd, and the non-conformist congregation found neither the substance nor the manner of his sermon alien.

It can be remarked, cynically, that the praise of God was a somewhat amateur enterprise. The extolling poet had no guarantee of his reward: rain would not fall; nor was he relieved of his scabs and haemorrhoids. The Welsh bards were professional in comparison. Their praises, if laid on beautifully thick, were suitably rewarded by Prince ap Mammon. Sometimes the flattery was directed towards a lady but then, too, the bard looked for and probably received love's honorarium.

The Song of Songs, which is Solomon's, the early theologians suggested, was religious praise-allegory. The 2nd century A.D. rabbis, in order to include it in the canon, maintained that it signified God's love for the people of Israel. The Church Fathers of the same century, also finding the poem lush and alarming, interpreted it as being Christ's declaration of love for the Church. Nobody would imagine the Song of Songs which is Huw Morus's, to be allegorical. 'In praise of a girl' was in praise of a certain seventeenth century girl, praise of a slip of loveliness, 'slim seemly, freshly fashioned, Moon of Wales, your loveliness prevails.'

Both poems – Solomon's and Huw's are... lovely; one observes yet again that the literary traditions of David and Dafydd are not separate entities. Simply, the older tradition permeates the younger, there is a dialectic, a development. A seepage!

Raymond Garlick and Roland Mathias suggest that one piece typical of Welsh-flavoured praise poetry is George Herbert's sonnet, 'Prayer'; that it owns, moreover, characteristic devices of bardic craft: compound words and the heaping up of comparisons. Not long before the publication of their Anglo-Welsh anthology, in short well before I read their introduction, it so happened that I wrote a sonnet based on Herbert's poem which I called 'Music'. It, too, consists of consecutive poetic definitions – though not of prayer but of music. Since both are brief I shall read them to you. First, 'Prayer':

Prayer

Prayer, the Church's banquet, Angel's age,
    God's breath in man returning to his birth,
    The soul in paraphrase, heart in pilgrimage,
The Christian plummet sounding heaven and earth;

Engine against th'Almighty, sinner's tower,
    Reversed thunder, Christ-side-piercing spear,
    The six days' world-transposing in an hour,
A kind of tune, which all things hear and fear;

Softness, and peace, and joy, and love, and bliss,
    Exalted Manna, gladness of the best,
    Heaven in ordinary, men well drest,
The Milky Way, the bird of Paradise,

    Church-bells beyond the stars heard, the soul's blood,
    The land of spices, something understood.

Now (excuse the impudence of following George Herbert) my own sonnet, 'Music':

Music

Music, in the beginning. Before the word,
    voyaging of the spheres, their falling transport.
Like phoenix utterance, what Pythagoras heard;
    first hallucinogen, ritual's afterthought.

A place on no map. Hubbub behind high walls
    of Heaven – its bugged secrets filtering out:
numinous hauntings; sacerdotal mating-calls;
    decorous deliriums; an angel's shout.

If God's propaganda, then Devil's disgust,
    plainchant or symphony, carol or fugue;
King Saul's solace, St. Cecilia's drug;
    silence's hiding place – like sunbeams' dust.

Sorrow's aggrandisements more plangent than sweet;
    the soul made audible, Time's other beat.

The question I would like to ask you here is what amalgam of influences are apparent in 'Music'? Because of its covert praise-component, its strategy of using a catalogue of analogues, should it be classed as an Anglo-Welsh poem? Is it of the tradition of David and Dafydd? Or, simply, is its influence only that of George Herbert himself?

II

When I was a schoolboy, my elder brothers Wilfred and Leo were already in their twenties, young adults. They became the most important influences in the direction of my life. Wilfred, when he himself became a doctor, newly qualified at the Welsh National School of Medicine here in Cardiff, came home one day to find me uselessly pushing a saucer of milk towards our sick cat, Merlin. I was a fourteen year old who wanted to play football for Cardiff City, rugby for Wales, cricket for Glamorgan.

'Better to become a doctor,' Wilfred suggested. 'I could put your name down for the new Westminster Hospital they're planning in London.' 'I wouldn't mind being a vet,' I said, looking at the cat.

I did not fancy shifting to London. I resented even moving the 1½ miles from Sandringham Road, Roath, Cardiff, to Windermere Avenue, Penylan, Cardiff, as we were to do the following year. For God's sake, who wanted to travel 160 miles every Saturday to reach Ninian Park or Cardiff Arms Park? And where, in London, would you get a better chip shop than the one opposite the Globe Cinema?

By the time we moved to Windermere Avenue, Wilfred, with my father approving, had responsibly charted my future. He persuaded my parents to put my name down for Westminster Hospital and, at school, I now turned to the science subjects – physics, chemistry and biology – with a more purposeful interest.

If Wilfred set me towards studying Medicine, my brother Leo, inadvertently, faced me toward Poetry. At school, at St. Illtyd's where I was taught by Christian Brothers, I did not enjoy our poetry classes. It was, I thought, cissy stuff. Daffodils, Lesser Celandines, Skylarks, Cuckoos, jug-jug, pu-we, to-witta-woo! That sort of thing did not seem of moment. There was a war going on in Spain; one of Leo's friends, Sid Hamm, had been killed out there fighting for the International Brigade; Mussolini was puffed out and ranting in Italy; Hitler, eyes thyrotoxic, dangerously maniacal in Germany. There was sloth and unemployment and depression in the Welsh valleys and the Prince of Wales had said poshly, uselessly, 'Something must be done.' But nothing was done, so what relevance, 'Cuckoo, jug-jug, pu-we, to witta-woo'?

At school we still sang, 'Let the prayer re-echo, God bless the Prince of Wales,' though I mistakenly believed that patriotic lyric to be 'Let the prairie echo, God bless the Prince of Wales', and wondered vaguely where the devil those grass-waving prairies were in mountainous Wales. At home, though, I read those left-wing magazines Leo brought back and, in them, I discovered poems of a political nature and of the war in Spain. How moved I was, for instance, when I happened on 'Huesca', the simple, direct poem by John Cornford. Not twenty one, John Cornford had been killed at the battle of Huesca while fighting for the International Brigade. How poignant his melancholy premonition of his own death; how terrible those lines of his, the last lines he ever wrote.

Poetry moved into the centre of my preoccupations gradually and that movement only truly commenced after I had read, in 1940, an anthology, *Poems for Spain,* edited by Stephen Spender. Here I encountered poets whose adult moral concerns and protestations engaged my own schoolboy wrath and indignation. Their voices had a passionate immediacy and their language was fresh, of the twentieth century. The raw, political poems of the Spanish peasant poet, Miguel Hernandez, especially, triggered me to try and express my own indignation about the horrors of the Spanish war in verse. Yes, naively, wanting to make political statements, I had begun to write verse voluntarily, not as an exercise for school. I showed my efforts to my elder brothers, and Wilfred, particularly, encouraged me.

The war in Spain ended and Hitler was screaming and given thunderous applause. It was not long before we heard our Prime Minister, Neville Chamberlain, utter on the B.B.C., 'I have to tell you that no undertaking has been received and that consequently this country is at war with Germany.' My sister had married, had already left home. In 1940 it was Leo's turn to leave Wales. He was called up for the R.A.F. Later, Wilfred joined the Army. Suddenly the house seemed larger. There was only father, mother, me and the dog.

Perhaps it was fortunate for me that my brothers had to go away at this crucial period: at least it allowed me to develop unimpeded in my own tentative way – dreaming most of the time or browsing in Cardiff Central Library or listening to Duke Ellington records or to the war news of the B.B.C., or playing games, or fumbling after girls, or preparing myself for a medical education, or writing a collocation of words that I wrongly called a poem.

III

Medical students, in their pre-clinical years, are allowed long summer vacations. In Cardiff, I spent much of my holidays in the Central Library reading poetry. First I reached for the books on the left hand side top shelf of the Twentieth Century Poetry Section: Richard Aldington, W.H. Auden. Then I worked my way across and downward. I read for pleasure, in this untutored way, alphabetically, not chronologically, without benefit of knowing who was considered by critics to be worthy, who to be scorned! One day I asked a girl called Joyce Herbert who was reading English at Cardiff's University College if she had heard of Dylan Thomas. My question provoked a little chuckle and a contemptuous, 'Of course.'

Dylan Thomas's poems powerfully engaged me – too much so, for a number of my own poems which can be discovered in my first volume,

After Every Green Thing, are touched by his manner. Certain phrases sound like Dylan's cast-offs: 'harp of sabbaths', 'choir of wounds'. Admiring his work as I did, naturally I became curious about the man who lived not far away from my own home-patch. I was most intrigued when Leo, soon after he was demobbed from the R.A.F., told me that he had met my hero and that, moreover, Dylan Thomas had related to him a remarkable dream.

It seemed that Dylan, in this dream, entered a huge cavern or chamber in which he witnessed a biblical scene being enacted: Job, head bowed in grief, sat on the ground, crosslegged, with his three bearded comforters in silent attendance. Dylan quit this chamber to enter another and here saw Absalom, caught by his long hair, struggling and swinging from the boughs of a great oak. Then the dreamer entered another chamber where frenzied crowds danced around a golden calf. He passed from chamber to chamber, cavern leading into cavern, going back in time, watching Jacob wrestling with the angel or Abraham, in rage, destroying the wooden idols. At last, Dylan came to the ultimate chamber. He entered into almost darkness. He peered. Something was glinting against the rock of the back wall. He approached. Two skeletons became visible: the skeletons of a man and a woman, hand in hand.

That dream was surely a waking vision, rather than one recalled from sleep, and perhaps it owed something to William Blake's memorable fancies in *The Marriage of Heaven and Hell?* No matter, Leo's recounting of it made me pause and wonder. I relished it and, soon enough, back in London, retold it to literary friends in one of the cafés of Swiss Cottage that, in those post-war years, I regularly visited.

I had lodgings in Swiss Cottage. It was a cosmopolitan area with a remarkably vivid café-life because of the refugees, mostly Jews, from Austria and Germany. They had settled in the district. So ubiquitous were they that the bus conductors, approaching Swiss Cottage, would bang the bell and shout out, 'Next stop, Tel Aviv.' In cafés such as *The Cosmo* or *The Cordial* loitered theatre and film people such as Peter Berg, Lotte Lenya, Peter Zadek; or writers like Elias Canetti (who insisted on being called Canetti since he loathed his first name), the poet Erich Fried (who happened to have an abnormally thick-boned skull and could thump it, bang bang bang, against a wall for our amusement) and Rudi Nassauer (who had been influenced by Dylan Thomas, even more than I had, so that he thundered out his poems in an arresting but unnatural booming voice that would have delighted Dylan Thomas's elocution teacher).

In this ambience I heard of European poets who had hardly featured in the Poetry Section of Cardiff's Central Library. I read some of these in translation and one, especially, became a passion with me: Rainer Maria Rilke. How exciting to read such praise-poetry lines as:

There is nothing too small but my tenderness paints
in large on a background of gold.

When I read Rilke's *Letters to a Young Poet* I felt he addressed not merely Herr Kappus but me: 'This before all: ask yourself in the quietest hour of your night: must I write? Dig down into yourself for a deep answer. And if this should be in the affirmative, if you may meet this solemn question with a strong and simple, *I must,* then build your life according to this necessity...' I responded, of course, with a strenuous, 'I must' and I have, though it may sound somewhat grand to say so, unconsciously as much as consciously, ordered my life ever since to allow for this central need.

The eighth letter addressed to Kappus from Sweden in 1904 stimulated me to write a poem called 'The Uninvited'. It is the only poem I am now willing to acknowledge that appeared in my first volume, *After Every Green Thing*. Rilke, in that letter, spoke of how certain sorrowful experiences alter us because of what they may engender. When we are open to important moments of sorrow, argued Rilke, then our future 'sets foot in us'. Though we could easily believe nothing has truly happened, our destiny begins and 'we have been changed as a house is changed into which a guest has entered'.

Rilke's influence endured and could set me ticking like a wheel of a bicycle going downhill. In 1954, I wrote a number of poems on existentialist themes, among them 'Duality' and 'The Trial' as a result of reading a passage in *The Notebook of Malte Laurids Brigge*. Here Rilke described an encounter with a woman who was deep in thought, completely sunk into herself, her head in her hands. 'At the corner of the Rue Notre-Dame-des-Champs,' wrote Rilke, 'I began to walk softly as soon as I saw her... The street was too empty; its emptiness was bored with itself; it caught my step from under my feet and clattered about with it hither and yon, as with a wooden clog. The woman took fright and was torn too quickly out of herself, too violently, so that her face remained in her two hands. I could see it lying in them, its hollow form. It cost me an indescribable effort to keep my eyes on those hands and not to look at what had been torn out of them. I shuddered to see a face thus from the inside, but I was still more afraid of the naked, flayed head without a face.'

Rilke not only triggered me to write a number of poems but taught me lessons which I took to heart. In his first letter to Kappus, for instance, he averred, 'A work of art is good if it has grown out of necessity.' I assented to that: so many poems that I admired most had sprung from the stress of a personal predicament or from an active emotion like indignation or rage or love. Had I not been turned on originally to poetry because of the urgent cries of help from some poets in beleaguered Spain – poets like Miguel Hernandez? Had I not been moved by John Cornford's 'Huesca' – or, going back through the centuries, by John Clare's 'I Am' and William Cowper's 'The Castaway'?

Again Rilke suggested that one should be committed to difficulty. 'We know little,' he wrote, 'but that we must hold to the difficult...' Poetry, true crafted poetry was scandalously difficult to write. And the practice of medicine, too, at least for me, was hardly an easy ride.

Some poems of Rilke, too, became guru-lessons for me. At a hospital bedside, in a consulting room, I have listened, as a doctor must, purely to patients – never having to silence the clamour that my own senses might make. But discarding the white coat, encountering strangers of interest, I have tended to talk too much, to display, rather than to listen. Then I have reminded myself of these lines by Rilke that I know, in Babette Deutsch's translation, by heart:

If only there were stillness, full, complete.
If all the random and approximate
were muted, with neighbours' laughter, for your sake,
and if the clamour that my senses make
did not confound the vigil I would keep –

Then in a thousandfold thought I could think
you out, even to your utmost brink
and (while a smile endures) possess you, giving
you away, as though I were but giving thanks
to all the living.

There are those who cannot bear Rilke – among them friends of mine, poets, whose opinion I generally value; and indeed there are many occasions when Rilke in his letters seems too sanctimonious, too high flown, phoney even. I thought this when I first read him. In the margins of my old copy of *Letters to a Young Poet,* years ago, I scrawled, 'Note here his evident insincerity.' Or I remarked on his patronising attitudes and pomposity. I argued in an abbreviated form (with question marks and exclamation marks) against the poetic ideas he proposed about such matters as the attainment of inner solitude, of the need to be alone as one was in childhood when surrounding adults seemed so busy and distant. Yet arguments with a mentor can be valuable in themselves, be productive. I disliked then, as most Welshmen would, the way Rilke, encountering others, thrust out his arm, as it were, to keep them away. His need to distance other people as if other people were vulgarly dangerous. Years later I wrote a poem concerning a lady with these Rilkean attitudes. If the poem that follows, 'Close Up' (N.B. no hyphen), is any good at all then my argument with Rilke was not entirely worthless:

Often you seem to be listening to a music
that others cannot hear. Rilke would have loved you:
you never intrude, you never ask questions
of those, crying in the dark, who are most near.

You always keep something of yourself to yourself
in the electric bars, even in bedrooms.
Rilke would have praised you: your nearness is far,
and, therefore, your distance like the very stars.

Yet some things you miss and some things you lose
by keeping your arm outstretched; and some things
you'll never know unless one, at least, knows you
like a close-up, in detail – blow by human blow.

What I could have learnt and should have learnt from Rilke was the value of experiences in making a poem. That I was to learn later when I began to believe poems should not begin with ideas but rather spring from true or imagined experience. One poet whom I met in Swiss Cottage, Denise Levertov, was more percipient than me about this. She has said in *Light Up the Cave* that her first lesson from Rilke was to experience what you live. I should have heeded, right from the beginning, how Rilke told the secret that verses amount to little when one begins to write them young. Rilke continues, 'One ought to wait and gather sense and sweetness, a whole life long, and a long life if possible, and then, quite at the end, one might perhaps be able to write ten good lines. For verses are not, as people imagine, simply feelings (we have these soon enough); they are experiences. In order to write a single verse, one must see many cities, and men and things... One must be able to return in thought to roads in unknown regions, to unexpected encounters, and to partings that had been long foreseen; to days of childhood that are still indistinct... to days spent in rooms withdrawn and quiet, and to mornings by the sea, to the sea itself, to oceans, to nights of travel that rushed along loftily and flew with all the stars – and still it is not enough to be able to think of all this. There must be memories of many nights of love, each one unlike the others, of the screams of women in labour, and of women in childbed, light and blanched and sleeping, shutting themselves in. But one must also have been beside the dying, must have sat beside the dead in a room with open windows and with fitful noises.

And still it is not enough yet to have memories. One must be able to forget them when they are many, and one must have the immense patience to wait until they come again. For it is the memories themselves that matter. Only when they have turned to blood within us, to glance and gesture, nameless and no longer to be distinguished from ourselves – only then can it happen that in a most rare hour the first word of a poem arises in their midst and goes forth from them.'

IV

In the structuring of experience into poems I have sometimes drawn on literary texts in a way that I suspect is not visible or audible to others. The texts generally are soluble in the poems. Sometimes they are not soluble and could be discerned if the reader happened on certain sources. For instance, I have in recent years, drawn on brief Talmudic or Midrashic lesson-stories. Here is one example: Rabbi Eliezer was sick. Rabbi Yohanan came to visit him. He saw Rabbi Eliezer lying in a dark house. Rabbi Yohanan bared his arm and the room lit up. He saw that Rabbi Eliezer was crying. He said to him, 'Why are you crying? Is it for the Torah in which you have not studied enough? We have learned, do more, do less, it matters not, as long as one's heart is turned to heaven...' Rabbi Eliezer replied, 'I am crying over this beauty of yours which one day will wither in the dust.' Rabbi Yohanan said, 'You are right to cry over that.' And they wept together.

Under the influence of that succinct anecdote I wrote a narrative

poem called 'The Silence of Tudor Evans.' I'll repeat the title because it
makes an important point: 'The Silence of Tudor Evans'. It goes like this:

Gwen Evans, singer and trainer of singers,
     who, in 1941, warbled
an encore (Trees) at Porthcawl Pavilion
     lay in bed, not half her weight and dying.
Her husband, Tudor, drew the noise of curtains.

Then, in the artificial dark, she whispered,
     'Please send for Professor Mandlebaum.'
She raised her head pleadingly from the pillow,
     her horror-movie eyes thyrotoxic.
'Who?' Tudor asked, remembering, remembering.

Not Mandlebaum, not that renowned professor
     whom Gwen had once met on holiday;
not that lithe ex-Wimbledon tennis player
     and author of Mediastinal Tumours;
not that swine Mandlebaum of 1941?

Mandlebaum doodled in his hotel bedroom.
     For years he had been in speechless sloth.
But now for Gwen and old times' sake he, first-class,
     alert, left echoing Paddington for
a darkened sickroom and two large searching eyes.

She sobbed when he gently took her hand in his.
     'But my dear, why are you crying?'
'Because, Max, you're quite unrecognisable.'
     'I can't scold you for crying about that,'
said Mandlebaum and he, too, began to weep.

They wept together (and Tudor closed his eyes)
     Gwen, singer and trainer of singers
     because she was dying; and he, Mandlebaum,
     ex-physician and ex-tennis player,
because he had become so ugly and so old.

I have plundered different midrashic texts to energise other poems, not a few of which have been portrait poems, a genre that has been favoured, according to Garlick and Mathias, for centuries because of 'Welsh curiosity about other people.' To be sure, there are no kept secrets in Wales. All women leak; all men are moles. Everybody knows Dai, the spy. Or to put it more diplomatically: we gossip so much because we are all so interested in the unfathomable strangeness of other human beings.

If what Garlick and Mathias say about portrait-poems is true, then it would seem, that in an odd way, I may have inadvertently once again tried to make the traditions of David and Dafydd confluent.

V

In February 1961 I became involved with the astonishing Poetry and Jazz concerts that were to take place with regular success in the theatres, town halls, school halls and public libraries of Britain during the rest of the decade. I had received a phone call from a young man called Jeremy Robson inviting me to read at the Hampstead Town Hall along with Jon Silkin and Lydia Slater who would recite her brother's poems in translation. (Lydia Slater was the sister of Boris Pasternak). Jeremy Robson did not inform me that he planned intervals of jazz between the poets' readings nor that he, himself, would read his own poetry especially written for jazz accompaniment. In addition, he omitted to tell me that the comedian of Goon Fame, Spike Milligan, would also feature.

I was, I suppose, a literary snob! If I had seen the advertisements, I doubt whether I would have accepted Jeremy Robson's invitation. I set out that evening expecting to participate in a genteel poetry reading with the usual numbers attending and thus I was baffled to discover, at the doors of the Town Hall, a huge crowd demanding entrance while a distraught porter shouted, 'Full up, Full up.' I had difficulty, in fact, in pushing my way through. Inside, hundreds sat on the Town Hall's upright wooden chairs, others sprawled in the aisles, leant on the side walls and back walls while jazz negligently blared. Soon Spike Milligan appeared in dramatic spotlight saying, 'I thought I'd begin with a sonnet by Shakespeare but then I thought why should I? He never reads any of mine.' The concert was not solemn.

Over the next six years Jeremy Robson organised hundreds more of these concerts, inviting a score or so of alternating, different poets to take part. Some, such as Vernon Scannell, John Smith, Jeremy Robson himself, read their poems to jazz; others such as Ted Hughes, Laurie Lee and myself, read our poems 'straight', unaccompanied, believing as we did that each poem had its own music and, for that matter, its own silences. (Stevie Smith sometimes *sang* her poems in a peculiarly flat voice.) The enthusiastic, large audiences clapped frequently and seemed to be genuinely entertained. Later they bought books (in the interval) to investigate in private, on the page, the poems they had heard publicly in the auditorium.

We always arrived in one or another provincial town at lighting-up time. I still feel that on entering such places as Nottingham or Leicester somehow the lampposts should all jerk into life, and on quitting them the hands of the clock should turn fast and turn again until the streets are late, deserted, the shops darkened except for the one, lonely, lit Indian restaurant that beckons jazz musicians and poets to eat and unwind.

Over the next six years, did the regular practice of reading poems aloud to large audiences affect, consciously or unconsciously, our strategy in structuring poems? When Dylan Thomas began to read to proliferating mass audiences the idioplasm of his poetry gradually altered. His poems, while growing more complex in their rhythmic orchestration, also became somewhat less dense, less recondite generally. There were seductive dangers in being exposed to large audiences and I daresay some poets sometimes succumbed to them and not in the way Dylan Thomas did. In my case, I know that my poems about this time became more conversationally pitched but I doubt if this was the result of performance and live audience. When I wrote a poem I did not usually consider reader or listener. The exception to that was in writing longer poems. Then, at a certain point in their maturation, I would become aware that I would actually enjoy reading this or that one out loud to receive a public response. When I wrote plays I had to be aware of audience, of allowing the narrative its tensions and relaxations. So, too, with a long poem which otherwise could freeze an audience into lassitude. In writing, for instance, 'The Smile Was', about 1965, after some drafts I knew I would read it out loud at a Poetry and Jazz concert. I became more aware of the problems of pace, density and humour than might otherwise have been the case. And I ensured that the rhythms did not become too monotonous, that the repetitions of sound patterns were appropriately varied. Once Eliot had generously said of a play of mine that it had the virtue of being both for the stage and the study. I would like to think some of my longer poems could be similarly characterised.

VI

Most of us hardly question what influences us and do not observe our barely fathomable metamorphosis steadily. We merely mark how our life situation may have changed or how our interests have been developed; how our children have grown up, how others we loved became much older or died. All authors, though, have visible concrete evidence of their own internal changes: they can turn to their artefacts – in my case, to my plays as well as to my poems – and see how these give witness to altering attitudes, preoccupations, arguments with oneself. They recall debts to other writers, textual influences, transient or repetitive experiences and moods, successes and failures, occasions and relationships. Poems on the page lie there and do not lie: their own progenitor can scrutinise them as if they were spiritual X rays.

Certainly my poems relate, in hidden narrative, my true biography. There is hardly an important occasion in my life that is not covertly profiled or overtly re-inhabited in my poems. So when I open my *Collected Poems* and turn, say, to page 107, I suffer almost an abreaction as I hold again my father's hand while he is dying in Llandough Hospital in 1964; or when the book falls open on page 131 I can remember, altogether less painfully, how with my wife and children, I attended a demonstration in Trafalgar Square, in 1968, against the war in Vietnam.

Poems can remind me of such things because they are rooted in my mental life, in my experience, some mundane, some dramatic. I recall the words of Rilke again: 'In order to write a single verse one must be able to return in thought... to unexpected encounters... to days of childhood that are still indistinct... to nights of love... But one must also have been beside the dying, must have sat beside the dead in a room with open windows and with fitful noises.' I have experienced such things as so many others have; and I have done my best to tell of these things in the best way I can, with what gift I have, sometimes going to other men's texts like a sleepwalker and sometimes wideawake.

Nor have I worried about such matters for I agree with Goethe when he remarked... 'We are all collective beings, let us place ourselves as we may. For how little *have* we, and *are* we, that we can strictly call our own property? We must all receive and learn both from those who were before us, and from those who are with us. Even the greatest genius would not go far if he tried to owe everything to his own internal self. But many very good men do not comprehend that; and they grope in darkness for half a life, with their dreams of originality. I have known artists who boasted of having followed no master, and of having to thank their own genius for everything. Fools! as if that were possible at all; and as if the world would not force itself upon them at every step, and make something of them in spite of their own stupidity... And, indeed, what is there good in us, if it is not the power and the inclination to appropriate to ourselves the resources of the outward world and to make them subservient to our higher ends... The main point is to have a great will, and skill and perseverance to carry it out.'

And here's the curious thing: after decades of writing poems, every poet, I believe, if he takes his own work seriously as he should, comes under the influence of it. When a poet begins to write a poem there is no reader; but as he concludes his poem he himself becomes the first reader. Sometimes the last! He receives his own words. Thereafter, in subtle ways, his poems even as they may recede for others, remain for him strangely active. They help to determine not only how he will write but how he will live. Some may argue that poetry is a useless thing. It influences no-one. But whatever else poems do, or do not do, they profoundly alter the man or the woman who wrote them.

'*Under the Influence of...*' was originally given as a Gwyn Jones Lecture at University College, Cardiff.

David Avidan

Eleven Poems

What Did Kurt Waldheim Expect from the Polish Pope?

A funny question: what did Kurt Waldheim expect from the Polish Pope?

Johanan Paulus, the second and not last, received him in his Holy Chamber, and what, in fact, was going on there?

The exhausted Austrian President was looking for a *priest*, simply for a priest, but certainly not for a *simple* priest.

He was, in fact, looking for the Father-of-Fathers, for the Super-Priest, to have a true confession properly discharged.

And that's what he did, Panie Papieżu, that's precisely what he did.

From the heights of his Austrian Highness, detesting Slavs, peasants, sausages in place of cakes,

he went down to his Holiness' floor, Polish peasant, ex-boxer, knows Hebrew, acquainted with Kurts,

then told exactly what had really happened, how all little screws were screwed and screwed up, and organized and orginized.

Suddenly amnesty was granted, like a radioactive lightfall, Hiroshima and Nagasaki and the Berlin Wall

and Hitler, who grasped his basic education in Vienna, and whose ideological masterpiece, Mein Kampf,

Israeli students are now eagerly looking for, in all bookstores, Hebrew version coming soon, for historical purposes.

The *Hit*-ler will obviously break down the entire book-market, the black square mustache will crack a thousand Black Boxes.

"A nation that doesn't fight once every twenty years is doomed to degeneration," he said somewhere else, in Secret Conversations with his GHQ

or on any alternative *Hit*-lerish occasion. And Israeli youth will carefully examine this assertion, a mindblowing axiom.

Hitler was a natal Taurus with a rising Aries, and he gored the Red Army all the way back to Moscow.

He hated the Jews for having originated Christianity, the latter having violated the ancient Hellenic Harmony (quote).

The Japanese (quote) had a forceful racial awareness, therefore Jewry couldn't penetrate their culture – the Germans had less of it,

consequently Jewry settled down in their cerebrum, having bioprogrammed, with the Theory of National Relativity,

both the Holocaust and the State of Israel, which seems to make a point of fighting at least once every twenty years. And if we'll argue that the Japanese have always had a perverted tendency to challenge giants (China, Pearl Harbor), contrary to all

classical Martial Arts' doctrines, something maniacal, Kamikazish, pain in the ass – then where are we

within the framework of this global characteristic, and where, for that matter, was Germany, and what is Austria anyway? And the President – yes the President – went down on his knees before the Polish Pope, and told him, "Forgive me, father, I've sinned, I've done evil,

I did not know what I was doing". And Paulus-Nie-Pierwszy was showering Holy Vodka on his balding skull,

birdhead, evil bird perhaps, definitely frightened to death – yet bird of prey, no doubt –

then waved over him the Greek Cross from the Harmonious Hellenism, far earlier

than the Christian Cross and faraway later than the Swastika, the latter which the Germans switched over, graphopolitically,

from the ancient original Buddhistic-Tibetan symbol, closely related to the Shield of David, a sunrising-marking Mandala,

a Sunstika, in fact, as I've already mentioned – to the symbol of ruin and destruction and decontaminating Europe of inferior races. And now in Rome

the Vatican's supreme authority is redecorating a dwindling career of the President of a cakes-and-electronics republic,

kind of German-speaking Italy à-la-Duce, only without the pizzas and the day-fighting Fiats that had bombed Tel-Aviv –

a floor and a half in the Women-Workers-Farm, around ten meters from
where I was standing, Keren Kayemeth Boulevard, fucked up, clumsy
bombardment,
having preceded the alarm signal by several seconds – then went back
home completely unharmed, ready to write within x years
this heavy-duty political poem, homage to Ezra Pound's Cantos, an old
story, a story in itself –
did for the twentieth century's poetry much more than his
contemporaries, including Eliot – his follower – and Auden
and Dylan Thomas and Allen Ginsberg who interviewed him at the end
of the 'Fifties or beginning of the 'Sixties (better check)
and granted him amnesty (pariah pitied pariah) and received in return
meaningless wording, terminal statement.

So what did Kurt Waldheim expect from the Polish Pope? And what
did the Pope expect from him? Interim:
probably the midpoint of last lost honor. Poland has not perished yet,
and Austria, Austria über alles.
Poor, dangerous world, still dominated – in all ranks and on all levels –
by good & bad plebeians,
post-war-criminals and future-war-criminals – and the intellectual élite,
writers, scientists,
is making comments, suggesting, signing petitions in squares and plazas,
no Cessnas –
Red Square is out of bounds. So that may be Gorbachev who remembers
Stalin who remembered Zhukov
who had ripped the Wehrmacht – might remind Reagan who remembers
Roosevelt, who got America
into the global frame (China plus Europe much obliged), that a *word*
should be dropped to the Polish Pope,
etwas stark, out of Dov Zakheim's vocabulary, to make him flash back to
his childhood and youth,
acolyte, blood-sausage, black magic up there in the cupola. Down on
your knees, Panie Janie Pawle, down on your knees,
and confess to the free and glasnostical world your sinful reception of the
Austrian Führer –
then a dipping in the Dead Sea and a prayer in Jerusalem, and the Holy
One keeps full view from above,
and the Vatican Veterans' congress in the National Buildings and Yad
Va'Shem and the laser beam and the glittery thundering starwar.

Lingual Politicians

People like myself, not like yourself,
determine the lingual policy
everywhere in the semantic galaxy,
every place on this planet
and outside it.

They are monitoring the soft, invisible, subatomic vibration
of the silent, extralogical, metapsychological,
subscientific and supergrammatical buzz.

We are responsible for whatever occurs in the language every single
       moment,
for people like myself and yourself are the lingual politicians.
It's for us to decide how humans will speak within ten, twenty, a
       hundred, two hundred,
ten thousand years from now.

We are engineering your understanding mechanisms,
tuning up your input-output devices.
We have neither money, nor power, nor political authority.
We have given it all up in favor of being
the first and last deciders of lingual policy.
We determine the policy of the language as well as the language itself.
We decide how you will perceive
pressure-situations, softness-situations, perceptional situations,
nonsensical situations, redemptive situations
within the language and the policy of language,
for we are the first and last decision-makers
within the realm of lingual policy.

We don't run banks, industries, agriculture, governments, political
       parties, military & police infrastructures.
We have no financing or managing boards, no administrative influence
    on other people.
But we determine the constant, hyperfast flight of all lingual stirs
every given moment, in any language and every place.
Each of us does it in his own language and occasionally in one or two
    more and it accumulates all together.

We determine interverbal communication.
We grasp semantics semiotics images shadows and sounds,
and we decide how you will grasp this graspingness.
For we are the lingual politicians,
the first and last decision-makers within the policy of language.

Don't think of us as megalomaniacs – for megalomania is just a word,
and every word is retrieved by us every particle of a second.
Megalomania is equally mega-communication, mega-semantics, mega-
    mega.

We are megalomaniacs more than micromaniacs,
yet we are far less megalomaniacs than you are,
for we know much more than you do about the language,
without having even one thousandth of the self-confidence you seem for
    no reason to possess.

We are the ideologists of global and cosmic semantics.
We know exactly what happens in your brain at any given moment,
while the policy of language
contacts the powercenters of brain and interbrain
of each of you separately and all of you together.

We are the lingual politicians, for we know
that language is policy and policy is language –
and still language is located out of all political boundaries
and out of all lingual ones as well.

Within the extralingual language and extrapolitical policy
we are simultaneously representing and represented,
away from your brain and the brains of your ancestors & ancestral
    ancestors & grandsons and great-grandsons.

For we are the lingual politicians,
the first and last decision-makers within the policy of language.
And we are possessed by hysterical happiness for what we are.

Yet hysteria is just a word, and every word is reinspected by us every
    particle of a second.
We are the hysterics of self-confidence, we are hysteria's unruffled
    subjects.
We are the hysterics of hysterical nonhysterical tranquillity.
We are hysteria's permanent stability.
For we are the lingual politicians,
the first and last decision-makers within the policy of language.

Biting and Kissing Angles

Any bite of a man dog shark anything that bites has an angle
a fixed angle for the biting creature and a changeable one adjusted to the
    bitten.
And for any kiss of a man kissing a woman a woman kissing a man a
       man kissing a boy and a girl a woman kissing a girl and a boy
there's one fixed angle for the kisser and one fixed angle adjusted to the
    kissed

And there is a clear link between the biting angle and kissing angle a
    kissed bitten angle.
The line between biting and kissing is thin flimsy measurable by atomic
    rulers

There are few such atomic rulers in Tel Aviv New York or Tokyo
and one can compute with them not only the result but just as well the
    reason
that is to calculate in advance the biting and kissing angles of any given
    creature
and also predict whether the mouth opening will eventually shut down
    into a bite – or kiss.

Current Observations

Judaism is the ceramics of the twentieth century.
It is written: make thyself neither an idol nor a painted image.
But it is not written: make thyself no ceramics.
Judaism is the ceramics of the almighty, who has suddenly desired
6 million objects from the oven.

That's the last thing I need – beggars of emotionality, beggars of
    sentimentality,
beggars of intellectuality, beggars of beggarliness.
That's the last thing we need in order to be emotionally bankrupt.

In a science-fiction reality on planet earth a way was found to duplicate
    humans –
on the condition that they be photographed in a certain sexual position.
The Women's Liberation Movement encourages females to find the
    compatible male,
to go to bed with him once, to take his genetic picture,
then reduplicate him into a humanoid,
so that he can fulfill all the remaining functions endlessly and without
    depreciation.
The catch is that resulting from this photograph the human power of
    virility
passes on to the humanoid, but the source remains impotent.
Millions of men find themselves victims of the impotence trap
after being dragged to bed by radiant beauties.
A young scientist declares rebellion and plan to stultify the scheme –
and to destroy this geneto-photographing gadget.

The Surrounding Aridity

A sudden satori flashed thru my mind in the height of Tel Aviv heat:
In view of the thermoneurosis, attacking most people in their desiccated
    brains, it should be quite clear
that one of the reasons for the conflict in the ME has been the climate, as
    no logical argumentative structure
has ever been capable of passing smoothly from man to man or from
    group to group above a certain degree of heat.
Simply, above such a certain degree the message does not go thru.
It is possible to suggest that the logical structure has actually expanded
    because of the heat and couldn't enter the slot
it was meant to go into.
The result might be that it was necessary to thrust it in forcefully, with a
    push and a scream, with belligerent actions.
Since the temperature in this region, on most days of the year, is much
    too hot
people simply aren't used to comprehending western logical structures –
    and each side thinks
that its heat-expanded message is the ideal one.
As soon as one side tries – and consequently fails – to communicate a
    logical structure to the other –
that other one goes mad.
Hada Hoo.*

*) That's it (Arabic)

The Legacy of the Serpent

Why do people all of a sudden die? What meaning does it all have,
if the operation is cut in the middle?
Are we all destined to be vipers, adders, sons of viperidae,
an Ammonite serpent that stands upright on its tail? The divine promise
    that was never fulfilled –
and instead he is licking the dust?
But this is precisely the state of man and the entire meaning of the
    matter.
Every man thinks of himself as a vertical serpent, standing on its tale
and directing the affairs of this world, but as a matter of fact we have
    neither
arms nor legs, and we are licking that dust and crawling.
What is left to man are the serpentine pretensions from the time of Eden
and the actual state of the serpent after the expulsion.
Not man was expelled from the Garden of Eden but the serpent.
If the serpent had remained in the Garden of Eden, man wouldn't have
    so much trouble getting along outside it.
The fact that the serpent was expelled is what complicated
our human situation, because it was our divine emissary that sinned.
The serpent was the only good insurance man had for eternal life.
But the serpent messed up – and when this uniped flopped,
what else could a biped do to correct the error?
One can wave one's arms and legs, but the serpent has already bitten the
    dust,
and that is the member that was shed in the Garden of Eden.
Ever since we've kept on trying to raise it from the floor, but the best it
    can do
is sting from time to time – this is the most a limb can do.
What alternative has a limb but to crawl on the floor and lick the dust?
So the serpent is the limb that was expelled from the Garden of Eden,
    and ever since man is bruising its head.

Campaign Speech for the Presidency of the US of Chinamerica

Now listen to me I'm speaking to you with the charms of rice with
    brand new steelwool Japanese microphones
I have every reason to believe you'll vote for me in the coming elections
    out of your own freewill.
My rhetorical capacity is merely part of your unrestrainable voting
    resourcefulness.
This time you will surely exercise it for me and for me only because you
    believe in me
I for my part trust your trusting I'm talking to you like a man to a man
    like a man to a woman a dog to a dog a dog to
    a bitch barking to you
crying to you with brand new steelwool in muddy ricefields in gasoline
    stations.
This particular speech I wrote for a change by myself.
Pay pay attention how these splendid lines are swiftly sifted right into
    your problematic hearing organs.
Right into your deserted hearing organs I am transporting healthy
    fluent food
your hearing organs and my braincenters and speaking technique and
    line cutting
I'm sipping your growing attention deep from your eyecorners with
    colorful straws
believing in myself and doubting you and doubting my doubt in you
    with plenty of faith.
You will elect me because I confess the crime and you're the
    accomplice.
This last stanza was for a change written for me by the Chairman with
    a starchy quillpen.
At the Peking airport the Kennedy airport the Ben Gurion airport you
    keep waiting for me.
You're shooting me landing recording me speaking shooting and
    recording yourself shooting recording me you're
    the media.
You are a newsman a steward insectologist literary critic x-ray
    technician customs officer.
You weren't born yesterday and nobody gives a fuck for you and you
    keep reproducing arms
I'm your salesman your woman of valor women's and men's lib
    organization.

Put something on the grill please scratch my back it's hard for me to
	talk to you on an empty stomach
I detest food and you're full of food so I'm trying to reach you on food
	frequency.
Dog to dog pig to pig Chinese to Chinese Indian to Indian ulcer to ulcer
I have something to tell you and the others which I have delayed for
	twenty years and more.
Wait for me across the street with a shiv sniperifle licensed gun.
Now for a change I'm bleating to you with my craziest ecstasy.
Well that will do for a while you dig me don't you and if you don't piss
	off
I return as usual to the less communicative words and you'll hear from
	me therefrom as well.
You'll receive me in your underdeveloped braincenters and
	supermonkeyish fingertips
with your subintelligent digits you'll rehearse a global lynching to
	become your never fulfilled fantasy.
From a security distance uncrossable by intercontinental missiles till
	further notice inclusive
from a viewpoint out of your visibility and a speechpoint out of your
	audibility
out of your initial nervous system way and above your tissue
	constitution and vibration hierarchy
the entire set of rights duties emotional contracts kitchen legality
I'm scraping the stubborn layers of fat around your scrap-mind with
	thin handy steelwool
I'm draining you programming you a mind wideopen to the next
	generations next speeches next presidents.
And you'll vote for me right before retiring cursingly singingly
I'll be a sophisticated negative slide in your gloomy family albums.
You'll resign from your job your sexlife your military service.
You'll browse and rebrowse and wonder how come you couldn't.
How the hell couldn't you get rid of me when you were still young and
	strong and around.
Well that's the end of my speech and this time for a change nobody
either ghostwrote it or ghostgave it or ghostheard it.
Therefore it'll remain just between us till the end of the century.
The white house the yellow house the Jewish state
I gave all these up when I was still a kid.
This last statement is made seriously for a change.

And now if you have a spare moment just notice momentarily
how I'm starting out in a speed much higher
than sonic rapidity velocity of light than brainwaves
without waterpressure without oilpressure all pressure groups
and the crying rice petroleum fields atomic reactors
and rocket bases input palps output extensions
way and above all possible financial predictions
and literary political strategic military norms
and insurance companies and family structure and evolution.
And equally notice how anywhere anytime
I constantly remain an army administration bookkeeping
and a mafia and interests open eyes open ears
with brand new steelwool Japanese microphones the charms of rice

Re Those I Irritate

Re those I irritate –
it irritates me
not only that they exist,
but mainly the realization that I irritate them in advance, by my mere
    existence.
It irritates me
that I irritate them in advance,
therefore I shall probably always irritate them in advance.
Such accounts can't be settled in one generation.
What appeases me most is not just the fact that they don't exist,
but mainly the fact that I am appeased in advance
while facing the fact that they won't be existing.
I'm appeased in advance facing the fact that they won't be existing,
therefore their nonexistence appeases me so,
no matter whether they actually exist or not.
And the multigenerational bookkeeping
will eventually take care of it all.

Well-Known Matters

Deeds are headlined by motivations.
Well-known
is he whom the One knew well.
Well-known artist,
well-known statesman,
well-known waiter.

I am interested in the facts of life with no connection or application to the
    facts of death.
I am perfectly ready to be interested in the facts of death with no
    connection or application to the facts of life.
These are the life and death basic facts of my interestedness,
therefore I am out of all life and death matters
of my interestedness.
Therefore I am out of all life and death matters altogether.
I represent the third power, neither life nor death,
vanilla magic, icecream magic, white-yellowish magic, hypercolor magic.
I am the representative of the third power, neither life nor death, neither
    black nor white,
neither before nor after, neither now nor then, ready to enter negotiations
    instantly
with all other parties – grey magic, yellow magic,
violet-red-green magic.

And now a new kind of magic: Futuristic TV.
When you broadcast what might happen an instant before it does –
it won't
simple as that.

Magnetic Bird

A magnetic bird attached herself to the edge of a plane.
She became an inseparable part of it.
Together with its enormous engines her wings were vibrating up above
the clouds.

What did she search for in those heights? She wasn't an intelligence
device.
She had no interests of her own or any interests to represent.
She searched for refuge, peace, power, at the edge of the plane she
attached herself to.

Now the reverse process has begun. She magnetized *it* gradually,
and then the plane attached itself to her, and she was navigating it up
above the clouds.
A big airplane attached itself to a bird and was flown by it to unknown
territory.

Don't underestimate magnetic birds on the edge of a big powerful plane.
A seemingly dependent, unnavigated bird
can carry hundreds to a blind landing.

A Sonnet

It slowed down gradually, then faded out.
I waited for myself on line, in time.
Not innocent and least of all sublime,
I was just seriously thinking about

the probability of never coming back,
just kept in here – a magic terminal –
not concentrated, tired and banal,
expecting nothing to retire or awake.

Then aeroplanes, like miracles, rushed high
from subterranean lanes in the sky,
and fled up to the chilly height, from heat.

I stood alone there, right beside the beach
that fastened to my body like a leech –
my mouth was shut and spitful, bitter-sweet.

Lingual Politicians, Biting and Kissing Angles, Well-Known Matters,
Re Those I Irritate, What Did Kurt Waldheim Expect from the Polish Pope?,
Campaign Speech for the Presidency of the *US of Chinamerica,* and *A Sonnet* were
translated by the poet.
Current Observations and *Magnetic Bird* were translated by
Hanna Inga Moishezon.
The Surrounding Aridity and *The Legacy of the Serpent* were translated by
Hanna Inga Moishezon in collaboration with the poet.
All translations are from the Hebrew.

Ernst Neizvestny

Conversations with Khrushchev

By 1962, when I encountered Khrushchev for the first time at the exhibition in honor of the thirtieth anniversary of the Moscow branch of the Artists' Union, I had a good deal of experience of life and art behind me. My family had suffered the horrors of Stalin. My father had been an officer in the White Russian army. My mother was a biologist and a Yiddish poetess. As a soldier and officer, I myself went through nearly the entire war as well as the harsh postwar years and university.

I had begun to sculpt in childhood, but for almost my entire life I swung back and forth between art and biology, and between art and philosophy. While I was studying in the Art Institute, I was simultaneously studying philosophy at Moscow University.

I must say that neither my friends nor I deliberately strove for nonconformism or any special path in art. In youth we tried to master the techniques of painting and drawing. Emerging from the war in which we all suffered, we kept trying to travel a straight path. So if I can speak of my own individuality as an artist and sculptor, it is something that evolved naturally.

I won recognition as a sculptor quite soon and by 1962 I had won a few prizes at All-Union Competitions.

However, this was not official recognition. Official recognition was reserved for others – the orthodox "masters" of socialist realism such as Vuchetich and Gerasimov, although they were in a dangerous position in the wake of the 20th Party Congress. The issue was that the auditing commissions of the creative unions were basically composed of people who had suffered imprisonment. They were considered the most unprejudiced judges in the liquidation of the consequences of the "personality cult" in art. And at first they did in fact take daring and energetic action.

Thus it was that the auditing commission of the Union of Artists exposed the activities of the "supermafia" of sculptors and artists. On the basis of documentary and personal testimony it was demonstrated that the most prominent artists of the Stalin period had deceived even Stalin himself. Now the situation during the Stalin era, and the sixties, has been summed up as follows in one of my previous articles:

'In the Soviet Union there is just one employer – the state. Everyone attempts to enter into this narrow niche because there is nowhere else to get a commission. There is a particularly bloody battle in the field of sculpture which assumes a truly gangsterish character.

If you examine the structure of the relationship between the sculptor and the state, you discover that, inside the so-called socialist state, the sculptor represents some sort of pre-capitalist factory: a contractor gets all the money so it is not so important to be a talented sculptor as a good subcontractor and manager. None of the leading sculptors in the USSR is a real master in the Western sense. Instead, they are masters at the art of scheming and at the skill of getting orders. It is thought that the work can always be done by hiring other less frequently employed but not less talented colleagues.

The struggle for the right to get an order sometimes assumes a truly dramatic character. This, in essence, is the Wild West, a Western set in Russia. What they usually say is that it is not so important what you have done but who unveiled your monument.

In sculpture there is a strict hierarchy. If you have portrayed Marx, the sculpture will be unveiled by the head of the Party of the city where the monument is located or perhaps by the head of the Party of the entire district. This means that you must be commissioned to do sculpture which seems destined for a Lenin Prize even before it is completed. And this involves much social experience, impudence, cleverness and skill.

In this regard I would like to suggest a little scenario which I shall call *The Monument*.

Among the artists, it becomes known that an order for an important monument is to be handed down from the top and here the intrigue begins. It is born in the studio of a sculptor and from there it moves into the inner workings of the Union of Artists, then up to the Central Committee. It takes in the Army and the KGB, spreads through the whole country from Vladivostok to Brest. In it become involved the Young Pioneers and pensioners, domestic servants and stool pigeons, steel workers and shepherds. The intrigue takes on a grotesque scope: the entire country has been divided into parties supporting different sculptors.

In the end the order is given to the cleverest, most unprincipled and sliest artist of all. He gets the order and, in his joy, has a heart attack. But that is no obstacle. The monument can be made even without him because he himself never worked. While he is recuperating in the hospital his assistants, unknown drudges, make the monument. At the moment of unveiling of the sculpture, he emerges from the hospital, shaves, and rushes to the celebration. Columns of Chekists and the Army, the tanks, the pensioners and the Young Pioneers, janitors and metallurgists, milkmaids and stool pigeons, march past. The fanfares sound. Black government limousines drive past. The most important man of all, bowlegged, salutes, goes up to the monument and removes its cover. Suddenly, there before the entire country, stands a tiny figure in a torn jacket, badly modelled, falling off his pedestal and pointing with his hand directly at the toilet. But all this is unimportant. To thundering acclaim, the sculptor is awarded the Lenin Prize. If it is necessary to make a genius, the Party will appoint him as one – so the sculptor becomes a genius'.

Of course, all this is a grotesque. But, particularly in Stalin's times, real life was often very close to this! It was proved, for example, that the sculptor Vuchetich, in a competition with his colleagues for the best image of the leader, went to Stalin's reception room and while looking at photos presented to Stalin, asked Poskrebyshev, Stalin's secretary, the following question:

"Which of these sculptures is likely to please Iosif Vissarionovich?"

To which Poskrebyshev replied:

"I think this one here."

This was a sculpture by one of Vuchetich's competitors, Kibalnikov. Vuchetich signed Kibalnikov's work with his own signature.

When Stalin confirmed this as his choice, a major scandal erupted, but neither Poskrebyshev nor anyone else was willing to report this daring and delicate deception to Stalin.

Thus Vuchetich worked on Kibalnikov's model and became Stalin's favorite. When he built the twenty-seven meter tall monument at the Volga-Don Canal, he carried out another astonishing gangster-like trick. After the sculpture had been executed by prison labor, a commission was unexpectedly convened which determined that the copper of the sculpture allegedly did not achieve the required standard of durability.

Vuchetich then reported to the top and was granted new funds and new copper. However, he did not make a new sculpture but merely left the old one in place. They divided the money between them and buried the copper. But an argument took place, among those who had shared the money, and one of the engineers allegedly in charge of the work was jailed by Vuchetich. When he got out of prison he testified about the deal which cast light on the entire story.

This sort of activity was carried out in all areas – financial, ideological, personal, and was all recorded in documents. I cannot vouch for their reliability but, after my conflict with Khrushchev in the Manezh*, the authors of these documents became terribly frightened. At that time one of them – an elderly man and a member of an auditing commission – secretly brought copies of these documents to me. He told me he had nothing to lose and said all this might help me in my struggle with the artistic supermafia. I sewed a big pocket into my jacket and carried these documents on my person at all times.

One way or another the situation in the Artists' Union at the beginning of the 1960's was by no means a simple one: on one side, new forces were entering art which would not tolerate the tyranny of the artistic mafias. Yet on the other hand, the mafia, which had enormous influence and connections, had no intention at all of surrendering their positions. When a group of young artists headed by Bilyutin was invited to take part in the exhibition in honor of the 30th anniversary of the Moscow branch of the Artists' Union, I grew wary.

The arrangement of the exposition itself was extremely strange. In prominent places were works by nonconformists who by no means enjoyed the favor of the Party. And, on the other hand, works of the mastodon classicists for some reason wound up in the shadows, in the background.

I was quite anxious about participating in this exhibition. I was worried about the purposes behind it and what this strange arrangement of works actually meant.

Yet Bilyutin persuaded me that new times had come and the Party and the Central Committee intended to delve deeply into artistic matters. All we had to do was to demonstrate our capabilities, and the Manezh exhibition gave us that opportunity.

The atmosphere was very tense. We worked all night long. Among the

*) Manezh – old nobles' stables converted into an exhibition building.

artists in the Manezh were many undisguised and camouflaged police agents. This became particularly clear in the morning when the chief of security for government leaders arrived. He looked under the tables, knocked on the bronzes, evidently worried about bombs or tape recorders. There was one rather amusing episode.

When I asked him, "Are you really so and so," he said "Yes, yes," not concealing the fact.

Then I pointed out the window, facing the opposite side of the Manezh and overlooking the University. As an army officer with some pride, I indicated that, if he were really concerned about Khrushchev's safety, he should realize it would be quite possible to shoot from that side, or simply see how government leaders entered our room on the stairway. He became very nervous and sent several men there to close off the window. But it was too late – the government had arrived at the Manezh.

We were worn out and unshaven. The Bilyutin Studio, which was rather prominently represented at the Manezh, consisted of people of various nationalities and there was no particular predominance of Jews. However, in some strange way, those invited to participate at the Manezh were mostly Jews and had typically Jewish faces.

At that moment I had some premonition of a provocation. In fact, I spoke to Lev Kopelev about it. He was standing with friends downstairs in the exhibition halls as the exhibition was being prepared upstairs. We strolled through the halls; I directed his attention to those present and remarked:

"I don't understand what's going on, Lev. Is this a provocation or not?"

He replied: "I don't understand it myself, maybe yes, maybe no. It's hard to judge."

By the way, I liked Kopelev very much indeed. We had become acquainted in the following way: In 1956 I participated along with other artists in a one-day exhibition of the Moscow branch of the Artists' Union. I was strongly and unreasonably criticized there. At that moment, a handsome bearded man arose and told the chairman, the head of the Moscow Branch, Shmrainov, to be careful.

He said: "You are criticizing an artist of the calibre of Mayakovsky and Brecht. Your words are therefore going down in history and I beg you to be careful."

When asked in whose name he was speaking and who he was, he replied impressively:

"In the first place I speak in my own name. I am Kopelev. And in the second place I speak in the name of the members of the critics' section of the Union of Writers."

This caused a certain commotion. After that I went up to him myself and said:

"You've given me such a large advance that I am simply obliged to work seriously."

And to both of us, there in the Manezh that day, came the thought of a possible provocation.

Finally Khrushchev entered the building with his retinue. We were upstairs but the sound of shouts and screams downstairs rose up to us. Some kind of a witches' sabbath was taking place down there.

What kind of a witches' sabbath it was I do not know because I took no part in it. But, after they arranged us all in a row at the front of the stairway on the upper landing, all my Jewish friends in a sort of a circle (and it was almost Birobidzhan) began to applaud Khrushchev climbing the stairs. Their applause mingled with the shouts of Khrushchev: "Dog shit!"

I did not yet know if this referred to us, but in any case he was enraged and everyone was aroused.

He began his tour in the room where paintings loaned by Bilyutin and several of my friends were displayed. Khrushchev cursed threateningly and was indignant at the sight of the "daubs".

Then and there he declared, "A donkey's tail could paint better." And then an amusing scene with Suslov took place. When he looked at works painted in Saratov, Suslov kept on muttering: "I'm from Saratov myself! I'm from Saratov myself – and it's not like that." And our friend Zheltovsky was told that he was a handsome man who painted monstrosities.

Then my own main clash with Khrushchev, which was a prelude to the conversation that follows, took place. This clash began like this:

Khrushchev asked: "Who is the main person here?"

They pushed Bilyutin forward in a state of dismay, confusion and depression. Possibly he did not expect a provocation. In fact, his dismay confirms that he was not a conscious provocateur even though this idea has persisted to this day.

Khrushchev asked him a puzzling question whose purpose I have still not divined: "Who is your father?"

Bilyutin replied: "A political official."

Then Ilyichev said: "He isn't the main one – this one here is!"

He pointed to me. I was forced to step out of the crowd and stand face to face with Khrushchev. At this point Khrushchev attacked me with a shout and declared that I was a homosexual.

This "joke" is famous and has often been repeated in the West. I excused myself to Madame Furtseva, the Minister of Culture, who stood next to me, and said:

"Nikita Sergeyevitch, give me a girl right now and I'll show you here and now what kind of homosexual I am."

He guffawed and then Shelepin, representing the KGB, declared that I was impolite to the prime minister and that I would soon get a chance to live in their uranium mines. I replied – and this is exactly how it appeared in the record:

"You don't know who you're talking to, you're talking to a man who is capable of doing away with himself in any moment. I'm not afraid of your threats."

I saw strong interest in Khrushchev's eyes. Telling him that I would now speak only in front of my own works, I went into the room where my pieces stood, not believing that Khrushchev would follow me. But he did, and so did his entire retinue and the crowd.

The real witches' sabbath began in the other room with Khrushchev declaring that I was squandering the people's money and producing shit! I said that he knew nothing about art. It was a long conversation which came down to the following: I tried to persuade him that he was the victim of a provocation and that he was appearing in a ridiculous light because he was not a professional, not a critic and not aesthetically literate. (I no longer recollect my exact words but this was the gist.) What was his reply?

"I was a miner – and I did not understand," he said. "I was a political official – and I did not understand. I was this and that – and I did not understand. But right now I am head of the Party and the prime minister and I still do not understand? Whom are you working for?"

I must emphasize that, as I spoke with Khrushchev, I felt that the dynamic power of his personality corresponded to my own. Notwithstanding the atmosphere of horror which all this aroused in me, it was easy for me to speak to him. It was a conversation in tune with my inner rhythm. The danger, the strain and the directness was something I could respond to. Officials usually speak foggily, rhetorically, in some jargon of their own, avoiding directness. Khrushchev spoke directly, without technical knowledge but directly, which gave me the opportunity to reply to him directly. I told him that this was a provocation not only against liberalization, not only against the intelligentsia, not only against myself, but against him as well.

This seemed to arouse a certain response in his heart – though it did not keep him from attacking me again as before. The most interesting thing was that, when I spoke out honestly, directly, forthrightly and said what I thought, I was able to drive him into a blind alley. But, as soon as I began to play the hypocrite, he immediately sensed this and took the upper hand.

For example, I said: "Nikita Sergeyevitch, you as a Communist are dressing me down, while at the same time there are Communists who favor my art, such as Picasso, Renato Gutuzo." And I went on to enumerate many supporters of the Soviet Union who were respected there.

He screwed up his eyes slyly and said: "Does it matter to you that they are Communists?"

I lied to him: "Yes!"

If I had been honest I should have answered: "I couldn't care less whether they're Communists or not. What's important to me is that they're great artists!"

And as if he sensed all that, he continued:

"Aha, so that's important to you!? Well in that case, don't worry. I don't like your works and I'm the Number One Communist in the world."

However, there were times when he said things which had never been uttered by the Party in general. For example, when I began again to refer to my successes in Europe and elsewhere, he said:

"Don't you understand that all foreigners are enemies?"

Now that was direct and straightforward in the Roman style.

The organizers of the provocation had not foreseen the possibility that I might be able to persuade Khrushchev of something. They wanted Khrushchev to roll over us like a tank, not leaving a speck to remember us by. But once he started to talk with me he commenced a discussion. And once he commenced a discussion, he was hearing things he was not supposed to hear. I threw caution to the winds and said what I thought. Somehow I wanted to show up the officials who were playing gangsters.

To General Serov I said simply:

"You bandit! Don't interrupt me when I'm talking to the prime minister! We'll talk to you later!"

When Shelepin accused me of being a homosexual, stealing bronze, speculating in foreign currency and, in some strange sort of formulation, indulging in forbidden communication with foreigners, I said:

"Before the Politburo of the Central Committee I make the following declaration: 'The person who is in charge of supervision of the KGB is giving false information to the head of state – either out of his own interests or because he is misinformed by his own people'. And I demand an investigation."

Later, there was an investigation. They did try to pin charges of speculation in foreign exchange on me and they did try to accuse me of stealing bronze and much else. But a year and a half later, when Khrushchev once again mentioned me at one of the ideological conferences, Shelepin got up and declared publicly that these accusations had been withdrawn.

Here is how my conversation with Khrushchev ended.

He said: "You're an interesting person and I like such people. But, at one and the same time, you have an angel and a devil inside you. If the devil wins, we'll destroy you. If the angel wins, we'll help you."

And he held out his hand to me.

After that I stood at the exit and, like Kalinin, I shook the hands of those who had gathered there. Many of the artists felt bad. I was in the eye of the storm and perhaps didn't feel how awful it all was. But those on the periphery experienced pure horror. Many of my comrades rushed up to kiss me and congratulate me because, in their words, I had defended the interests of the intelligentsia.

Then a short pale man in a wrinkled suit and with a wart on his nose like Khrushchev, came up and said:

"You're a brave man, Ernst Iosefovich! If you need me call me."

He gave me a telephone number.

In the heat of things, I did not grasp who this was, but later I learned that he was Khrushchev's assistant, Lebedev; with whom I subsequently conferred at least twenty times. Khrushchev assigned Lebedev to demand that I publicly recant, that is, give Khrushchev a letter of recantation to be printed in the Soviet press.

Evidently this was a Party assignment. Like the good functionary he was, he would break my arms while offering me a sugarplum to get what he wanted.

I wrote Khrushchev a letter, but it did not satisfy the Ideological Commission of the Central Committee, according to Lebedev: "Nikita Sergeyevich read your letter with great interest but it did not satisfy the Ideological Commission because it cannot be published as a symbol that you have taken the criticism to heart."

What was my first impression of Khrushchev? I must admit that I felt ambivalent about him. I felt sympathy for his dynamism as well as for his liberal steps. Yet, I was absolutely flabbergasted by his almost total lack of culture.

In my whole life, I never met a man with a greater lack of culture. At the same time, I could sense his biological power and psychobiological ability. In any case, this man had some of the qualities of an outstanding personality. Unfortunately, his personality remained unstrengthened by culture which is so necessary for the leader of such a great state and I think this always plagued him.

As for my further relations with Khrushchev, Lebedev summoned me to the Central Committee and conducted endless conversations on the subject of my repentance. Although these were interesting, a great deal has remained unclear to me even now. For example, whenever I let down my guard Lebedev would point to his ear and to the ceiling, letting me know that we were being bugged. Then he would take me into the corridor and say "What are you doing, Ernst, what are you saying? If this should become known to someone after Khrushchev is out of power, they'll hang us both from the same tree."

Once he called to tell me that Khrushchev had insomnia and had phoned him several times from Yugoslavia to ask how I was. In other words, he flattered me, telling me that Khrushchev loved and respected me and, on the other hand, he demanded that I do what my very nature made me incapable of doing.

Yevtushenko and, sadly, Shostakovich were sent to persuade me to write a letter of recantation. Yevtushenko himself even undertook to compose it.

Several times I sat down to write such a letter, for "the sake of my work," as Shostakovich told me. But it simply did not turn out right, not even because it was against my ideology. I rejected it completely and I tore up these letters.

There was an amusing situation when I was in Vladimir Semyonovich Lebedev's office and he demanded I write it all out in longhand.

I asked: "What is there for me to write?"

He said: "Sit down and I'll dictate it to you."

This is approximately what he dictated:

"Nikita Sergeyevich, I assure you of my loyalty and respect. Nikita Sergeyevich, I am grateful to you for your criticism. It helped me in my work and in my creative growth."

I did not want to write this and told him I was making spelling errors.

"That's all right," he answered. "Nikita Sergeyevich himself sometimes makes mistakes in spelling."

He was comforting me.

My next encounter with Khrushchev took place at his country house. My essential works of sculpture were brought there. Ilyichev and Promyslov were once again in charge, and I insisted that the exposition would include such works as "The Cosmonauts" and the proposed plans for the Novosibirsk Science City (I had taken part in its planning) as well as my designs for sculptural reliefs at the Artek Children's Camp – in other words, works which, so it seemed, might be correctly understood by Khrushchev.

I went to Promyslov and said: "Why have you deceived me? Why are there none of those works I asked you to include?"

He laughed cynically and said: "They're going to exorcise the devil from you and you still complain?"

"Where is your vaunted Party conscience?" I asked.

"My Party conscience serves only the Party's cause."

What happened at this much-publicized ideological conference?

Each of the participants at this meeting concentrated on his own problems. Therefore I felt that everything revolved around me, which was indeed the case.

This was a very insipid dinner accompanied by weak drinks. Yevtushenko was sitting next to me and I asked him: "Why are things so insipid?" His reply struck me as an apt joke:

"What do you expect? The lowest-ranking cook in the place has the military rank of captain. Cooking and the KGB are totally incompatible."

After dinner we were invited to enter the large auditorium where some of the attending audience were already present. In the center of this circular hall stood a pedestal obviously put there to show off sculpture.

Impulsively, I entered the hall and stood next to that pedestal, ready to defend my works. Evidently this was not planned by those who had organized this affair, because I was supposed to be a defendant charged with crimes, and not allowed to speak.

Here an amusing bit of staging took place. While everyone sat in the amphitheatre, I stood there in the center of this mob. Khrushchev appeared with his retinue, the whole Politburo. When he saw me he stood in the doorway, said something, waved his hand and went out.

Then and there orders were given to move the meeting into the hall where we had dined. I did not understand at the time what had happened but later it all became clear. They seated me alone right in front of the Presidium, behind a table. The rostrum stood literally a meter and a half from me.

Beside me was empty space. No one wanted to sit next to me. Interestingly enough, a bit later Yevtushenko and the Minister of Culture, Furtseva, did sit down beside me.

Furtseva kept hold of my knee during the speeches of Khrushchev and others and, whenever I tried to shout from where I sat, she pressed it. Yevtushenko did the same, repeating: "don't be bitter."

Thus we were seated. The entire Politburo entered and their young toughs brought in the works of sculpture and filled the table with them right in front of the Politburo. Thus the Politburo was fenced off from the hall by my sculptures. This ridiculous effect somewhat spoiled the scenario which had been prepared earlier when Khrushchev entered the hall, but by now it all had a grotesque and comic character.

Khrushchev looked particularly ridiculous, peering out from behind my work entitled "A Boy with a Mouse," the largest of the sculptures. Finally he summoned someone to set the sculpture on its side so that Khrushchev could be seen. He then stood up and read a boring ideological statement in typescript which teemed with threats: "We will not permit, we cannot allow..." In short, he was brandishing an ideological club but, while reading his report, he would suddenly put down the typescript and speak extemporaneously, and here everything was reversed. It was strange and awkward. For example, directing his remarks at me (as he did much of the time), he said:

"He's sitting there and thinking that we are against culture and against the intelligentsia and he wants us to loosen all the screws at once – but in Chekhov the mischievous boy only loosened every other one." Then he resumed his reading: "We will not permit, we cannot allow."

All of a sudden he cast aside the written text and said out of a clear sky:

"They say I do not like Jews – that's not true! Even so, in reality, there are situations where you don't have a choice. I can remember, for example, in Kiev how a young officer, a Jew, was walking along and behind him were two hooligans. They kept shouting 'Kike' at him. And instead of laughing it off he shot them. Naturally the public makes pogroms."

Or, for example, he told his story about Pinya quite out of context. I heard it with my own ears and even jotted it down when I got back home.

He said: "I am going to tell you a story. Some thieves in jail were afraid of each other and yet they had to elect an elder to represent them. And whom should they elect as elder when they were afraid of each other? There was a Jew among them, so they decided to elect him. He's a quiet chap and he'll be obedient. So they elected Pinya. And Pinya became a very tough boss who kept everyone in line. The thieves began to plan an escape. They made a tunnel, but they were all afraid to go first because they figured the first one to pop out of the tunnel would get a bullet in his head. So Pinya said to them: 'I, as elder, will go first.'"

"And so," concluded Nikita Sergeyevich, "I am that Pinya!"

Then, without any pause at all, he read a threatening ideological statement which contained many strange accusations against me. For example he said that I was not an artist but the leader of a Petöfy Club, and that I was eager to take their places and kill off the Politburo of the Central Committee. And he demonstrated this vividly poking his finger at his heart and his forehead to show how I would kill him. I shouted from my seat that this was stupid and that I wanted only to sculpt as I wish. But they didn't let me speak. There were other amusing moments, such as when mixing up the role of the medium and that of the hypnotist, he suddenly shouted out: "Yevtushenko! Get away from that man. He'll hypnotize you!"

Then he thought for a moment and began to shout: "Medium, Medium! Go off to your spiritual fathers in the West! I am prime minister and I guarantee you a passport and travel money!"

I stood up and said: "Nikita Sergeyevich, stop uttering stupidities. It's not for you to choose my Motherland for me."

Amazingly, he embraced me and then went on affirming that I was enemy number one and there was no place for me there.

Later, I thought all this over and understood that, given Khrushchev's spontaneity, there was a logic in his conduct. This man repealed Stalinist terror, but was unable to guide the apparatus of government and country because he had not changed its structure. How could he govern without terrifying people? It was his inconsistency that gave rise to fears. No one knew what he would do at any given moment! Thus, there was horror on the faces of the members of the Politburo who were apparently amazed by his side-comments as he read his statement. I think he did all this on purpose, so that everyone would be in a continual state of terror and ignorance. Many of his acts which are explained as libertarianism were egotistically and politically justified. He split up the ministries and reunited them. He merely wished to cut up and reshuffle those mafias that had been building up for decades so that he could manipulate them, injecting his own egotistical and bureaucratic logic into that insane apparatus.

This was his style of leadership. Khrushchev was a person who wanted to leap over the abyss in two jumps. But this was impossible.

In the meantime all this brought horror to me personally and to those about me: afterwards many of my closest acquaintances refused to shake hands with me, but many people I didn't know kissed me publicly. Everyone thought it necessary to react in some fashion and selected that mode which he considered in tune with Khrushchev's mood. At the time Yevtushenko defended me and I am grateful to him. I do not wish to make a profound analysis: many people said he was playing it cleverly, that he knew this would impress Khrushchev. Strange as it may sound, even Vuchetich, the great courtier and fox and my main enemy, took an ambiguous position at that conference. For example, he said he would give his own personal guarantee for my good conduct and that I could work for him. During the intermission, I approached him and said: "Yevgeny Viktorovich, how can I work for you if I win all the competitions from you?" To which he replied cynically: "If you had no talent why would I need you?"

After the conference, Vladimir Semyonovich Lebedev tried forcefully to squeeze a recantation out of me, for the Party needed that. They don't need the body so much as the soul – the recantation and the soul of the sinner! And it was especially in the battle for my soul (it would have been no trouble at all for them to take my body) that Vladimir Semyonovich Lebedev as well as Khrushchev suffered a defeat.

Then came the day of Khrushchev's removal from office. A woman friend of mine, who did research for the staff of Keldysh, the President of the Academy of Sciences, phoned to tell me that Khrushchev would be removed. This was not yet known to the general public. I immediately phoned Lebedev, but there was no answer. The next day I phoned and Lebedev answered.

"Vladimir Semyonovich," I began, "you wanted me to tell Khrushchev that I respect him and much else, and right now I have the opportunity of doing just that. I consider our conversation as public."

He snickered, knowing that the telephone was bugged and that I knew it.

I continued: "So inform Nikita Sergeyevich that I really do have deep respect for him for exposing the personality cult and for letting millions of people out of prison. In light of all that I consider our esthetic disagreements unimportant and I wish him many years of health."

There was a pause and then Lebedev said warmly, though ordinarily he was a very cold person:

"I expected nothing else from you, Ernst Iosefovich, and I will inform Nikita Sergeyevich."

Lebedev died two months after Khrushchev's death. I doubt he received many such calls on the day of Khrushchev's removal from office.

Khrushchev was removed from office. Three times he sent me someone to convey his apologies and to invite me to visit him at his country house. I did not, but not out of cowardice. Yevtushenko visited him from time to time and he saw others as well. I did not go simply because I did not think it possible to develop our esthetic discussions further. I knew myself and I knew Khrushchev and I knew there was no way of getting around that. But at the moment all that was meaningless and, anyway, I had no desire to hurt him.

Hence the legend that I met with Khrushchev at his country home has no basis in fact. I never had any encounter with him after his removal from office. But it's true that his wife, Nina Petrovna, did send me an excerpt from his memoirs in which Khrushchev, seemingly indirectly, apologized to me. But that did not satisfy me. Even here, perhaps because of his psychology or perhaps because of a certain natural craftiness, a partly dishonest cunning always peered through in Khrushchev. He apologized especially for mocking my family name. Big deal! I never even paid any attention to that. He should have apologized for something else!

I learned of Khrushchev's death from a taxi driver. As soon as he told me, a mysterious thought flashed through my mind that I would be making his grave monument. How this thought arose I cannot say, but it did.

After Khrushchev's funeral two men paid me a visit: Khrushchev's son, Sergei Khrushchev, whom I had not known before, and Mikoyan's son, also Sergei, with whom I had been friendly and who had supported me during my most difficult moments. Several times I had been beaten, once even to unconsciousness, and then had been brought to the apartment of the former Ambassador to the United States, Menshikov.

There I learned that I had been picked up by the Mikoyans, who had come to me at the moments of my most acute disagreements with Khrushchev.

The young Khrushchev and the young Mikoyan entered, looked around and kept hesitating.

"I know why you've come," I said.

They said: "Yes, you guessed it. We want to ask you to make the grave monument."

"Very well," I replied. "I agree. But on condition that I make it as I see fit."

To which Sergei Khrushchev replied: "That is as it should be."

"I am aware," I said, "that some people will attack me for my decision. I consider that this is the revenge of art on politics. But in any case those are just words! In reality I do consider that the artist should not be more malicious than the politician and therefore I agree. Those are my reasons. Now let me hear yours: why am I the one to do this?"

To which Sergei Khrushchev replied: "This was the wish of my father."

We never returned to this subject. It was confirmed that Khrushchev in his will asked that the grave monument be made by myself. This was also confirmed by a Polish Communist woman at the unveiling who came to me and said: "Nikita Sergeyevich was not mistaken when he asked in his will that you should make his grave monument." Khrushchev's widow, Nina Petrovna, also confirmed this.

The top leadership, of course, was flabbergasted by Khrushchev's decision. No one there had the slightest idea that things would take this turn. For three years I was denied the right to install the grave monument in its proper place. In this case, I had to use all my knowledge of the structure of Soviet society. The Khrushchev family also knew that structure, but it knew it from the top, and when they were on the bottom they had no idea of how to act. My experience as a man always on the bottom, on the other hand, helped me enormously. Eventually I used personal terror. No one along the bureaucratic chain would give the final word. What I had to do was steer that bureaucratic ship cleverly. At the very last I maneuvered things so that the order to set up the monument – which was already ready but with no final signatures – came directly from Kosygin. This was a complex, characteristically Soviet piece of work. The money appropriated for Khrushchev's monument was enough only for a stone with an inscription. No one was afraid of this, no one supposed they would come to me, no one supposed I would agree to make such a large and costly work for such a small fee. And no one supposed that this work would not be a simple neutral bust, but that it would express my attitude to Khrushchev, an ambiguous figure in the dividing line between two periods, a figure who contained within himself the contradictions of the age. So the grave monument turned out to be controversial. And of course it encountered opposition. What happened? The top shot the decision down to the bottom and the bottom waited for an order from the top. My task was to provoke the top to make a decision, which I did so well that the chief architect of the city told me: "You're using blackmail."

"Yes," I replied.

What kind of blackmail?

I explained to the various links in the decision-making apparatus: "Your refusal to permit me to install the grave monument does not mean that you have an order not to permit it to be installed. If that were the case, you simply would not talk to me at all."

But they did talk to me and demanded that I change the grave monument. They demanded, for example, that I make it white and not black or maybe just gray or, even better, simply a portrait on a pedestal. Best of all would be to remove the portrait and leave only an inscription. In a word, they proposed a thousand different variations.

So I said: "Since you're still conducting talks with me, that means there has been no decision from the top. I'll tell you what you have to be afraid of: if you go on dragging this whole thing out, and Brezhnev is going to visit the West soon, I will give an interview stating that he is forbidding me to install Khrushchev's grave monument. But not a word has come from him. And when the scandal explodes, I'll say that the Main Architectural Administration headed by Posokhin was to blame. And at that point they'll be looking for scapegoats. That's what you have to be afraid of – so make a decision."

In the very end these bureaucrats frankly explained to me that they were really frightened and advised me to appeal to the top myself.

I asked Nina Petrovna Khrushchev to write to Kosygin. When she appealed to him he gave permission. I imagine that for all these small "apparatchiks" this was a bigger holiday than for me. They almost kissed me because they had finally received orders from above to install the monument.

The unveiling of the monument took place in the rain on one of the anniversaries of Khrushchev's death. All his family and several foreign correspondents were there as well as a guard. The public was not allowed in. Yevtushenko came and tried to be the center of attention. No one delivered any speeches.

We recalled Khrushchev. His family doctor declared that he was not as simple as he seemed. I insisted that he was very primitive.

"No, no, that was only a mask," he insisted.

And he cited several examples of his exhaustive knowledge of his subordinates.

The family left because they did not want Yevtushenko to deliver a speech when they themselves were silent. I went with Sergei Khrushchev and five of our friends to Sergei's apartment. Sergei Khrushchev got out a bottle of cognac which de Gaulle had given his father and said:

"My father could never bring himself to drink this bottle of cognac. So now we will drink it ourselves."

And we did.

Published in Russian in VREMYA I MY, Tel Aviv, no. 41, May 1979.

Translated from the Russian by the author and Barbara Harshav.

Gabriel Josipovici

Writing, Reading, and the Study of Literature

I

Mr. Vice-Chancellor, Ladies and Gentlemen,

Some of you may have been present on another such occasion, three years ago, when Jonathan Harvey delivered his inaugural lecture as Professor of Music at this University. If you were you will recall that Jonathan began his lecture with a massive disclaimer: 'I am a composer first and foremost,' he said in effect, 'and so you will have to forgive me if I do not talk very well, for talking does not come naturally to one who works primarily with notes.' Actually he began even more disarmingly, for before he said a word he switched on a tape-recorder and played us the opening bars of his most recent composition. It was only *after* he had done this that he made the statement I have just quoted.

I listened to the lecture, as you must have done, with intense interest and admiration. It isn't often, after all, that we have the privilege of listening to a leading modern composer talking about his work. But I listened also, I must confess, with a certain amount of envy. For I thought: 'Yes, a composer can start a lecture in this way, but a writer can't.' And yet I, as a writer, feel myself to be in a position very similar to Jonathan's. I too feel that I am better, or, at any rate, more at ease, in *making* artefacts than in *talking about* them.

But surely, you will say, that is absurd. A composer, after all, works with notes, so that it is perfectly understandable for him to say that he is not very good at speaking. But what excuse does a writer have, since his medium is words?

I am not sure about excuses. But what I want to insist on is this: that making an artefact with notes or paint or words is the same *kind* of activity, and it is quite a different kind of activity from *talking about* art or life or anything else.

In saying this I do not want to suggest that art is made out of some sort of 'pure' language that is unconnected with the rest of life. That is part of a Romantic dream, the same kind of dream which led to the assertion that all the arts aspire to the condition of music. That, it seems to me, does a disservice not only to the verbal arts, but to music as well. For composers too work with a language which has its own history, its own tendency to turn into cliché, its own syntax and grammar, which must be understood, respected and renewed. No. When I say that all the arts stand on one side of a line and discourse about art stands on the other it is not out of any wish to uphold fin-de-siècle notions about the intangibility of art and the ubiquitousness of some entity called Genius. In fact what I hope to show in the course of this lecture is that it is only by taking that divide seriously that we can actually understand the central place of art – of all the arts – in our lives and in the culture of the community.

However, I do not want to approach the subject through theory. Clearly the issue is a central one in aesthetics, but I am not a philosopher and I have no head for sustained rational argument. Moreover, I am not sure that the philosophical way is the best way to deal with this issue. It may be better – it certainly suits my temperament better – to deal with it on a more personal and exploratory basis. For what I have just said about the unity of the arts and their distinctness from any talk about art is to me both blatantly true and profoundly puzzling. What I want to do this evening is simply to try and share my puzzlement with you, to argue with myself, so to speak, in your presence. And if I cannot come up with any answers I hope at least to persuade you that there are interesting issues at stake.

II

I start then not with an idea but with a *need*. Not the idea of literature but the need to write. For me this need to write is an imperative which cannot and does not have to be explained. At times it feels almost as biological as the need for food, sleep and sex.

When I say 'the need to write' I do not mean primarily the physical urge to put words down on paper. It is more the need to *utter*, to talk, but to talk in such a way that I say just what I mean and that the words don't simply evaporate. Writing for me is largely to do with finding a tone, a voice, and then following it where it leads. In the end this voice or these voices have to find their own balance, their own pattern, arrive at a kind of stasis where the whole is more than the sum of its parts, is, in fact, something quite new. And writing words down is the only way I know which makes this possible. And when it is all done I have the sense of the finished work not as an *object* but as a living thing, a living shape, a shape which can be brought to life again and again, as often as the work is read.

At the same time, in my case, the recognition of this need to write goes hand in hand with the *impossibility* of satisfying that need. I would go further and say that the work of art only starts where that sense of impossibility makes itself felt.

Why is there that sense of impossibility? Where does it come from?

At one level it is easy to understand. Every undergraduate meets it every week in the course of trying to get his or her essay written. He is bursting with ideas. He knows just what he wants to say, yet as soon as he comes to write the first sentence down he is filled with a profound sense of dissatisfaction. He cannot seem to say what he wants. Suddenly every move he makes seems slow, clumsy, unbearably awkward. He finds himself using phrases and expressions that belong to other people, other places, other times. What has happened to all his exciting ideas?

Everyone who has had to write anything at all has met with this kind of frustration. With the writing of fiction the feeling is compounded. I am not sure if we are dealing with something of a quite different order or only with something of the same kind but more complex. Let me give you some examples.

Here, to begin with, are five different versions of the same tiny fragment of dialogue, as one might encounter it in the pages of any novel. (Strangely, after writing this I found that Umberto Eco had used precisely this sort of example for precisely this purpose in his Postscript to *The Name of the Rose*. There is a *Zeitgeist* after all.)

1. 'Shall we go then?'
   'Well... All right.'
2. 'Shall we go then?' said Jack.
   'Well... All right,' said Jim.
3. 'Shall we go then?' asked Jack.
   'Well... All right,' answered Jim.
4. 'Shall we go then?' asked Jack hesitantly.

Jim was tight-lipped. 'Well... All right,' he said at last.

5. 'Shall we go then?' asked Jack, letting a note of hesitation creep into his voice.
Jim was tight-lipped. His face remained expressionless.
'Well...' His voice trailed away. Then, pulling himself together, he said firmly: 'All right.'

You see how many choices are involved, even in a simple exchange like that. And you see how different is the *feel* of the narrative in each case. As we read novels we are mostly unaware of the writer's having to make choices, but if you're writing you have to be.

But if I can write a tiny fragment of dialogue in so many different ways, how am I going to decide which is the right way? If each decision merely depends on how I happen to feel the day I am writing, or what books I have read, or (which amounts to the same thing) how I imagine novels *ought* to be written, then what happened to the desire to speak with which I began? For that was something intensely personal and urgent, which seemed to have nothing to do with books and to be too deeply rooted to be dependent on daily fluctuations of mood.

I suppose this doesn't much matter if you think of yourself as a professional writer, that is, as someone who happens to write to earn a living as others might mend roads or deliver milk or teach in Universities. But if you have turned to writing because of a *need* then the implications of this are very worrying. For there seems to be a need but no way of satisfying it. Is there any way out of this contradiction?

I think there is; or rather, there are as many ways as there are real writers. Let me try and explain this by presenting you with another example, not one made up for the occasion this time, but an autobiographical one.

When I wrote my first novel, in 1966, I faced a crisis. I didn't know if I had it in me to do what I had always felt I would one day, that is, write a novel. At that point many pressures converged which ensured that the novel did in fact get written, not the least of which was *fear*. Yet even when I could see my subject clearly, felt the shape of it, knew the different characters and the setting, I still couldn't get the opening right. I knew just where I wanted to start: a solicitor arrives at a house to take an inventory of the possessions of a man who has just died. There he meets the man's family, and the book is about the relations of these people to each other and especially to the dead man whose possessions lie about, waiting to be inventoried.

I could visualise the house and exactly where it stood. I knew where exactly I had to go from there. But every time I tried to write the opening scene I found it collapsing under me. Other novelists, as far as I knew, had never had that sort of problem. They might rewrite a scene several times, spend days, even weeks, searching for precisely the right word. But with me it wasn't a question of the right word. There seemed to be an unbridgeable gap between what I visualised, what I sensed was *needed*, and my ability to put it into words at all.

Was I not a writer then? Perhaps I had been fooling myself all these years? Perhaps this was the moment to recognise the fact and give up. Yet the need to speak, and now to speak about this particular subject, was overwhelming.

My problem seemed to have to do with description. Should I describe the house in one sentence? One paragraph? Two? Ten? I had never given this any thought when I was coming to grips with the theme of the book, but now here it was, blocking my way. The trouble was that whatever it was I wanted to do, I was not doing it. Yet surely I was only writing in the first place because it was something I wanted to do? So what was going wrong?

The question I had to ask myself was: what was it I *really* wanted to do? And it seemed I could only answer that negatively. I found that each time I came to describe the scene I was doing something I *didn't want*. At first I thought it was that each time I found myself mimicking the tones of all the other descriptions I had ever read, and I didn't want to say it in other people's phrases. But what were *my* phrases?

And suddenly it came to me. It was not that I didn't like the *forms* of description that I was using; I didn't like any form of description. What's more, I didn't *need* it. What had happened was that I had adopted not just the tone and manners of every book I had ever read, but also the assumptions. Chief among these was the assumption that if someone, in a novel, arrives at a house or enters a room or meets someone for the first time, then that house or room or person must be described. But why must they? Was this an absolute law of narrative? No, of course not. It was a convention. But, as my struggle with it has just demonstrated, conventions are never 'mere' conventions. Till you have moved outside them they seem absolutely *natural*. But now I *had* moved outside this particular convention. I saw that all the time I had been struggling in vain to climb over a wall when I could simply have stepped sideways and walked round it. I could in fact get on with what really interested me, which was the introduction of the solicitor into the family of the deceased *without* having to describe the house at all. All I needed to do was to start the characters talking. (In the end this scene became the opening not of the book but of the second chapter.)

'Mr. Stout?' said the woman who opened the door.
'Hyman,' said Joe. 'Mr. Stout's on holiday. In Corsica.'
'Gill said it would be Mr. Stout,' said the woman.
Joe shrugged.
'They could at least have sent one of their permanent staff,' said the woman.
'I am one of their permanent staff,' said Joe.
'You look like a student,' said the woman.
'As a matter of fact,' said Joe, 'and if you want me to be quite precise, I *am* their permanent staff.'
'You'd better come in,' said the woman.
'Thank you,' said Joe.
'I'll lead,' said the woman. 'Close the door behind you and give it a push or it won't stay shut.'
'I'm afraid,' he said to the woman, 'I stepped on something which gave a kind of squeak.'
'What kind of squeak?'
'Well, sort of high-pitched I suppose.'
'Don't worry,' she said. 'That was probably one of Mick's toys. He leaves them about everywhere. I hope you broke it.'
'I rather think I felt it move,' he said.
'Some of them even do that,' she said. 'But it may have been Oscar.'
'It felt more like Oscar,' he confessed.

I had made a fantastic discovery, you see. I had discovered that I did not *have* to do what I didn't *want* to do, and at the same time that I could do something which a moment before I had had no idea I *could* do. I could actually create my characters *and* move my story forward using nothing but dialogue and – I suddenly realised this too – my inventory lists. So that instead of being something lodged within me which I couldn't get out, the novel had become something which I found a growing excitement in *making*. The challenge was what spurred me on and brought me pleasure: the challenge to create a novel using no description but only dialogue and lists of objects. And of course as I slowly made it I found myself growing in understanding of the theme which had set the whole thing off: the relations between subjective fantasy and objective fact, between invention and inventory.

III

The first lesson I learned then was that there are no short cuts where art is concerned. You have to discover everything for yourself and each time you have to go all the way back to the beginning. It is not a struggle between convention and sincerity, as Romantic theories of art suggest, but rather a struggle to discover what it is one wants to be sincere about. And to do that no amount of thought or reading will help, only work, the making of things.

And yet, of course, while other artists cannot ever act simply as models, they provide an indispensable help. Their own struggles, their own solutions, the paths they *didn't* take even – all these can help. Just as one discovers who one is not by introspection but through acting, and not only through acting but through love and dislike and friendship, so one discovers what it is one wants to be sincere about at least partly through what one reads.

Often this is negative. I *don't* want to do this. And indeed, looking back now I see that the main impact of other writers upon me was entirely negative. I read Tolstoy and Stendhal and George Eliot with different degrees of interest, but they failed to engage me at the deepest level. And the same is true of the paintings of Leonardo and Rubens and Delacroix, the music of Beethoven and Wagner and Brahms. At the time I didn't realise it. It was only when I encountered works of art which really *did* engage me that I realised what I was missing in the others, just as it is only when one really falls in love that one realises that what one had taken for love was not the real thing at all.

The moment of truth for me came with the reading of Proust's great novel. As soon as I began it I knew that it was *real* for me in a way that Tolstoy and the rest had never been. And for one simple reason: it dared to talk about failure. Not simply talk *about* it either, but to demonstrate it occurring in the very writing of the book I was reading. Proust conveys miraculously both the sense of pleasure Marcel takes in the world about him and his intense desire to transmute that pleasure into something permanent by writing about it; but he also conveys the *failure* of such attempts. I cannot tell you how exhilarating I found this. Instead of feeling that the failure *I* was encountering daily was a purely personal one I now saw that it had to do with the nature of the project itself. And, if that was so, then it was something that could be lived with and, by being accepted, be overcome. Overcome not by being left behind but by being *incorporated* into whatever had to be said.

You see, in those works, by Dickens and Conrad, Jane Austen or George Eliot, which I was told were the summit of art, there was a closed, a sealed-off quality. They shut me out. There they were, supremely confident, supremely articulate, even in their narration of failure and frustration and incomprehension. But Proust was different. And I felt, reading him, that he was talking about things that were familiar to me; not, as I felt with the other great novels of Western culture, that I was listening in on the rites and rituals of some utterly remote tribe.

Years later I came across the later work of Wittgenstein and realised why philosophers of many different persuasions warmed to him. For here too was someone willing to say: 'I don't know', 'I can't', 'When I try to think this through I grow dizzy'. The long tradition of Western philosophy which has, at least since Plato, taken it as axiomatic that if the mind encounters problems then its task is to *overcome* them, was here being quietly put in its place. Wittgenstein was in fact saying: 'If the mind finds problems coping with this particular subject then that *in itself* is perhaps interesting and meaningful.' In a similar way I found Proust saying: 'There is the desire to speak and the impossibility of speaking. That is a fact about human life. Why does it exist? How do we cope with it?'

Of course one only responds to a writer if one finds one can trust him over details. It was because Proust was such a marvelous observer of human nature, such a superb mimic of human speech, such a wonderful craftsman with language and narrative, that I could take courage from his central insights. In a similar way I found, reading Kafka and Eliot, that they were speaking to me in a way that suggested that they understood *me* in a way I felt no writer I had previously read, did. 'Someone must have been telling lies about Joseph K.' 'On Margate sands./ I can connect/ Nothing with nothing./ The broken fingernails of dirty hands.' 'Words strain/ Crack and sometimes break, under the burden,/ Under the tension, slip, slide, perish,/ Decay with imprecision, will not stay in place,/ Will not stay still...' What a relief these words were after the great, confident – and of course magnificent – novels and poems that are the staple of the European and English heritage. Not all writing, it seemed, belonged to some great tradition to which I did not have the key.

Let me read you a poem. It is a short poem by the Israeli poet, Yehuda Amichai. Its qualities survive I think even in translation:

When a man has been away from his homeland a long time,
his language becomes more and more precise
less and less impure,
like precise clouds of summer
on their blue background
which will never pour down rain.

Thus all those who were once lovers
still speak the language of love, sterile
and clear, never changing, and never
getting any response.

But I, who have stayed here, dirty my mouth
and my lips and my tongue.
In my words there is garbage of soul
and refuse of lust and dust and sweat.
Even the water I drink in this dry land
is urine recycled back to me
through complicated circuits.

This poem, like most of Amichai's, is at once simple and profound. The poet has stayed in Jerusalem, 'in this dry land'. Here there is nothing new and even water is recycled. But of course, no less than Yeats's 'Circus Animals' Desertion', which it resembles in many ways, the poem is both lament and celebration. More celebration than lament. The poet has remained close to his roots, his feelings, however confused and inarticulate these may be. Those who move away find a more precise language, but this very precision is a sign of its artificiality, like those summer clouds which are in a way not really clouds at all since they bring no rain.

In this poem, as in so much of Amichai and of the Israeli novelist, Aharon Appelfeld, I find again what first moved me in the work of Proust and Kafka and Eliot. Here is something which connects with my own experience as Keats's 'Ode to Autumn' or 'Lycidas' or even *King Lear* do not. Here is something which speaks to me and gives me a sense of how I might myself speak in turn. There is no key here to a mysterious power, 'genius' or 'tradition', but rather the acceptance of a lack of key;

words are recognised not as clear, forceful and exact, but as parts of the 'garbage of the soul'; and the life-giving water, I realised, could still be life-giving even if it was only my own urine recycled back to me through complicated circuits.

IV

I come now to a crucial question. It is one I have often asked myself and to which I still don't have an answer. The question is this: how far was my response to the work of the writers I have just mentioned due to purely personal and arbitrary factors? Was it just because I was born in one country and have had to move on to two others, because I am a Jew with a typically Jewish ancestry – with ancestors, that is, coming from many different countries and cultures, none West European – was it because of this that I was touched to the core by Kafka but not by Milton, by Proust but not by George Eliot, by Amichai but not by Hardy?

There is of course nothing wrong with that. We all find pleasure and comfort in authors who speak to our condition, who write out of traditions we have been brought up with and about places and people we are familiar with. That is why the whole notion of a *canon* of literature is nonsense. A Victorian gentleman will respond to Horace and Pope in a way that a child from a Northern mining community or from a Sephardic Middle Eastern family obviously will not. An Anglican will respond to Herbert and Coleridge in a way that a Moslem or a Jew will not, and so on. So perhaps my own response to Kafka and Proust, my sense that here were writers speaking to me as George Eliot and Tolstoy never had, was simply the result of my own historical circumstances.

But that of course is only half the answer. Art is precisely that which speaks *across* cultural divides. I can respond to Dante and Herbert though I don't share their system of beliefs. And though Proust was indeed half-Jewish I am not going to commit the absurdity of suggesting that he is a Jewish writer.

Historical circumstances, while they can never be discounted, are not paramount. But I would put it more strongly. I would say that while historical circumstances may blind us to some areas of art and culture they may also help us to see what had been hidden to those with different backgrounds. We should, I am suggesting, think of our personal circumstances not as disadvantages but as a privilege. In other words there were perhaps forms of art which my personal circumstances had given me insights into, insights which might have come with more difficulty to those who, for example, had never left their native country except to go on holiday and spoke only their native language. (Incidentally, if I am right here that is also why the only good criticism is likely to be positive criticism, criticism which says: 'Look, you didn't realise this was good but...' Negative criticism is always overtaken by history, and those who don't like something would do best to leave it alone rather than trying to prove why it's bad.)

So, what had my particular circumstances enabled me to see about the art of the past which the scholars and critics I read as a student failed to see, or, seeing, had misunderstood?

V

The *Sunday Telegraph* reviewer of my last novel, the novelist Thomas Hinde, reprimanded me severely for abruptly changing track in the middle: 'The author arrives in one chapter,' he wrote, 'to wander about the setting of the novel, tediously complaining that till now he hadn't been able to get a word in. If this were true... it would be a confession of failure, since speaking through his characters and their actions is the novelist's business.'

Thomas Hinde may not be a bad novelist, but he is certainly a bad reader. Because a character says 'I' in a novel it doesn't necessarily mean he's the author, as every schoolboy knows. But why I quote this passage is because of the sentiments with which it concludes: '... speaking through his characters and their actions is the novelist's business.' But why should Hinde think that he has a monopoly of what is and is not the novelist's business? Imagine a music critic telling a composer that it's his business to write good tunes (actually such reviewers existed until fairly recently), or an art critic telling a painter it's his business to produce life-like portraits (we haven't heard from those for a long time).

My answer to such accusations is that if this is indeed the novelist's business then I am happy to be in another sort of business. In that first novel I was telling you about the issues I was concerned with were issues like: what is left of us when we are stripped of our possessions? What kinds of creatures are we, who put clothes on our bodies and live in houses and accumulate objects about us and who, when we die, expect to be buried or burned? Why do we live more forcefully in the hearts and minds of those who are closest to us when we are dead than when we are alive? Looking back at the six novels I have published since *The*

Inventory I see that these are the questions that have gone on obsessing me. Like recent French historians I am interested in the *longue durée*, in seeing human beings and their actions in a longer perspective than that of a single set of actions, in trying to catch the slow transformations wrought by time but not normally perceptible. Not that I am interested in *romans fleuves*, for one can speak about the work of time in quite short books, as Virginia Woolf has done, or even in a page or two, as Borges has done. And not that I am uninterested in stories; but there are stories and stories. Braudel still thought he was a historian even though he wasn't much interested in recounting the political intrigues of the court of Philip II, and I still think I'm a novelist even though I don't want to write the kind of novel Thomas Hinde writes.

Let me remind you of an experience you must all have had. You come down to breakfast on an early summer morning and in the fruit-bowl in the kitchen you see a melon. It is early, very quiet. The light is uniform, slightly misty. One side of the melon glints as the light catches it. Why does your heart leap? Why does it go out to the melon in the way it does? Why do we want to draw the fruit or put down the experience in words?

I think that the answer is that by doing so we would in some way *possess* it. But there are many kinds of possession. There is the buying of the melon; the eating of it; and this other thing I am talking about. And I think artistic possession is the most satisfying. For what happens when we sit down in the silence of that early morning and start to draw the fruit? We begin to discover its *otherness*. We begin to learn, in our bodies, through our fingers, what its breath is, we begin to feel the stream of life in which it floats. We begin to experience the stream as *other* than ours, and yet by the activity of hand and eye and mind and body we begin to partake of that stream. And as we do so we are more possessed *by* the melon than possessing it. And in that state we start to discover something about ourselves, about the stream of life in which *we* float. We start to experience ourselves not, as we ordinarily do, from the inside, but from some point outside ourselves, we start to sense ourselves as having no more but also no less right to exist than the melon before us, the cat lying asleep on the table beside it, the tree that can be seen through the window.

But, it will be objected, that is all very well for the painter, but what about the writer? Surely, as Thomas Hinde says, the novelist's job is quite different? But why? Does it have to be? If I am drawn to the melon, to that early morning scene, and if my gift is for writing and not painting, why should I hold back? If I feel that the melon calls forth a certain confused speech within me to which I desperately need to pay heed, why then should I deny myself just because Thomas Hinde tells me to?

But I want to go even further than that. I want to say that the kind of novel Hinde is advocating is one which leaves out too much. I want to insist that most of our experiences are *closer* to the one I have just described than to any we find in the traditional novel. I want to assert that the kind of novel Hinde appeals to actually imposes on its readers a thin and unreal view of life. John Mepham, in a beautiful essay on Virginia Woolf, has put it better than I ever could:

> The traditional novel [he says] is a form of representation which involves the creation of an imaginary but well-ordered fictional space... The orderliness of the fiction involves not only this internal orderliness but also an orderliness in its telling. For a story to be told there must be, implicitly or explicitly, a teller of it, a narrator, or a narrative voice, the voice of one who knows. The narrator who tells the story does so in order to speak his knowledge. The story is thus teleological both formally and substantially. The fiction has an end in terms of which its beginnings and middle make sense. And the telling of the story has a purpose, a purpose which is prior to and independent of the fiction itself.
>
> But what if we lack this sense of epistemological security? What if our experience seems fragmented, partial, incomplete, disordered? Then writing might be a way not of representing but of creating order. This would be a specifically literary order and it would not be parasitic upon any belief in an order existing prior to it. For example, think about the memory one might have of a person one has loved. It is possible, quite independently of literature, to give shape to, to fill out, this memory. Or it might be assimilated into some religious vision of life... But without such frameworks, without such means of thought and expression, we might have the feeling that the remembered person escapes us, is ungraspable, cannot be contained in our minds except as a disordered flow of particular fragments of memory... Then we should feel, as it were, that there is something that needs to be said but that we lack the means of saying it. If writing could be the means of completing the half-finished phrase, or bringing together and thereby enriching the fragments, then writing would not be primarily the telling of a story, but the search for a voice.

Narration would not be the embodiment of some pre-existing knowledge, but the satisfaction of the desire to speak with appropriate intensity about things of which our knowledge is most uncertain.

This puts marvelously well what I have been striving to say. It may be that few people will feel that need or will respond to the forms of art which articulate it. But it may be too that the dominant traditions of art in the West since the Renaissance have, for complex reasons, played down or denied outright this need, and so made us forget that it exists in all of us, and forget too that there are other traditions of art which do recognise it. It may be that the interest of Proust in medieval cathedrals and the paintings of Vermeer, of Eliot in Dante and Donne, of van Gogh in Japanese prints, of Webern in late medieval polyphony, of Stravinsky in riddles, charms and the ancient rituals of the Orthodox Church, of Picasso in African and Iberian art – it may be that these things were not haphazard but grew out of the sense these very different artists all had that if they were to discover what they really wanted to say then the dominant traditions of Western art since the Renaissance would be of no use to them. They would have to look behind and beyond for models and inspiration. And by doing so they have made us, their public, aware of the fact that for four centuries we had been living with an unduly restricted and impoverished view of the *possibilities* of art.

VI

The first thing everybody learns about the history of art is that some decisive change occurred at the time of the Renaissance. Exactly what that change consisted of is more debatable. The old story went that it led to the rise of realism, the acceptance of the human form and the disappearance of an inhuman, church-dominated art. But that story has looked more and more unconvincing as we have learned to look at other traditions than those dominated by the Renaissance ideals themselves. I simplify but I don't think I distort unduly when I say that in painting the change led to the development of the window-effect – that is, the viewer is placed centrally and looks into the painting as if through a window at a drama being enacted in an enclosed space outside; in music it led to the expressive use of the voice in opera, the development of the key system and the forward drive of sonata form, with its dramatic clashes and eventual resolution; in literature it led, in the end, to the kind of novel

Thomas Hinde was appealing to. In all these instances the two key points are: 1) the teleological drive of the work, and 2) the careful excision of anything that might ruin the illusion.

These two developments were enormously powerful and mutually reinforcing, and they help account for the masterpieces of Western art between 1600 and 1900. But there was a price to be paid. I have already mentioned one: the inability of fiction to deal with what John Mepham called 'the satisfaction of the desire to speak with appropriate intensity about things of which our knowledge is most uncertain.' But there were others. Take opera. In the nineteenth century more and more elaborate sets and costumes were made to body forth a drama which was growing more and more improbable. But do we need all these cardboard ships and temples and palaces, all these rich costumes, in order to respond to what happens on a stage, even in so unrealistic a medium as music-theatre? When Stravinsky wrote *Renard* and *L'Histoire du Soldat* he required no set, the minimum of props and, above all, he used singers to sing and actors to act. In so doing he was going back to an age-old tradition of popular drama, where travelling players would set up a simple stage in a village square and perform upon it, showing the audience their skills but never trying to swamp them with illusion or exoticism. The audience, needless to say, had no difficulty in responding. The great early film comedians worked in much the same way, in contrast to the producers of the Hollywood spectaculars, which continued the operatic tradition. When Harpo and Chico move away from the wall against which they have been leaning and it collapses on top of them, we love it. We respond at one and the same time to their own sense of shock and to our own foolishness at having forgotten that this was no real wall but only a stage prop. Soon, though, they are up again and with no difficulty at all we too grow involved again in the plot of the film.

Since the Renaissance Western art has been obsessed by the twin notions of imitation and expression. What Stravinsky and the Marx brothers do is remind us that art has always and everywhere, apart from a brief span of time in a tiny corner of the globe, been seen less as the imitation of reality or the expression of profound truths than as a kind of *toy*.

The idea of a work of art as a toy is one that may offend the more highminded among you. But I think I need hardly invoke the name of Winnicott or any other child psychologist to remind you of the fundamental, perhaps sacred, importance toys had for us in our childhood. And what is a toy? It is and it is not. A toy bear does not pretend to be a bear; it *is* a toy bear or teddy-bear; a toy horse does not pretend to be a horse, it *is* a toy horse or hobby-horse. As such it can be invested by the child's imagination with the properties both of animals and of inanimate objects. It can be named and hugged, but it can also be thrown about and kicked.

It is of course no coincidence that two of the greatest modern poets, Baudelaire and Rilke, have devoted essays to toys, and that one of the greatest modern writers of fiction, Kleist, has written an essay on puppets. There are really three aspects of the toy analogy I would like to bring out.

The first is that both toys and artefacts are always double: objects and living beings. A novel is words on a page *and* the world those words evoke; a painting is marks on a canvas *and* the world those marks evoke; a piece of music is sounds made by instruments *and* the form those combined sounds create. Recently it has become fashionable for both artists and theorists to insist on the material side of the equation: a book is *only* words on pages; a painting is *only* the marks on the canvas, etc. This is of course part of a reaction to the nineteenth century insistence on the opposite. What that gave us was the aesthetic of realism; what we now have is the aesthetic of abstraction. Neither in its pure form seems to me very interesting. The works I respond to are those which move between the two, those which, like toys, can take on a full life, can engage our imaginations fully precisely because they acknowledge that they are made objects, precisely because they do not try to hide the materials from which they are made.

Once this doubleness is accepted a new sense emerges of the possibilities of art. Art is no longer a poor imitation of life; it can do things life cannot. Why for example force a good singer to act when he will do it badly? Why not, as Stravinsky did, double singer with actor? Why limit what goes on in a painting only to what one would see looking out of a window? Why not, as in medieval paintings or in R.B. Kitaj's magnificent *Cecil Court* painting, include past and present, those who could have been there and those whom one wishes might have been there? Why try to reproduce in words a description of something which will always be infinitely richer than words? Why not use the possibilities of narrative to talk about the intermingling of past and present and future which occurs in dreams but not in our normal existence? Why, on a stage, stick to one plot, one story? Why not have five quite different stories existing simultaneously?

And this brings me to the second aspect of the toy analogy. A wooden toy is a complicated little object. It is more than the sum of its parts but its parts and how they are put together are clearly visible. So with artefacts. Actually I dream of a novel not so much like a wooden toy as like those great nineteenth century machines you see in the Science Museum or the Brighton Transport Museum, those gleaming pistons and spinning wheels. Why should a novel not be as complex as that and yet made up of such essentially simple elements? As we work on it we discover that it can do things we never dreamed it could; yet this is the result not of genius or inspiration but of quiet humble work with nuts and bolts and levers. If there are thirteen ways of looking at a blackbird there are also no doubt thirteen ways of making a mechanical blackbird, and each way reveals a new aspect of the blackbird to us.

But ultimately – and this brings me to the third aspect of the analogy – toys, no less than tribal masks, are mysterious and powerful presences. They are mysterious and powerful because of, rather than in spite of, their materiality. Picasso's great portraits of the thirties, Stravinsky's *Octet* or *Symphonies for Wind Instruments*, the early novels of Robbe-Grillet and the chilling later plays of Beckett pack an enormous, a frightening power into quite a small compass. Yet there is nothing hidden about their production. Everything is there for us to see. Yet there is of course a miracle here: the miracle of the artist's skill and resourcefulness. As we look we respond to the object but we also come to see that with a little effort we too could make something of the same sort: not as good, obviously, but of the same kind. It brings us to an awareness of all the wasted potential in our lives and shows us how to use it.

VII

Now, if it is true, as I have been arguing, that the predominant art traditions of the West have for the past four hundred years taken a direction quite different from that of other cultures, and if this has meant the shutting out of certain possibilities as well as the dramatic development of others, then the question arises: why should this have happened?

That of course is a big question, and many of the best historians of ideas and culture have written big books trying to answer it. We have been told about the printing revolution, the religious revolution, the scientific revolution, the rise of the bourgeoisie, the rise of the novel, and so on. The real difficulty lies in the fact that we are the heirs of those revolutions and so find it very hard to think in any terms other than those they have made current. Some of the best recent work on the subject, such as Svetlana Alpers' book on seventeenth century Dutch art or Peter Brown's collection of essays on society and the holy in late antiquity, have been successful precisely because the authors have managed to project themselves imaginatively into cultures not dominated by assumptions derived from these revolutions.

I hope that my first critical book, *The World and the Book*, flawed and often naive as I now frequently find it to be, belongs to this tradition. In it I set out to explore what had got lost when the Renaissance turned its back on the Middle Ages, and how some of those elements survived, though in transmuted form, in a few writers, and then resurfaced in this century. I tried to show how writers like Rabelais, Swift and Sterne had kept before us the idea of a work of art as a toy in a culture which was progressively narrowing the boundaries of the concept of play.

I do not want to rehearse these arguments here. I mention that book because it is part of my theme that it is out of my own preoccupations *as a writer* that my criticism has emerged. Any insight I might have had in that book into Dante and Chaucer, Swift and Nabokov, as well as its central theme, was the direct result of discoveries I had made in the course of struggling to write the novels, stories and plays which I was mainly interested in producing.

All artists are solitary beings. All artists have to find their own way. But none of us can do that entirely on his own. So we look around for help. And we become rather good at sensing what will be of use to us and what won't. I said earlier how much we owed to the great Modernists not just for their own wonderful works but for making it possible for us once again to appreciate forms of art which had been forgotten or ignored for centuries. Proust and Eliot are among the greatest critics as well as the greatest writers of our century just because it was vital for them to understand the past in order to go forward in their own art. When Schoenberg was asked how he had come to work out his compositional methods he answered: 'I was thrown into violent seas and I just had to swim.'

The critical and historical insights of a Schoenberg or an Eliot cannot be taken out of the context of their own struggles. Unfortunately that is exactly what happens when these insights are transferred to the academies. When that happens personal insight and polemical position are reified into a canon of literature or a great tradition. And this is perfectly natural, for academies perhaps need to think in terms of fields of study and cannot tolerate the idea that the nature of the field might itself be in question. Thus the Oxford English syllabus in the 1920's would have made sense to Matthew Arnold. It made no sense to Auden, who did no work and got a bad degree. The very same syllabus didn't make much sense to me either, thirty years later, though it did leave me plenty of time to read the books I wanted.

Perhaps that is the best a writer can expect from a University. Perhaps there will always be a conflict between literature as an academic subject and literature as a living force. But there is also a historical dimension to the problem. Though Universities emerged in the Middle Ages, the attitude we associate today with the study of the Humanities in Universities itself goes back to the Renaissance. In other words the study of the Humanities in the Universities is itself *complicit* with those attitudes to art whose limitations I have just been trying to sketch in. No wonder Eliot said [of what seemed to him to be Oxford of his time]: 'Oxford is very beautiful but I don't like to be dead.'

Though, as I say, Oxford left me plenty of time to read what I wanted, I was glad to get out. Its values were too much those of George Eliot and Matthew Arnold, and though I could respect and even admire these, I did not feel they were mine. How fortunate I was though to have Sussex to come to. For what I found here and what I have tried to perpetuate in my own teaching was an openness *within the academy* to precisely those kinds of re-evaluation I have been discussing. The arts syllabus here does not reflect the vision of George Eliot or Matthew Arnold – a watered-down version of which lies behind Thomas Hinde's remarks – but – in spite of all the revisions of the past 25 years – that of Proust and Eliot and Kafka and Stravinsky.

I don't know how many of you realise how extraordinary this is. How much we at Sussex owe to the vision of men [...] imaginative enough to see that the Renaissance Humanist traditions in which they themselves had been educated were, despite their virtues, severely limited, and that here, in the first of the new universities, there was the chance to introduce into the academy some of that rethinking of both the history and the *function* of art and culture which Modernism – the thought and work of Kierkegaard, Nietzsche, Proust, Eliot, and Kafka – had brought with it.

That is why teaching here at Sussex has meant far less of a clash between my own concerns as a writer and my duty as a teacher than I could ever have thought possible. I have found an atmosphere here open to the views of art expressed above. And, amazingly, I have been able to teach here what I love and not what I have been told I should admire. I hope I have been able to persuade my students also to love and not simply to make gestures of obeisance towards a range of works and authors no-one would have dreamed of putting on the Oxford English syllabus in my day: Biblical narratives, Dante, Kierkegaard, Thomas Mann. I hope that in spite of these times of Government-induced crisis in the Universities, in spite of the blindness of the UGC, who are making every effort to undo all that Sussex has created and turn us into just another University, safe, solid and dull, a place no artist would want to come within a hundred miles of – I hope that in spite of all this Sussex will be able to go on offering its students just that.

VIII

But it would be wrong to end there. I began, after all, by asserting that there was an unbridgeable gap between the making of art and all talk about art. I have tried to show that every artist has to be a reader; has, that is, to find what help he can in the masters of the past. But I have also insisted that the critical activity must come second. And that is the danger of talking about the subject as I have done this evening. And it is of course the danger inherent in all teaching, even when that teaching is most congenial. For there is knowledge and knowledge. Each work is a struggle to discover what it is one knows, what it is one wants to say. And when it is done, it is all to do over again. And if artists are better than scholars at rediscovering the riches of the past, they also secretly long for amnesia. History, for all of us, is a nightmare from which we are forever trying to awake. If the work I am currently engaged upon is to be any good then I have to forget all I ever knew. Then, in time, the work itself may teach me to remember.

That is why I should now like to stop talking *about* art and end by reading you a story. It is the shortest story I have ever written, barely a page long. I want to read it partly as a commentary on this lecture and partly as an experiment, to demonstrate that though it will still be my voice that you will be hearing, and though that voice will still be speaking words intended by me, the story is both much more and much less my own than the lecture. The precise nature of that 'much more' and 'much less' is what I hope you will ponder as you leave this hall.

The story was sparked off by the title of a picture by Paul Klee, 'At the Edge of the Fertile Land'. I didn't know the picture, but when I came across the title I found I couldn't rest until I had somehow made it my own. When I had finished the story I found that Klee's title wasn't quite right for it, and so changed it from 'At the Edge of the Fertile Land' to the simple 'In the Fertile Land'. Not very logical, you will say, if the story was only written to try and make sense of Klee's title. But whoever gave you the impression that making artefacts was a *logical* business?

In the Fertile Land

We live in a fertile land. Here we have all we want. Beyond the borders, far away, lies the desert where nothing grows.

Nothing grows there. Nor is there any sound except the wind.

Here, on the other hand, all is growth, abundance. The plants reach enormous heights, even we ourselves grow and grow so that there is absolutely no stopping us. And when we speak the words flow out in torrents, another aspect of the general fertility.

Here, the centre is everywhere and the circumference nowhere.

Conversely, however, it could be said – and it is an aspect of the general fertility here that everything that can be said has its converse side – conversely it could be said that the circumference is everywhere and the centre nowhere, that the limits are everywhere, that everywhere there is the presence of the desert.

Here, in the fertile land, everyone is so conscious of the desert, so intrigued and baffled by it, that a law has had to be passed forbidding anyone to mention the word.

Even so, it underlies every sentence and every thought, every dream and every gesture.

Some have even gone over into the desert, but as they have not come back it is impossible to say what they found there.

I myself have no desire to go into the desert. I am content with the happy fertility of this land. The desert beyond is not something I think about very much, and if I occasionally dream about it, that contravenes no law. I cannot imagine where the limits of the desert are to be found or what kind of life, if any, exists there. When I hear the wind I try to follow it in my mind across the empty spaces, to see in my mind's eye the ripples it makes on the enormous dunes as it picks up the grains of sand and deposits them in slightly altered patterns a little further along – though near and far have clearly a quite different meaning in the desert from the one they have here.

In the desert silence prevails. Here the talk is continuous. Many of us are happy even talking to ourselves. There is never any shortage of subjects about which to talk, nor any lack of words with which to talk. Sometimes, indeed, this abundance becomes a little onerous, the sound of all these voices raised in animated conversation or impassioned monologue grows slightly disturbing. There have been moments when the very abundance of possible subjects and of available directions in which any subject may be developed has made me long for the silence of the desert, with only the monotonous whistling of the wind for sound. At those times my talk redoubles in both quantity and speed and I cover every subject except the one that obsesses me – for the penalty for any infringement of the law is severe. Even as I talk, though, the thought strikes me that perhaps I am actually in the desert already, that I have crossed over and not returned, and that what the desert is really like is this, a place where everyone talks but where no-one speaks of what most deeply touches him.

Such thoughts are typical of the fertility of our land.

An Inaugural Lecture given at the University of Sussex on 6.3.86.

Anthony Rudolf

Shhh Golem

(i.m. Borges – his rhyme)

Surely it is curious, if not actually disturbing, that whereas typical numbers (9, 42,73 etc. etc.) form part of an infinite total, typical letters (Q/q, T/t, the Scandinavian Ø etc. etc.) are members of a finite series, in my language 26 – if we exclude *th* and *ch* and similarly honorable ones. What a restriction on our liberty – as writers, speakers, citizens of a so-called democracy! I am Blake, I am Lautréamont! I shall not be brow-beaten in this way. I am certainly not the author of the Zohar, blessed be he, for whom the antinomian doctrine I am about to propound was repellent. And if, as indeed I am, I am indebted to G. Scholem (in the capacity of Shhh Golem), I am in good company. Yes.

What I propose, in the interests of freedom, is the existence (or at least the lack of proof of the non-existence) of another letter. I shall wander the face of the earth until I find it, and finding it, why, I become God, or at least his outrider. For, on that day, his name will of necessity be changed, the unknowable name eternally changed by the hitherto undiscovered letter, and not only *his* name, but all names, words, vocables, utterances, speech, discourse, dialects, ideolects, languages: and I shall turn the curse of Babel into a blessing. I would not go so far as to say that the very fact that the potential existence of another letter can even be conceived *proves* that it exists, but I *would* argue that this fact is presumptive evidence in its favour. Science, as we know, is hypothetico-deductive.

I will build a house of worship and once a year I shall enter into its innermost sanctum and speak *the name*. And yet, I must not allow myself to fall into the trap of my opponents. Let me empathize with them: if I seek another letter, is there not an anti-me somewhere, seeking the last number, seeking to prove the finitude of number? And if I empathize still further, am I not that seeker? For, is not the existence of an infinite "total" of numbers an affront to my reason, a futile attempt to catch it with its trousers down? Surely, as satellites encircle the earth, as poetry and mathematics meet behind the mirror, surely the very idea, let alone the existence, of an infinite total of numbers is completely ridiculous, beyond belief, the ultimate in discredited superstition?

I have worked for many years to refute the definition of number found in *Principia Mathematica*. The way is open! I shall seek the last number, up continuum and down spectrum, avoiding the false trails laid by aficionados of spurious Parisian dialectics. When I find it (and faith in reason is not to be dismissed as paradox) I shall not be God, that is not in reason's nature, but I *shall* be numbered among the immortals for having unlocked the door to one of those mysteries comparable to the square root of minus one. All the school text books will be fucked up. Not to mention...

There is a further possibility: that in some way the last number and the new letter are one and the same thing, one and the same signifier. That my two quests are one. That the rose and the flame are one. That somewhere in South America the prophet knows the answer but is not to reveal it to the novice. There are no short cuts in the wilderness. He slaps my face with one hand, and claps with the other. He too is imagined by me (even as he imagines me), O foolish reader.

Claude Vigée

Two Poems

Jerusalem Wind

Celebrate what world, language of our loss?
Clothe what triumph in the purple of ruins?
High in the cold the linen of the clouds
flaps above the house in the winter storm.
Jerusalem wind, you run across the mountain
like the rumble of the day about to be.
We had little joy; and yet a festive
dawn is upon the earth.

Returning from Tel Aviv

Returning from Tel Aviv, in the night coach...
Empty grottos of the evening, by the sea. Fog, streets wandering amid
    the debris. Jaffa. Ruins in the distance.

And, once again, that cry emerges from the sea.

Cold black sand. Frozen, radiant turbulence of the song.

With the children grown up, you become living water once again, for
    there is nothing, but nothing, which can prevent
    you from dying.

Returning from Tel Aviv in the night coach, on the road strewn with
    crushed jackals.

Translated from the French by Anthony Rudolf.

Mordechai Geldman

Six Poems

The Plant

In the vase a plant took root,
I planted it by a pillar of my house, watered it,
fertilized the soil and it already took root.
Fearing for the pillar, the neighbor came and tore it out, so
I planted what was left behind the house, near the window,
I said, I'll guard it against the wicked.
But the cleaning woman threw a rug into the yard and it broke.
I mourned and talked about it with a friend, a woman and the dog
    Toot,
I wanted comfort and they gave it.
But I was not consoled.

For a plant holds a hint of the forests, the plant reminds me
that I am from the forests, the forests of Poland,
I am from the snows, from my grandmother's village.
There she sat in the window watching the snow fall
on the pear tree, the raspberry bushes, the black fields.
When lightning flashed the cows calved in panic
and rain rapped as if the curtain of seas in heaven had torn loose.
In spring the river turned silver from the scales of fat fish.
In the summer the delicate fowl mated in glass air.

And I am from the sea, I remembered,
from the Mediterranean I thought would go on to the end of the world.
Every summer, every morning, I went with a bag of food
to the blue peacocks as to school,
I saw how bodies turn gold
how charm ripens into beautiful flesh,
examined the eternally possible changes of blue.

Boats happily lost in good-hearted azure,
white balls did not fall from the sky.
I was a narrow-waisted lifeguard
whose generosity matched his beauty
(I hoped he'll save me).

For girls have different beauty with damp hair,
in the wave lies the mystery of strength and weakness –
Desperate longings turn to foam approaching land.
In the foam the gulls were born emerging suddenly,
little fish practised their descent to the aquarian avenue of Keren
    Kayemet
in sifted depths of light.

I sought girls from the provinces.
Girls who knew the names of plants.
Girls who studied the plant guide, the bird guide.
I loved a boy born in the hills,
My cleaning woman brings me flowers from her garden every week
– Is that sentimental?

I come from the tropical forest
where I have never been.
Where beauty and wildness are bound together.
Where love is wild, heavy and lithe as beasts,
and shine like dewy flowers laden with color.
I am from the land of hot feelings
where the sun grows blood-filled fruits
where beauty borders the monstrous
where sky is sky and land is land and night is night
and love is love and death is death.
If you lend your ear you will hear how in a moment,
this moment, everything grows and fades as one.

In my room are books, pictures and a mirror.
In my hall a dog, and my work is regular.
The girls are lovely when dressed, and lovelier naked.
Many choices are open before me and many closed.
Many times I schemed to go away next summer.

Alexander the Great

Alexander the Great of the mind
reached India, as far as the wisdom of Yogis,
and there he stopped.

Naked Indians, under a horrid sun,
becoming spirit with savage self-possession
transmuted before his eyes an illusion of reality into the illusion of
    illusions.
In the distance, strange dark Platos awaited him,
in love with light, with the Idea of Ideas,
haters of the real.

From there on countless walls blocked his sword.
From there on he conquered no more.
Empires ruled by barbarian kings
opened in his depths.

A Bird

A bird between her sheets enticed me
and I was enticed, in her bed I thought Sabbath
for soul, a bird between her sheets
will calm me, with plumage vanquished face
alive perfumed and tickling, hues
like a glowing rainbow, big as palm,
a bird, I feared between her sheets to crush
the fineness of her life, I also feared lest beak
grow large between her lips, to gouge
my veins bloody.

Fruit

Rash and mottled summer horses will come
and love his glowing soul
transport his laurel-scorched back
to a cool turquoise tending toward blue,
then will his mouth fill with laughter
ripe, the fruit of hours will please
his grasp will be full with a blossoming
perfect green.

Apollo 2

A gold lion on the basketball court
sucks cola through a white straw.
Sweat leaks a sweet stream issues from his armpit
becoming a wet stain on his shorts.
A ball at his feet, his friends' bodies steaming,
Sun in the south of the court.
Roundness radiating to blindness.
They said: dumb as a floorboard
tossed from school to the street,
without knowing in their middle brain
that he retired to ripen to Apollo.
– Muscles stretched in scorching garages
and half-naked among tires and engines
anointed with lubricating oil.
Honey and sun merged in him
to flesh whose wisdom's more ancient and complex
than that of the best of his teachers.
Honey and sun coalesced in him
into solid gold.

Mister Death

Strange, but the scarlet fever I contracted late in my life
brought to my house Bitter Death, Mister Death.

And he spoke to my heart, in varying volumes –
soft, liquid, and seductive, even dry as pebbles –
that I should come to his kingdom of darkness
where because of the darkness you don't notice
the vanity and futility of action.

Mister Death exploited the scarlet fever and spread his net.

"Where is she?" I thought, as he walked through my rooms,
"I should phone her from my heart."
It is she who can scatter the dusty fogs
from objects in the room of faded meaning,
she who can call for Grace, for connections, for the lightness of birds.
By the shine of your eyes she'll know
your fever is gone and a leaf of hope is sprouting from the branch.
She knows you've never failed
– you simply were what you are –
and bring flowers.

And Death urged his well-ordered arguments
propelled his telegrams to desolate consciousness
promising over and over the sleep of the just:
"Be a grain of dust in wide plains, in mountains and towns.
Be a particle and a wave in the big heavenly light, in unspeakable
    thusness,
be in the element of immortality, in the perfect round.
Silent words in stone."

No doubt Mister Death exploited the situation.

But that same landscape flashed as well
like the song of flutes in shadowy groves:
that olive valley between Piazzale Michelangelo and Forte Belvedere
I watched from a quiet café;
and in my hand the hand of a girl
who, at the end of Mass at San Mineato
where I happened in as a tourist,
put her hand in my hand, and looking into my eyes,
said, "Peace," as did all the other prayers.
They gave peace to each other as if passing
a tiny bird or a tune or a necessary check
from hand to hand. Shedding the gloves of estrangement.

The Plant was translated by Karen Alkalay Gut.
Alexander the Great was translated by Barbara and Benjamin Harshav.
A Bird, Fruit, Apollo 2 and *Mister Death* were translated by Harold Schimmel.
All translations are from the Hebrew.

Rachel Chalfi

Nine Poems

Changes

The petals of the rose
shut out the rain.
Hail will smash the gates of the pearl.
One hard woman rebukes the wind.
Soon she will fade

Waste

So many years of wasting the blue.
What simplicity what kingdom
could have seeped through this decay.
What green light
could have shone
out of the chlorophyll of dreams
and blue
that never existed
in all this vegetation of oblivion.
What waste what loss
it was all my life
not to have worn that blue dress
for the air could have thinned
rarefied and thinned
toward the angels

Spell

The sea calls her
hole in the ground invites her to fall
crack in the wall opens, speaks to her,
stone trips her and tempts the whole
body, lizard smacks red lip from inside wall
volcano mouth passes soft tongue along its lips
come come   fall

Tiger-Lily

Once upon a darkness
I was a tiger-lily.
Pallor preying,
pallor preying orange pursued
in mottled light,
speckled, speckled,
pollen falling from the tip of a rare
long-necked
lute.

Tiger-lily.
In those other places it's a fearsome flower.
In our cruel region,
it's a fear of wonder, wonder of flowers; lily of prey.

Dark tiger in the lily of a valley.
All a plant could desire
from a beast.
A pistil pealing in the mouth of a cruel bell, stirring
within the stirred, throbbing
within the flame.

And I would climb
with him
there
through thick sea – vagabond wandering,
large   lonely,
blood between us,
leading at a gallop,
a flailing fall,
then tunnels   tunnels of
light.

A lily within a radiant mountain tiger.
All a plant may, all a beast may.

Once upon a darkness

Traveling to Jerusalem under a Full Moon

The window is traveling clouds are traveling I am
traveling the road is traveling the moon the trees the
bus traveling the moon is traveling windows are traveling travelers
are traveling thoughts are traveling earth is
traveling
time is traveling
light is traveling stones are traveling glass is traveling the
galaxy is traveling the universe is traveling the galaxy is
traveling the moon is traveling
and God is
forever
still

Chameleon

Shreds shimmering in the drugged dream
of a chameleon
your lies bear enchanting colors
violet and azure enveloped in darkness
they are lies and they are not
transparent
a lie cannot be transparent
let no one tell me a lie is transparent
for each lie has the flesh and the hue and the tremor
of its own and each lie surrounds itself
with a small tangible world of
a living truth

★

Last day of
grace
last feather in the golden
tail of summer's peacock

Painful Yellow Breaks the Stretch

Painful yellow breaks the stretch
of the sea
The rocking of gulls will not break the barrier
of words
The pain of the painful pain
pains
On a lovely day in the city of lovely seas,
From the dome of the ceiling delicate flecks
of plaster flake and sway
Flocks flocks of gulls lull the water away
The sea does not know today
Tomorrow
It will froth
with wrath
How can a man dwelling under a dome
know the cycles rocking of
yellow   white   blue
blue   blue   blue
dark see-through rocking
sea-through

Cypress Will Forever Arise

And I say to you
a few nice words
and the rest indirectly

And I say to you
Will nothing bring back the days

And that skin   and the sweetness
and that cold fire
                              is
and that simplicity
                         is it
lost

You say

Changes, Spell, Chameleon and *'Last Day of...'* were translated by Linda Zisquit
and Zvi Terlo.
Waste was translated by Linda Zisquit in collaboration with the poet.
Tiger-Lily was translated by Alexandra Meiri, Myra Glazer Schotz and Zvi Terlo.
Travelling to Jerusalem Under a Full Moon was translated by Myra Glazer Schotz.
Painful Yellow Breaks the Stretch was translated by Karen Alkalay Gut
in collaboration with the poet.
Cypress will Forever Arise was translated by Karen Alkalay Gut.
All translations are from the Hebrew.

Harold Schimmel

Poems from Lowell

★

Among the names accompanying you remain
"Robert Lowell" in the childish signature on your letter
and dedications in two thin black volumes
it's your official name under which follow the poems
in any event the "Cal" you arranged for yourself
after unsavory heroes like Caligula
Caliban (and Calvin your first wife said
considering your religious experience)   I heard
Lizzie call you to the phone once
by the nickname but when she was forced
to speak with family she reverted to the Bobby
of childhood mother and father   your students
called your Mr. Lowell if not Professor...
freckle-faced intense bespectacled   with a woodpecker's-look

★

The orchard extends through the heart's reach
heartscape our at-ease into strangeness
the deer we move toward on the road
across the quarry at the foot of the hill
we'd climbed for its summit are still
to our slow approach   eyes angled
something a little in the shoulders turning
or a pair still at the same between-space
wandering off to a bordering
heartscape of grapevine along the path
and the everpubescent almonds   also the figs
could never speak with more force or more impress
all of which here we take in as if
through a straw with a swivelling movement through eyesight

★

I'm in uniform fresh from basic training Frank
all leanness of thighs moves to a bass-beat with a glass
of Jim Beam (his partner) on ice   Edwin presents me
(*this* anonymous soldier) and we speak of a mutual philosopher-
friend's fairness and decency   "And when he feels like a boy"
     O'Hara
attacks... "Wham!" I come-to after through splintery seconds of
     catching on   deer
like river minnows nipping at my toes   Jane Frielicher
descending her ladder smiles wily sexy and Frank
devotes himself to pulling at his absent dinner tie   In all
of this were are you   In the corner
in the Whistler's rocker   heterosexual and learned
holding court with both your hands..."ten dollars"
"car keys" and "thigh" in your poems were arranged with
Chardin-like precision of the floral exhibitions (set to the botanic-
     calendar) at the Isabel Gardiner Museum

★

Boston's all history and recall
New York's out ahead of you
elsewhere the spirit of encouragement's
more rare   no one's too big for it
and in any case I admit there's something
frightening... to widen the poem so as
to include without compromise what one felt
and knew in one's lifetime   we
speak with many false voices   sometimes
with a little luck we find one true one
in our poems   a poem should include
the contradictions in a person
all our compulsions and inclinations have to be there
so that in the end our intentions are unrecognizable

★

Opposite uptown is
downtown where Edwin lives
with a table-on-which-he-writes-(in pencil and
on separate sheets of paper)-poems   a cat or two
and against the wall several paintings he's collected or had given
him over the years   From time to time Rudy shows up to
work in the dark room. Next to the door a pile of what
Edwin's labelled "intellectual trash" his friends
are invited to pick from... about your poems Edwin
was negative preferring (East Village legacy)
to hand me a slim volume *The Hotel Wentley Poems*
of John Wieners   I defend you as well as I'm able
Edwin (gentleman) China-born and a Berlin dancer in the 20's
isn't impressed by the blue blood Beacon Hill society   Jim Bean he
   buys by the flask

★

I rub my eyes seeing metal
pop-tops to infinity as something fallen
from the sky hail of aluminium having hit
the grapevine hard destroying it unripe
early-summer fruit robbing the grapes
of sun-shielding foliage   I'm back here from my
warmcountry for a short while and stroll up upper
Broadway toward Columbia department of rare books and mss
to fill out a form which will procure me Crane
across the way Eisenhower in academic gown someone's portrait
fifteen feet long in oils I meet Cunningham
(chairing the MLA) popping across the street
to a bar between prefatory remarks for beer and baseball
on the big screen   JV of the Hawk's nose and great brilliance

★

We spoke for two hours Erev Yom Kippur
I had to leave at five for the pre-fast meal
at the City Tower   "I'd guess" you said
"that it's just as difficult to believe in a chosen people
as in a divine messiah"   "The New Testament?"
"You should keep in mind it's a Jewish story
it has the same flavor... It's just now we're
beginning to understand that the Old Testament
isn't an English book that it was written in Hebrew
It's the most perfect translation ever made! The book
that's most perfectly been translated! It's impossible
to outdo the King James... At the moment I'm translating
Aeschylus which allows me the same lush diction
Is it much different in Hebrew?"

★

One day noon thirty fourth street a little up from Macy's
across the street a terrible screaming rises powerfully
up through the pedestrian throng in the August typically
humid midtown thousands of passersby freeze to locate
the source of the scream which walks on screaming
a few minutes ago I saw the jackhammer crews among the
group of bronze men bang out "twelve-noon"   happily
a passive study and here comes a woman's summer ordinary dress
stopping the blood in our veins... which means what   madness?
despair? ancient-Greek-landscape-Pan might have understood
a bluish waterfall at Grand Central Station continues
bathing the feet of menthol smoking vacationers
and on one one of the columns at Penn Station there's a green stain
from the wing of a day-old Buick somewhere within the grains of
      marble   as all we'll know of forever

★

Little elegy for my father run over on Columbus Circle
crossing the street toward Lincoln Center
it was a delivery van he
crossed with the light   fifty years
he walked the length and breadth of her streets from end
to end and river to river   he knew intimately
the pattern of surrounding highways   her bridges
tunnels and city exits he loved her
restaurants wine shops and the Metropolitan Opera
with its panoply of singers at the opening of the Kanovitz show
at the Jewish Museum we met Irving
with his second wife Arien a well-turned blonde "my former student
      Harold"
he talked to strangers like to eat in company the glitter
of the famous was for him an indispensable part of the city decor

Translated from the Hebrew by Peter Cole.

An Interview with Isaac Bashevis Singer

Conducted by D.B. Axelrod, S. Barkan and J.C. Hand

DBA: Concerning reference to supernatural, and even mystical, elements in your work, as well as to unconscious and conscious psychological drives, what is your view of Freudian psychoanalysis? Perhaps Freud's terminology also refers to the same phenomena of possession, and the possession by the 'dybbuk' and schizophrenia may be regarded as nearly identical?

IBS: I know that Freud, before he created his theory of psychoanalysis, was interested in hysteria. He even published a book together with Breuer. He was also interested in a way in psychic research, but in his later years he abandoned this kind of research. He really believed that by analysis he could cure the human soul. In this respect he was not a mystic because the mystics don't find cures so easily. A real mystic knows that the human tragedy, if there is a human tragedy, is not going to be cured in the consulting-rooms of a doctor. I wouldn't say that Freud was a mystic. His role, rather, was a mixture of mysticism and rationalism. This is my personal opinion.

DBA: Certain terms that you use – or words that I see occurring – in your autobiography, for example, refer to a notion of Spinoza that anything can become a passion...

IBS: Yes. That is true.

DBA: Then you make a comment that perhaps passion is all there is, and that to allow passion to occur is not so bad. It's the use of the word "passion" that I am interested in.

IBS: Yes, Spinoza also uses the word "passion" or "affection". Spinoza believed that all emotions were more or less bad. I don't have this feeling.

DBA: Then "passion" was feeling in the negative sense of the word. He doesn't celebrate passion.

IBS: He says that even if you do something – let's say you help a poor man because you pity him – it's not as good as if you helped him because you understand that he should be helped. In other words, everything should be done from a point of view of understanding. I don't agree with him. I think that without emotion a human being is really not much more than a vegetable, no matter how much logic he has. Take the emotions from us, the passions, and we are nothing. I think that although the passions have done a lot of damage, we cannot live without them, we cannot exist. Even logic itself becomes worthless once the passions are gone. In other words, if we would lose all our emotions, science wouldn't be worth a penny, because it would have no meaning for us whatever.

JCH: It seems as though your characters are captives of their passions, like Clara, like Asa Heschel, Hadassah, Zipkin.

IBS: They did not have a good death!

JCH: Yes!

IBS: Passion is actually like a knife. You can kill with it and you can cut bread with it. The question is how it is used. Of course passions are always dangerous. In this respect Spinoza was right. But human life itself – or I would say life generally – is a dangerous business. Why, passions can lead us into the abyss; they can also lead us into heaven. This is how I feel.

DBA: That's why many of the things that occur in your books – not as a fault but as a frequent occurrence – seem to come by accident. A child is as often conceived, or more so, by accident; a marriage is made by circumstance or accident. Does this reflect the illogical tendency of things or the passions which can seize us?

IBS: No, I don't say that there is a contradiction between logic and emotion. Since logic without emotion has no meaning, the passions are the basis of logic. And also, as far as accidents are concerned, this is a different question altogether. I personally agree in this respect with Spinoza: that there are no accidents; that behind the accidents there is a law.

JCH: You say in your autobiography that there is a thin line between sanity and madness.

IBS: And insanity, yes – this is really what the Jewish moralists always taught, and this is what you find even in the Bible. Once you make a mistake and you leave the right road, you are on the way to the abyss.

JCH: Like in *Satan in Goray*?

IBS: In *Satan in Goray*, and in life itself, because why should we speak about books and not about life?

JCH: But you know, your characters who go crazy in "Black Wedding," in *Satan in Goray* who absolutely plunge into the abyss, are beyond any psychoanalytical rescue. But some of your characters say, "Maybe you need a psychiatrist"; and one of them answers, "If I need a psychiatrist, every Jew in the world needs a psychiatrist...".

IBS: He meant every *modern* Jew! Not the old-fashioned Jew who didn't need a psychiatrist. Our grandfathers didn't need a psychiatrist. But our generation needs them very much. The only thing is that the psychiatrist himself needs a psychiatrist.

DBA: That leads us to another question. The orthodoxy, the structure of the *shtetl*, the old country, all these more or less disappeared. Are the modern Jews suffering any less, or are they better off for the abandonment of orthodoxy? They've given up what we could call superstition.

IBS: I'll tell you, they are better off in a material way but I wouldn't say that they are better off from a religious point of view because Jewish religion has done better in the *shtetl* than it's doing in the big cities. People were together, and they didn't demand so much. Their passion for wealth and for material happiness was not as strong as it is today. However, I think that the *shtetl* as we knew it is gone, and there is no going back to it; we can never go back to it. The saying, "you can't go home again," applies also to the *shtetl*. We have to make peace with it. Other generations will come, and they will have their own way of life. The basis of Judaism is that, despite our passions, we still have free will. There is still a spark of free will left in us. And this spark can become a flame if people make use of it. But people seldom make use of free will.

JCH: In what sense? Could you explain how we make use of it?

IBS: Once you fall in, the deeper you fall into the net of passion or, I would say, into the fire of passion the less free will you have. The less you can make use of it. But what the sages of the future will have to find is how to combine passion with free will. This is, I would say, the crux of the matter: if you can be a passionate person and still choose between good and evil, you are more or less on the way to paradise.

DBA: You made a remark that we are not as well off spiritually as the orthodox Jews (for example in America), although, being dispersed and secularized, we have gained materially (Brooklyn perhaps excepted). But what is it that has lapsed: simply the structure, the orthodoxy, the ritual?

IBS: More than this. More than this. First of all, the modern man, not only the modern Jew, is a terribly greedy creature which our grandparents were not. No matter how much he gets or she gets, it's not enough. And there are other things in modern life which are, in comparison with the *shtetl*, less ethical, less sublime. But again, you can be greedy and still be a decent human being; if you exercise free will, if you are greedy for the good things, not for the bad things. In this way Judaism is different from Christianity. The Christians believe that once you believe in Jesus, you are already redeemed. All you have to do is to belong to the party, to the collective. And we Jews don't believe in this. You are not redeemed by belonging. You have to exercise free will, and free will is something you have to use every minute. It is not only a matter of using free will once a month or once a year. At every moment there is some dilemma and you have to make decisions. I would say that Jewish ethics fools itself less than the ethics of others who have found a certain kind of nonsense, and say "dee" like this and you are already "doh." Our grandparents knew that the temptations for sin and for evil are constantly with us. Neglect one moment and you are doomed. It is like driving a car – if you fall asleep for a half second, you can already kill someone or be killed. The same thing is true in life in general. We are always in danger, and we always have to make choices. We see that in the case of the automobile it is possible: a man sits there at the wheel, and he makes choices every half second, and sometimes he takes hours. It is possible to do the same thing in a spiritual way, where you know that the danger there is as great as on the road.

JCH: Do you believe that Jews are more moral than Christians?

IBS: I don't know if they are more moral, but I believe that Judaism has more basis for morality in its teachings. It also has more reality than what the Christians teach. They say that God sent his son to die and because of Him we are redeemed. We don't say that we are redeemed; we say the opposite. We say that at any moment we can fall into worse misfortune if we are not careful and watchful all the time.

JCH: And yet it's so understandable that the poor people of Goray would embrace the false messiah having gone through what they went through.

IBS: Of course, the poor people; but they did not embrace a false messiah. They thought he was a true messiah. They made a mistake. It's like when someone gives you a check and you think it's a good check.

JCH: But they suffered for their mistake.

IBS: Of course they are punished!

JCH: To what extent do you believe that the Jew, if he is not in love with his own suffering, he at least tends to endorse it?

IBS: Well, I suppose that there are Jews who, if you told them that "this man is an anti-semite," their eyes light up: they have found an anti-semite. I don't belong to this class of Jews.

DBA: They say this proves the point.

IBS: Yes, yes, they say that proves their point. I think this is a very dangerous thing because any human being can make a mistake. People can just fall into a rage and then say something abominable. How many bad things did I say about the *goyim* in my lifetime? Still, I wouldn't say that I am an enemy of gentiles. Sometimes you say things. In other words, we shouldn't go out and search for anti-semitism. Modern Jews are, in this respect, rather masochistic. The old-fashioned Jews understood that they were not friends of the peasants; the peasants were not great friends with them. They didn't demand this sort of friendship. I would say that the religious Jew, even here in America, is more realistic and understands life even better than the modern Jew with his millions of theories.

DBA: My grandmother came from a mud hut – all my four grandparents basically came from a mud hut, a dirt floor, from the *shtetl*, from somewhere near Rostov. And they came to America and suddenly they acquired wealth, they owned property, and they founded a synagogue in Beverly, Massachusetts. And now I have children and I live on Long Island. I've moved away from even that, and I don't teach my children anything in the direct sense of the *cheder*-based religious study; they won't go on to a *yeshiva* subsequently. I wonder if there is any hope for Judaism without the cultural reinforcement.

IBS: I would say, if you have children, you need something like organized religion. If you are already a ripe man, a man of sixty years, you can say, "I am religious in my heart, and I don't have to go to the synagogue." But with small children, you absolutely need it. Without any Jewish education your children will never embrace a viable sort of Judaism.

DBA: Isn't Judaism at a certain level an absence of certainty? Like the ten commandments themselves – you define things by negatives. 'Don't do this, don't do that'.

IBS: Yes, but the person who wrote the ten commandments said, "You should teach your children." If you neglect to bring up your children by telling them that certain things are good and certain things are bad, they grow up with the idea that might is right. And anything they can do is fine. You do great moral damage to your children if you don't teach them.

DBA: They don't lack an ethic. They lack a culture, my children.

IBS: The truth is that real culture and ethics go together. If a culture has no ethics it is not really a culture; it is a barbaric culture.

SHB: John Steinbeck has said, "Perhaps the major problem in modern-day America is the losing of any sense of direction." In view of the passing of the *shtetl* and the traditional codes of behavior – and in view also of Eliezer Ben Yehuda's success in revivifying Hebrew – what do you see to be the place of Yiddish in modern Jewish children's education?

IBS: I would say that Yiddish has succeeded in creating a culture which has been with us for the last six hundred years. You cannot erase Yiddish from our history because we are living at a time when all people are looking for their roots. They understood finally that without roots a human being is not a good plant. In Yiddish are our roots. Of course in Hebrew we have roots that are four thousand years old, while in Yiddish we have roots that are soft and can still grow. I think that they made a very big mistake in Israel by neglecting Yiddish and by fighting Yiddish. Now, lately, they have begun to see their mistake, and they have tried to correct it, and they have begun to because it is never too late to correct a mistake.

SHB: So you feel that the language may yet be revived as Hebrew was by Eliezer Ben Yehuda?

IBS: The people may not speak Yiddish for the next two hundred years, but, if they forget Yiddish, they forget their roots, and these are not just roots – folklore roots - but they are roots of ethics and human conduct.

JCH: May I ask you a question about the women – your women characters?

IBS: Yeah, how's about the women?

JCH: They seem to me to be more victims, more victimized by the men and more entrapped.

IBS: Because women by nature are highly emotional, and if the woman gives in to her emotions, has no direction, has no moral comfort, she really will suffer more than the man. But I would say it's true about all of us; in a way, what is true about women is true about men and vice versa. Of course, if you tell your daughter, let's say a fifteen-year-old daughter, that she can sleep with any man she meets, she will listen to you and pay a big price for it because the woman was not created to be so promiscuous. When she has relations with a man, she gives him not only the body but a part of the soul. A woman who spreads her soul all over the world is a kind of lost person. In a way, from a sexual point of view, she is more of a victim than a man who is doing the same sort of thing.

JCH: So, because of the woman's biology, she suffers. But you also said that if we could go back to the *shtetl* where there was more structure we wouldn't need psychiatrists...

IBS: But we can't go back completely to the *shtetl*. We have to create something between the *shtetl* and present civilization. You cannot bring up your daughter to be like your great-great-grandmother was. Neither can you bring up your daughter the way, let's say, some of the girls in New York or on Long Island are brought up, that everything is kosher and that a girl of sixteen should already have the experience of an old prostitute. Again, it's terrible. You have to give them a choice, but you have to teach them that good and evil are not just words that old-fashioned people created. They exist today. Evil brings more evil, and vice versa.

SHB: Speaking of good and evil and your references to the Kabbala in your books, what is your view about actual existence of evil and representations of it in the form of *dybbuks* and so forth?

IBS: According to the Kabbala, evil is not something positive, but negative. The Kabbala teaches us that since man should have free will, God's face should sometimes be hidden from him. If man were to see God every minute of his day, he wouldn't have free choice. He would just do what God told him. In other words, we have to be blinded in a way so that we have free choice and this kind of blinding is the source of evil.

DBA: In the conversation we are having, you appear to be a religious man.

IBS: I consider myself a religious man although I am not a man of dogma. I don't think, for instance, that I must have a *mezuza* on my door. In this respect I am not religious but I believe that world, the cosmos, is not a chemical or a physical accident. I believe that there must be a plan behind it.

DBA: An actual plan? Not spirit only, but a plan?

IBS: Absolutely. A plan from every point of view. And if a man tells me that evolution has created the world, I say, "Who is evolution? What is evolution? How has evolution learned to do all these things?" They use a lot of words today which are, so to say, substitutes for God, such as "nature" and "evolution." They would say "God has created the world? Impossible!" But evolution? This is possible! What is evolution? They cannot really say what evolution is. The only thing is that it has lasted a long time. But things that have lasted a long time also have to be planned.

DBA: But the basic mystery that you reflect on is how much cruelty there is, that it abounds in us. Do you go so far as to say that man is the cause of that? The characters that you design...

IBS: I would say that man is the cause of much evil. I would say that all evil is not made by man. Cancer isn't, and when there is a flaw, when there is a fire, it is not always man's fault. But I would say that generally nature is not as cruel as men can be one to another. The more civilized man becomes, the more potential there is for cruelty and the more man has to curb himself. If people stop exercising their free will, they might also raise new Hitlers and Stalins!

Abba Kovner

Sloan-Kettering

Sloan-Kettering

Sloan-Kettering (full name: Memorial
Sloan-Kettering Cancer Center) is a building grand
and growing all who come in
are undressed between its walls
naked
each one separately and all together
suddenly caught
in a transparent cage

Amazing silence on all
the many floors
and one who loses his guide
finds himself running
from room to room

not knowing which way to turn
peeping
into gleaming corridors
half
open doors
or half
closed

Sloan-Kettering is an encounter with a wasteland
pathless
between yellow arrows
and blue signs.
Something mysterious emerges
in the feverish
cells of his brain
in front of a triple elevator
before
it opens its gaping maws
like a desert
that begins to evolve
inside him.

Transparence

Drip
Drip
Drips from above into his veins
atropine colorless
like death. Like the spelling of his name
in a foreign tongue

Dripping into any telephone receiver
to get an American answer caressing
an alien heart
      You're welcome, sir,
doesn't cost a cent. He wonders:
the fingers of the black nurse on duty
like Mother's velvet cushions
she kept   her needles
in a velvet cushion worn out like the color
of chocolate – –
Looks at him and doesn't see:
your pulse, sir, is perfectly OK.
Thank you.
You're welcome.

Beyond the Screen

Beyond the screen lies a Thai
pouring his grating breath
into a plastic sleeve.
    If my geography is not wrong
he comes from Siam, the former
land of free men.
No need to look beyond the screen
to see how the last
family members of the old
man who spit his breath
into a plastic bag surround him
like the hoops of his life.

We built magnificent metropolises –
how empty is their splendor beside
the loneliness of people outliving
their dead world.
    A parchment lost in the desert,
its yellow faded gray, a Thai man spitting
his breath into a plastic sleeve
until the soft steps of his wife, sons, daughter-in-law,
run over his face glimmers of life returning
like an imperceptible reflection,
till they are swallowed
in the octopus arms
of the great, cold
stone city.

In Their Infuriating Confidence

In the infuriating confidence of the Memorial doctors
there is something of the mystery of
the mountains of Jerusalem.
– You're just passersby, that's all!
Say the mountains of Jerusalem:
Move on.
Move on.
To the edge of
the border
  Ahead!
Dangerous turn.
Warning!
Slow down!

They come in. They go out.
Walk on.
Walking on
nothing worse
than a corridor in the middle of
laughter –
On. On!

Road cutting through
Samaria;
Sloan-Kettering
corridor
cutting through life.

Sarah

Sarah appeared to us like a loss coming back from the sea.
We didn't think we'd find kin in New York.
When we arrived she was waiting for us
among the gigantic presences
with sooty light in her hair
in upper Manhattan.
We are a generation starving
for relatives. And even if this one is a shade doubtful
or needs further inquiry we cherish
this sudden relation
because many other things
began dying out
and when Sarah came to the hospital to say good-bye
I was very excited
for her time was short. Tomorrow, I'm going to say good-bye
to everything that was my voice and at that same time
Sarah will raise her voice in Africa
against Apartheid – no,
Sarah won't set foot on the soil of Apartheid
itself
only from beyond the border
she'll raise her voice, from one of the neighboring states
of South Africa. I feel a great kinship
to Sarah, to that stubborn thing inside her, a woman
of the tribe of rebels, if only she knew Hebrew
she would still sing: *Don't listen, son,*
to the ethics of your father / And don't heed
the teaching of your mother / a song of our stormy youth
unwittingly put in our mouths
by the proper Hebrew poet David Shimonovitch –
But Sarah knows only English
And English is heard from the end of the world all the way
to Manhattan, feedback in mighty volume.
And Sarah knows by heart speeches
from all the congresses.
Barefoot she would sit in front
of the fireplace (not lit. For Sarah has no time
for such trifles) and tell you about the protest

meetings, as on Passover telling it
all night long, not like my firstborn son
who was born at the end of the congress that gave birth
to the Jewish state and gave it Jerusalem
for a capital of Israel. I was honored to be
in one (Zionist) congress, my father dreamed and did not get there
but my son who lives in Bak'a Jerusalem, for him
Congresses are *alte zakhen*, and the son of my son
won't even learn about it in school
for our modern school is a comprehensive school
including the future and would not face
the past. Living Jews don't have to
live on the dead. There are plenty of dead
in Jewish history anyway.
When I look at Sarah I think
that she is always on tiptoe. For always
she looks only forward.
If only we too
could always be intent like that,
forward. So typical of generations
of Jews gone by
lifting themselves out of the immediate moment
and now the immediate moment
is stronger than the Jews.
      I look at Sarah
as at a looking-glass: in her, the cycles of beauty,
of the sublime. What I mean is something
that our experience will not destroy:
Like light returning
light ever returning,
even deceptive light.
      You could envy Sarah,
no longer young
 a thin woman, with no masks,
no splendor. And so much overflowing
vitality – – – Not that I dared to ask
but a slip of my tongue: And Afghanistan?
Is there no congress for Afghanistan etc.?

And Sarah's heart grew heavy for a while and she recovered
and she said: My dear, the world may be small
but there is more suffering than we can bear...
we must choose. And so, for right now
Sarah will go to Africa
not to the country of Apartheid, as we said,
but to a neighboring state, where there is no Apartheid
nor any
black hope.

Like a Seal on His Heart

1
How little we need
to be happy:

½ a pound of weight gained,
one double round in the corridor
of Sloan-Kettering
in slippers
a morning without aspirin
silence like a delicate abyss
a distant
sand dune
beyond the Green Bridge
a patch of grass
and she next to him beginning
to knit a new sweater.

2
In the rhythm of the knitting
needles in her fingers
the rhythm of *ay-li-*
lu-lu-
li (for me).
Sounds that live on inside you
with other unreal things
that were not wiped out
in the exterminations.

Drugged

9 o'clock. Norma will bring the pill to smooth his sleep
if one can say pleasant sleep on a night exhausted
from a dream insane recurring time and again
with minor variations, like caressing
the thighs of a sinking ship that pulled them out into
the vast expanses before the port was blocked, at 2 a.m.
Night filled with caresses. So he stood caressing the blurred
photo with faces of his grandchildren, later
caressed one hand with another
and the wind strong and cold and the snow whips. And he sings.
Moves and sings.
And the stones that tore the skin of his hands and feet. The sharp
edges of big stones from the land of our fathers
and he knew well that there is no land of our fathers
without people hence he ran
on his hands and feet over stones
hurt all over his body and screaming
in pain and pleasure
for his scarred skin was enveloped
in waves of a salt sea.
And he screamed mightily
and only the sudden appearance of the Puerto Rican nurse
standing there between the doorsill and the screen, embarrassing,
unreal, saying:
"You rang the emergency bell, sir?"
forced him to ask: "What time is it?"

Xenophon among Jewish Partisans

1

And they cracked their lice at the edge of the bonfire and
the potatoes for supper they roasted
on the same fire and they boiled
their tea from the water of the green-eyed
swamp and the frogs watched the spectacle.
Every man on his weapon. And they spent the night
in the earthen burrows, dug out, well camouflaged,
women and young men together
and no rape here, they only make love.

For cold is the earth of Lithuania and the winter is harsh.
And Russian partisans who came from far away
lusted after the daughters of Israel. For famed are
the daughters of Israel all over the forest and the Jewish
Partisans were at war
front and back.

2

And Cyrus fell in the battle of Kunaxa. And they cut off
his head and his right arm. And the arm and the head
of Imka were hanging with his guts on the electrical
wires and the electrical wires were torn by the blast.
Imka whose brother Danko was brought from the place
where he fell beyond the river
just yesterday, was not yet eighteen
and he did not start this war and on the mine
the boy's feet did not step in order
to conquer the kingdom of Persia

3

Like the men of Sparta you never heard of Partisans
crying. But when they finished covering the grave of
the two brothers,
ends of a family that was, you could register
the sigh of pinetrees rising
from branches heavy with
snow

4
When there is no Xenophon. No Imka. No
Danko here only he circles
among the trees wafting
the smell of novocaine
trying to put himself in the right perspective
for what... My god!
To wake up mute
in a foreign bed
    and without the fear of the forest!

Translated from the Hebrew by Barbara and Benjamin Harshav.

Michael Benedikt

The Kapos
(or Arnoldt)

Germany, 1939

And so the Kapos came to our little town, let out
for a while, from that crazy Nazi camp; & they rounded us up
saying we could be Kapos, too, in their "Gray Announcements,"
if we rendered ourselves up to join them, "At Once, Early, & Without A
    Fight";

For otherwise, just as sure as we were born, they said – close to one late
    midnight,
the muffled roar of convoy trucks would come
when we weren't dressed & it was inconvenient.

– And my husband, Arnoldt, too, proclaimed to me that surrendering
    was a damn sight
better than being awoken one night looking into a muzzle or a gunsight
or worse yet, being hunted down when we both were bedded down
hiding, maybe, in the basement behind the wine-rack, in that old broken
    bathtub
which for so many months now I'd thanked Jähweh yes Jahweh Himself
    that no one else had found.

– Not even the neighbor's children who when we two weren't around
came back from their monastery school, or their butterfly hunt that fled
    through the field

so close to that Camp, every afternoon, every afternoon.
– Not even the neighbor's children, who used to make a "game" of
     searching thereabouts with flashlights, at twilights
with their puppydog, "Fritze"; & sometimes, even, with our other dear
     neighbors' dogs & children...

...And so, suddenly, there was a commotion of motorcycles stopping,
& Arnoldt & I laughing, with that poor old broken bathtub far, so far
     behind us
& We two (in two Kapo sidecars) carrying two light packages

Containing two toothbrushes & two combs one hairbrush & two new
     pajamas plus one nightgown
plus one bottle of good Mosel we'd taken, all for our overnight stay.
– "Experimentally," as we understood it – for truly it had to be
"experimentally," for just as Arnoldt said,
to get us to come to Camp that way, & to give up & go so easily
it was clear that they just had to agree.

And beyond even that, there were two gift packets of cigarettes which, as
those two drivers themselves pointed out, were given generously.

Yet it's true that as soon as Arnoldt had marched upstairs that very
night, with
     that very first copy
he said, of the "Gray Announcements" given out

– Arnoldt holding it in his *teeth*, & with Arnoldt also holding up both
arms as if in surrender as if for a joke & with a laugh.
Then pointing with one hand through a window downstairs to two *other*
figures crouching beside two old bicycles, two soldiers there who were
taking a Newspaper Photograph – Oh, how that bright sudden flashbulb
hurt my eyes
like a burning gas explosion; Oh why Oh why for the sake of Jahweh
     Why

did Kapos have to do that, too, for it wasn't yet midnight.
– Yes I remember it was just after dinnertime & our light was already
     out...

K.Tzetnik

Quintessence

'The fifth essence (after fire, air, water and earth); the one of which heavenly bodies are composed – the pure concentrated essence of anything.'

Gate One

(Taping:) LSD treatment of Mr. De-Nur,
first session at my clinic,
Psychiatric Department, Royal University of Leyden,
July 8, 1976.

Professor Bastiaans switches on the recorder, running through his routine preamble. Failing daylight had made room for shadows. I lie naked in bed, my legs trembling, aware of what had brought me to Leyden: there is a scene I must confront once and for all. But on the threshold of this confrontation, now, the seizure of horror in me is far worse that what I had experienced back Then. There where the nightmare was reality. Suddenly I want to shout: "Not yet, Professor Bastiaans, please not yet! I'm not ready yet." I'm so afraid of what's about to manifest itself to me.

But rather than the shout "Not yet!" the four Hebrew letters א.ד.מ.ע. "E.D'M.A!" came crying inaudible. That voiceless combination, again trying to escape, as it had every time Death confronted me in Auschwitz; that mute combination getting no further than my clenched teeth denying it exit. The secret of its omnipotence was that it outdid vocalizing; that never unlocked, it was in no danger of decomposing in the outside air; that it was as the ember's contained flame. Dr. Mengele saw it emerge from my eyes. It stopped him from lifting the Index Finger to signal the scribes to slot me with the others in their ledger book: "Crematorium!"

He appeared stunned that from the bony eyesockets of a mussulman[1] could issue a look like mine. Naked skeletons by the hundreds were in line behind me, and by the time Dr. Mengele regained his orientation, I had been shoved aside by his subordinates. Tick-tock, tick-tock, time is short. Hundreds more in line, waiting.

A fiery planet called Auschwitz. Countless selections. Countless deaths. And I, surviving them all for two Auschwitz years by finding refuge in the hush of these four Hebrew letters; I still believe it was the unvoiced power-combination that saw me through Auschwitz. In 1945, still wrapped in the striped shrouds of the Auschwitz campling, I first committed Auschwitz to writing in *Salamandra*. It was then E.D'M.A. was written by my hand of its own volition next to the book's title. Since then, the four Hebrew letters have headed my every book, in every translation, always next to the title on the first page.

Now, watching Professor Bastiaans approach me, syringe in hand, the intimate sense of danger was back: Will I live through this? Combination, can we survive the Nightmare again? –

And suddenly –

– I am marching in the procession, I watch myself from a distance. The Gestapo has granted the Jews one hour to vacate their Jew Quarter and move into the ghetto. Black Uniforms go from house to house shooting down dawdlers. I am part of the procession that I watch. The procession is petrified like a mid-scene film freeze mid-motion on the screen.

I see myself a detail in the procession. Given no more than one hour, everyone had grabbed whatever came to hand. Vevke the cobbler marches ahead of me, his workbench on his back, his head drooping like the head of a horse pulling a heavily laden dray. I myself hadn't made it to thc violin case when the shooting began; this is why I'm carrying my violin in my arms, bared. Vevke, head lowered, downcast eyes shooting side-glances to those flanking him, mutters: "Jews, don't weep! Don't give these hangmen the satisfaction. Jews, put your faith in God!"

The horizon prisms into all the colors and the procession reflects those colors. I walk in back of Vevke, my eyes riveted on his cobbler's bench which changes from blinding yellow-green to ultraviolet, and transforms itself from one shape to another. The procession is in total freeze, static, but Vevke's cobbler's bench is perpetually moving. Bit by bit, my eyes watching, the bench pours itself from Vevke's shoulders, elongating like that clock of Salvador Dali's which spills from the table's edge to the ground. While Vevke holds onto the bench, with both hands spread left and right, his palms appear nailed to the wood which bit by bit becomes a crucifix, aflame with infrared rays, incandescent. So Vevke drags along with his crucifix in this procession of the Jews. To the ghetto. Once upon a time the city's garbage center.

"Don't weep Jews, don't weep! Don't give the hangmen the satisfaction!..." And every whichway Vevke twists his head I catch a glimpse of his face in its nonstop transmutation. For one moment he had the face of Reb Nahman the Bretzlaver, causing a voice from heaven to thunder down: "Make way for the Messiah, Son of Joseph, make way!" Another moment his face is the Rabbi of Shilev's, the way I saw him locked in the Isolation Block before our transport was let out for the crematorium. And concurrent with his facial metamorphoses are the color-metamorphoses of the procession which marches forward while it stays put. Static, it is suspended cloudlike in the sky. The sky rains down the letters of the scriptural verse: "Like the Son of Man come with the clouds of heaven..." I read the words vertically like Chinese script descending onto the petrified procession, whose center is Vevke nailed to his shouldered cobbler's bench which one moment is Dali's clock and the next is Jacob's ladder, angels up and down on it, and then a crucifix. Great awe overcomes me. The procession is frozen. I am the breath in mid-asphyxiation of the immobile-marching mass. And locked in this no-exit stranglehold, I must breathe while we proceed to the ghetto, formerly the city's garbage center. "Breathe. Breathe." I rasp.

"What do you see, Mr. De-Nur? Tell me, Mr. De-Nur!" the voice reaches me like thunder rolling down from the skies, distant, so distant...

"What! – – Do you! – – See! – – –? See – –? See – –?"

I see Vevke's cobbler's bench grow into an altar, I see the Old Man of Shpuleh[2] in the High Priest's vestments and I see the face of Vevke, now the Bretzlaver rabbi's. He stands in the city's garbage dump, now ghetto, the altar borne on his back, the voice hurtling down thunders from on high: "Messiah, Son of Joseph – Make way!" And the Old Man of Shpuleh in the High Priest's vestments calls out to him in Arabic: "Mahrum!... Mahrum!... Mahrum!..."[3]

---

1) *Mussulman* – A campling (häftling – concentration camp inmate) whose bones were all that held him together.
2) *The Old Man of Shpuleh* – 19th century Hassidic-Polish rabbi, by inherent authority the excommunicator of Reb Nahman the Bretzlaver.
3) *Mahrum* – outcast.

And I ask my soul: are we-procession, with Vevke shouldering his cobbler's bench in our midst, doomed to stay stuck together like this forever as a frozen parade at the heart of the garbage-ghetto? Vevke's now bound to the brick stove in Franzl's Auschwitz block. Faceless to me, because he's arched over the brick-stove, head down, arms yanked out at his sides right and left, each hand bound to an iron hook, one crucified. His pants dropped, cover his bare feet. Terror seizes me. Block Chief Franzl has brought Vevke to The Binding. The sacrifice is ready.

"What do you see, Mr. De-Nur?"

The voice searching for me rises from a deep pit.

I see Vevke's two naked buttock hollows casting white fire into every nook of the dark block. A thousand camplings hold their breath.Any moment now Franzl will step out of his cubicle, the pure-white cane in his hand, and he will count off twenty-five strokes, one by one, into Vevke's withered buttocks. The sacrifice is ready.

This is the cane Franzl had removed at the unloading platform from a blind man's hand as he came tumbling into Auschwitz out of the packed cattle cars. Like a wood-chopper raising his axe to split a log, Franzl lifts this cane. And every time the cane crashes into Vevke's naked buttocks salvos of sparks in all the colors of the rainbow come spewing out, glowing stars bursting like fireworks to disperse throughout the block's darkness. Soon the block orderlies will remove Vevke's carcass to toss it onto the pile of corpses behind the block, the ones awaiting the next round of the Corpse-Kommando who will load them onto their pushcarts and deliver them to their destined cremation. Never yet has the soul of life remained in a mussulman's body after the twenty-five strokes of the Block Chief's white cane. An unbreakable cane. What would a blind man want with a cane, Franzl had quipped; his truck knows its way to the crematorium.

Suddenly darkness in the block. Vevke has been unbound by the block orderlies and removed out to the corpse pile and all the lights went out. Vevke will soon become ash now. I see smoke rising out of the crematorium chimney, twists of smoke interspersed with sparks. I stand and stare, expecting to see Vevke the cobbler within this sky-bound smoke. Day and night, night and day, this ceaseless delivery of smoke, crematorium to heaven.

"Rabbi! Rabbi!" I cry out, "Is it possible that the smoke goes up to heaven and just vanishes there?"

"What do you see, Mr. De-Nur? Tell us —"

I see millions of sparks shooting out of the smokestack from a pipe joined, as to a mystery fire-lab, to the furnace-core underneath: I see one and a half million live children, millions of maidens in the bloom of innocence, millions of mothers whose young breasts burst with milk, millions of youth in their prime, age-worn men and women – and each, each of them, cast like coal to feed the fiery maw of a racing locomotive, to feed the heart of the oven in the mystery of Auschwitz.

"Rabbi! Rabbi! What is manufactured by this oven whose flames are fed by bodies in the millions? Non stop, non stop. What is this plant's product?"

"Rabbi! Rabbi! I see the ash residue from the bodies, but what about the souls of the millions who passed like heavy water into the furnace-core – what do they produce? Rabbi! What will be the end product manufactured from the souls of one and a half million children of the pyre?"

Around me is day. Around me is night. Around me is week. Around me is year. My hand feels the fracture of a moment. I see the color and the light of the moment's fracture. I see time. I have the power to draw it; face and form. I taste time, eat it, it comes inside me. Time is in my insides. I can see it. I know there is no seeing Time's face so I snap its picture for a keepsake: it is photoengraved on the pupils of my eyes. Time is within me, I am Time; and, as Time's stand-in, I stand in Auschwitz, between block 14 and the roll-call area, my eyes on the ascent heavenward of this crematorium smoke, waiting to catch sight of Vevke the cobbler, who's supposed to be in these twists of smoke. With my own eyes I witnessed the Corpse-Kommando arrive to toss him on their pushcart; with my own eyes I witnessed how their pushcart became a cobbler's bench, and the cobbler's bench I saw become an altar; an altar whose likeness was fashioned as divinely prescribed by God to Moses in the Torah. Furthermore, the altar of Auschwitz shines with more radiance than the biblical altar.

Once the block orderlies tossed Vevke on top of the corpse pile behind the block, I came out to touch the white fire his body emanated. I wanted that fire to brand my hand with its stigma. This may allow me the grace of sharing his lot. Vevke is greater than Isaac, who got away from The Binding on that altar – no angel materialized in the Auschwitz block to stay the white cane in Franzl's hand. It was his white fire I wanted to touch. I didn't know if I would be graced with such a fire when it was my appointment with the Corpse-Kommando pushcart. And I witness the manner in which Vevke's skeleton was being tossed, a burnt offering on the altar, my ears echoing with verses channelled from heaven: "And take an unblemished lamb... and sacrifice it..." "And I will judge between lamb and lamb." Now I expect to see Vevke ascend with the smoke, and I stand and stare, and I am Time, and the way Time still stands in Auschwitz, so do I stand still in Auschwitz. And I stand and I watch and I witness:

No, it's not Vevke ascending from the crematorium smoke but He Himself, none other, Ashmdai,[4] King of Hades, to his right Shamhazai, to his left, Azael[5] as I came to know them through the Book of Enoch the Negro. I shake with terror. I scream. I want to hide my face, be unseen. It's because of the indigo. It blinds my eyes. In Auschwitz there is nowhere to run to, no place to hide.

"Tell us, Mr. De-Nur, what's frightening you?" The voice comes reaching for me from four-corners-of-Auschwitz. "What is frightening?... Frightening?... Frightening?..."

Auschwitz a single great blazing pyre. I knew I had been summoned to witness this fire-breathing sight of Auschwitz. King of Auschwitz, Ashmdai, Here He is! I see Him with my own eyes: emerging from the furnace-core in his ascent from the chimney, from the hidden holies of His abode, cloaked by smoke He wafts to the heights of heaven with Shamhazai and Azael unfurling an umbrella over His head. Mushroom-like, the specter looms in the sky; Shamhazai and Azael are about to anoint Ashmdai as the new King of Kings, Lord of the Universe. By blowing horns they declare to the four corners of the earth that the new name of the Sovereign King of the Universe is from now on to be no longer Ashmdai, but Nucleus!... His birthplace: furnace-core Mystery Lab, Auschwitz factory. Manufactured of a new substance, an altogether unique matter, Nucleus is the concentrate of the souls of a million and a half breathing children.

My eyes are lifted to the skies of Auschwitz and I see Nucleus on His throne, under His majestic Mushroom Dome; and the Dome – a mammoth umbrella in the sky – outgrows Auschwitz, His birthplace, and is borne to the four directions of the celestial compass till it has completely blotted out the sun and the firmament.

I am shaken by the terror of utter darkness. The voice calling: "Son of

4) *Ashmdai* – Hebrew. Satan's name.
5) *Shamhazai* and *Azael* – servant-angels to Ashmdai.

Man, eat this scroll!" and I, crying and crying: "God, Why? Why?"

I turn away to avoid the looming specter, and what my eyes run into on the horizon is the hanging *shivitti* and, at its hub, the letters of the Holy Name *Y H W H,* squirming like a tangle of vipers with my face under the SS cap imposed on all of it... *SHIVITTI* changes like a digital watch that alternates date and hour: opposite the Mushroom of Nucleus the letters of the Name of God catch fire; but as soon as the Hebrew letters change into a tangle of vipers superimposed by my face in the SS cap – *shivitti* is gone into hiding and Nucleus the King wins the upper hand. I raise my voice, shouting across to my own face on the hiding *shivitti:* "Oh God, God! It was Vevke the cobbler I asked to see in the smoke, not Satan! God, oh God! In your war with Satan don't turn Your Face from me! Don't surrender me to Franzl's white cane! My God, my God, don't forsake me!...

("What do you see, Mr. De-Nur? What hurts?")

"Oh Lord, let me be left over. Leftover... leftover... leftover... I took an oath, a vow made to them to be their voice. Spare me, Lord, spare me! No one here will be left over. Oh, God, I'll be a witness to Your Fulgent Presence in the letters of your Name! I'll be a witness to Your Face in Auschwitz, Lord!... Lord!..."

– An electric jolt, and I am tossed back into my body, in bed.

I open my eyes. Professor Bastiaans is seated in the chair by my bed, while next to my head is the unfamiliar face of a stranger, squatting.

Soaked in tears and perspiration I hear: "What did you see, Mr. De-Nur? What are you still seeing? What images keep surfacing in you?"

Translated from the Hebrew by Eliya Nina De-Nur and Lisa Herman.

Emil Habibi

Your Holocaust
Our Catastrophe

My first public appearance was at the founding meeting of the "League for the Struggle against Nazism and Fascism" in Jerusalem, 1942. This league was established by Palestinian Arabs who saw enlightened patriotism as the antithesis to "traditional Arab behaviour," which, in its political narrowmindedness, believed that Nazi Germany was likely to help those fighting British colonialism. Rommel's army was then approaching El Alamein and, on the eastern European front, Stalingrad stood heroically against the Nazi army. My friends and I felt that it was impossible to postpone the founding meeting of the League any longer. We selected the spacious Rex cinema as our venue. The hall and the balcony were completely full even though many of our people grumbled against the arrogance of "these young people." I was then 21 years old and was working as a newscaster in the Arabic division of the Mandatory broadcasting station, a functionary who could express his political feelings only by placing the news from the "eastern front" at the beginning of the program or at least before the news from the "western front."

The educator Abdullah Bandak noticed my excitement and embarrassment and offered me some cognac to calm my fear, not of Rommel's army but of the audience. My consolation was that there were three well-known speakers with me: Abdullah Bandak, the lawyer and later judge Jafad Hasham (both of them no longer alive) and the veteran anti-Fascist Hamdi El-Husseini (who lives in Gaza). Arabic newspapers reported the meeting and the speeches extensively and sympathetically. I do not know what the Hebrew press wrote about it; but I do remember that our meeting was noticed not only in the local Arabic newspapers but also in the Egyptian *Wafd* and in Communist dailies in Syria and Lebanon. Who expressed opposition to anti-Fascist activities among Palestinian Arabs? None other than the director of the Mandatory Information Office, Mr. Edwin Samuel. Two days after the inaugural meeting of the League, the director of the department informed me that Mr. Samuel had summoned me to a confidential conversation.

Even though forty-four years have passed, I still remember the details of that conversation between that tall, important, poker-faced official and the young and foolish newscaster. I had a similar feeling subsequently, in 1954, at a meeting with a senior official in the British Home Office in London. I came to him to protest the decision of his office to reject my visa to the UK. The official replied brusquely to my appeal with a decisive refusal and stood up. I understood that the conversation was at an end and I stood up too. Since I knew that Europeans are polite, I offered him my hand. He looked at me in a panic and did not offer me his hand.

While Mr. Edwin Samuel did offer me his hand, the meeting with him was also very short. He explained to me that my appearance at the meeting was a political activity, forbidden to government clerks. I replied that I saw it as participation in the war effort of the Allies. He smiled and simply repeated his previous words.

"And if I continue, you'll fire me?" I asked.

"Those are the regulations and the prohibitions," he replied.

I thanked him briefly in "Pinglish" (English in Palestinian dialect) and did not cease my activity.

This personal memory came back to me when I was asked to write on the Arab understanding of the Holocaust. I admit that I saw the subject as a challenge. It is no secret that, on this point, official education in Israel – directed by Zionist ideology – blackens Arabic history and tradition (if it recognizes it at all). Indeed, the Israeli Prime Minister allowed himself, in 1982, to compare the invasion of the Israeli Defense Forces into Beirut to the entrance of the Allied armies into Hitler's Berlin at the end of World War II! Only the distorted picture of the function of the Soviet Union during the War and the Holocaust, presented by that education, is similar to that outrageous distortion.

When I asked Arab educators to tell me what Arab youth in Israel are taught about the World War and the Holocaust, they showed me George Salama's book, *Modern History of the Israeli People*, a required twelfth-grade text. The Soviet Union – which lost twenty million sons and daughters and without whose help the Nazi monster could not have been destroyed – is mentioned only twice in that book: once in connection with the secret agreement between the Soviet Union and Germany (p. 115) and once concerning the recognition of the Jewish Anti-Fascist Committee (p. 125). Even the importance of the partisan movements in all occupied nations of Europe, which were led by Communists, is reduced by this educator to "Jewish partisan movements." And if this is how history is portrayed to Arab youth, it is not difficult to imagine how it is portrayed to Jewish youth.

I do not intend to ignore the attempts of German and Italian Fascists to exploit the Jewish-Arab conflict for their purpose – access to the Middle East – by relying on the superficial slogan, "The enemy of my enemy is my friend." But it does seem to me that Arabs were not the only victims of these attempts. Similar attempts were made by the Fascist powers in various countries (in Indonesia, too, for example) and, in my opinion, the Zionist leadership was hardly sorry in those days to have this stain sullying Arab "traditional leadership" in Palestine.

But most Arabs felt differently. I remember May 9, 1945. I was in Haifa. Crowds of Jews danced in the streets of Hadar-Ha-Carmel, in genuine joy at the end of the War and the victory over Nazi Germany. In our club, on the Street of the Maronite Steps in the lower city, we set loudspeakers on the walls and broadcast partisan songs and slogans. Crowds of laborers, teachers and students gathered at the club and then, in red letters on a piece of white cloth, we wrote the slogan: "Freedom Cannot Be Divided! Free the Political Prisoners!" With that slogan, seven of us youths went down to the marketplace and returned to the club with hundreds of demonstrators. Thus we celebrated the victory over Nazism and Fascism. It was not merely a Jewish victory. It was not a victory of one people over another. It was a celebration for all mankind, for all the peoples of the earth. A celebration of the victory of culture, a celebration of the victory of the accomplishments of the human being from the day he first stood erect and blessed the dawn over the powers of darkness that tried to destroy these accomplishments. It was a celebration of the victory of the slogan, "Freedom Cannot Be Divided."

How is the Holocaust seen by the Arabs? Like this – but not only like this. There is no people that has not suffered, to some extent, from the Nazi threat to the future of mankind. There is a direct relationship between the force of that suffering and the place of the peoples in the human struggle for progress. Hitler's warriors began by burning progressive literature before they set fire to the world. They destroyed the German Communist Party before they invaded the Soviet Union, the first country where the Communists had come to power and held it. Hitlerian antisemitism is not only a cruel continuation of the pogroms encouraged by the governments of darkness to distract the minds of their peoples from oppression and torment and to split popular movements; Nazi antisemitism was an inseparable part of the ambition to destroy the achievements of human culture and to turn history backward. Before and during the War, masses of Jews in Europe stood in the front lines of the human struggle for progress. The terrible suffering caused by the Nazi beast to the Jews is measured not only in the six million who were murdered in concentration and death camps. It is also measured by the negative influence of the terrible price paid by the Jewish people for the highly praised Jewish tradition and by the threat of corruption of what is called "the Jewish heart." In my humble opinion, it is hard to find a more difficult mission than opposing that threat, the task of the forces of moderation in Israel. Certainly, it is impossible to compare the suffering experienced by the Jews of Europe and the suffering of the Palestinian people. But the latter are still suffering and the existence of the Palestinian people in their homeland is still threatened. In the eyes of the Arabs, the Holocaust is seen as the original sin which enabled the Zionist movement to convince millions of Jews of the rightness of its course. I cannot imagine that, if it were not for the Holocaust, the brothers of Heine and Maimonides, Bertolt Brecht [sic!] and Stefan Zweig, Albert Einstein and the immortal Jewish-Arab poet Shlomo Ibn Gabirol would allow a Jewish government to expel another Semitic people from its homeland. If not for the Holocaust, a man like Rabbi Meir Kahane could not have appeared in the history of the Jewish people.

Thus the Holocaust is seen by the Arabs. Thus it is seen by the Palestinian Arab nation.

Antisemitism is a European phenomenon, an inseparable part of colonial governments. According to the textbook I mentioned earlier, the history of antisemitism begins with the blood libel in Damascus. That is egregious; and, even in Damascus, it was not Moslems who carried out the blood libel but French monks who blamed the Jews for the murder of a Christian. Arabs suffered from the Spanish Inquisition as did the Jews, perhaps even more. Arab history has known many diseases but antisemitism is not – could not be – one of them.

The division in this country is not between Arabs and Jews. It seems to me that the people with the older and richer heritage of the two peoples should be the first to take the path of patience and compromise that will lead both to a common life of peace, freedom and equality, out of the recognition that this is a land of two Semitic peoples, each of which has suffered in its own way from Fascism, colonialism and antisemitism.

If not for your – and all of humanity's – Holocaust in World War II, the catastrophe that is still the lot of my people would not have been possible.

Translated from the Hebrew by Barbara Harshav.

A critical comment on some aspects of E. Habibi's article will be published in the next issue of *TR*.

Maya Bejerano

Six Poems

Salammbô

Not that I wanted the amber necklace
fastened to hips and falling to her loins,
not the ankles laced with one gold
buckle;
And the snake crossing her head pressing
    her limbs carefully
preparing her.
I want to clasp the ancient horizon
in Salammbô's eyes,
to cradle warriors armed with swords in awe
and forget the Molech therein.

Salammbô wanted to kill Matos.
Matos loved Salammbô.
No one recorded it then.
They fought hard then,
hard as lions and lions-to-be
and tiger-striped tigers.
Salammbô is a Carthaginian princess,
what a wonderful name,
Salammbô daughter of Hamilcar the judge,
sister of Hannibal the strategist
maidservant of the goddess Tanit the white.
Enemy of Molech.
From all she had there remains
her illustrious name – Salammbô.

Data-Processing no. 15

The influence of movies on poetry is tremendous.
Fascinated I pressed close to the trunk of the anemone
as I went out to my lofty deeds
tormented by light, banishing the cars off me
with the breath of my mouth.
Casually we fell to the valley and the silence
covered my head green and sweet.
A beautiful scarecrow, a horseman and me, without provisions;
we remained behind, three hunters.
The work flowed on around when a tiger emerged from
the leaves. I therefore pressed on into deep slumber, properly dressed.
And above us the sky took our pictures:
with hair blowing, gloomy faced
and trembling in the end. The fishermen arrived
at three. Three refined men each on his way shaking hands
sniffing in horror. And the bells were ringing,
and the mustard flower and the cyclamen were given their due.
When I left the weak spot
everything shrank in relief. Returned to its course.
The ants began dancing a foolish ship-dance and the weeds
flared up.
I fell among them and the tiger outran his time.
My heart went out to him at four o'clock, consumed with lust.
Like an amethyst, breathless, I was gathered
with the last rays unto tomorrow
glittering on hilltops
in an unfinished whisper,
that the influence of poetry on movies is tremendous.

Gainsborough

Whore of Lilliputians. Spiritual spy.
Your unattainable knowledge is full of dimness.
Your body a sweet afikoman*.
We may deduce that Gainsborough is what we'll call the girl.

Gainsborough was cut from a yellow curtain
bluer than blue with utter insolence.
Vain chambers collapsed,
or perhaps by houses you mean chambers.

The juice of your mind is in gloom
rolling back the skin of spring,
plaiting sun's rays into braids at the ball,
roofs smoking with ardor, the blazing honey of roofs,
and the red roof tile is a sandal for my feet.

Gainsborough, velvet lad. Parlors upon you,
Gainsborough. Influences from all sides,
from every limb,
and perfect wholeness ripens, bending and
bowing to you.

*) A piece of Matza which is hidden during the Seder evening at Passover,
to be found and ransomed by the children.

Ostrich

Let me nest-
le as an ost-
rich. Let the shut-
ters on my face be
shut. Con-
ceal them with a flowered plastic co-
ver.
When au-
tumn comes it will pe-
el off.
I simp-
ly look we-
ary, what a wonder-
ful mask-
ing of the face and bo-
dy. Women! Hel-
ena Rubinstein de-
ceives you! that wear-
y look is calming.
Removes all sus-
picion, domestic peace is maintained.
But when her day comes the ostrich
rai-
ses her head, lo-
oking at her suitor, begs pardon
and goes.

The Tibetan Princess

The Tibetan princess. Mine. Born from a painter's brush
in a drizzle winding and black he took from her ears
roses and lilies,
and pomegranates creating shields of wreaths around
                                         her elliptical head,
all its pretty openings are close and concentrated
for expressing a dream of the moon
where the sun is a couch for her back as she sits
where the soles of her feet and her fingers whisper to each other
on veils and the perfect lotus leaves
while the colors in the imagination fill spaces
with such a very dancing movement of the spaces
green-white-pink –
yellow-blue

What boring pretty laziness in the pose of the flower,
and the hands idle with the movement of pomegranate leaves
and above all birds drunken from their natural course
hanging on clouds curled by a barber
and rocks softened with covering rugs
and only the arches of the waist behind the veils –
Round round smooth no protrusion –
white, served as first fruits in a basket.

Data Processing 48: The Heat and the Cold

(*Tell Dan* landscapes)

The Heat

From above comes the heat: first seen then arrived taking
form; whipped into shape.
Grasped in sweaty palms in a changing vaporous haze.
The grass and the brown sand hovered clinging
to the crotch of Tabor oak branches, the mastic tree.
Their distant slenderness is sunk in the oppressive heat –
Melting nests high above.

The chirping expired: a heat cushion strangled their shrieks,
and the defeat that has been troubling me; the fall of the oak.
From inside the empty acorns
insects jumped out in disgust: witnesses of thirst,
far from the source of water.
Poverty of existence and satiety: acorns have been and will be
food for squirrels.
Babies slumber, mothers' breasts;
kiosks distribute clean servings
with hungry flies,
to the seated diners who dropped down onto the steps
of a central station in the field.
Crumbs shining on the edges of mouth and neck.
Bits of gold that hand out heat and light lie uncollected.
We smiled at ourselves; decadence sweeps everything away
like filthy black money; abundance of information and memories;
with no remorse stripping off their covers
into the mix of heat, far from the pendulum clocks,
with no white clothes and drawers of polished vessels.

The waterfall sprays our backs.
Falling into slumber, amid faded grass, swallowed by breath
far from rain and storm and will of volcanoes,
kissing and crying in the heat, bare bellied
and eyelids shading a neck, feet
resting against the head, the neck, on the neck,

shoulder to shoulder;
the maragose trees above with claws of shading leaves.
With the slender funnel (transparent) we hear the lashing of the sun's
    rays
without sharp pain things are born,
abandoned and imposed on one another; no parents, no children,
no lover and beloved, and even some haters.
Supine on cotton cloths, wounded with quarreling,
asleep; their interchanging sleep. Bandaged in towels,
their wrists transfuse their dreams to others;
portions of a passing holiday that won't return;
a creature trapped in ironing.
This is the routine obligation to earn a living from some warmth,
among people in a frame of wood and flower,
plaited curtains; there by the hot border, far
away. Unclear if far from here or there. Where to?
The heat will shade (please),
will melt completely, accompany us,
flat in the body and skin,
up to the edge of the cold lakeshore,
in peace.

The Cold

All at once the cold jumped out of the river bed
in a sudden spasm;
and above, close over the recumbent water.
The cold different from any other substance;
cold air; cold water; chilled stones; shade of land
moist and cold; toads in cold blood and fish.
A clear flat river covers the ankles,
movements frozen deliberately up to the hips
surrounded by fig leaves and a plane tree and common ash
and wild grape vines;
eucalyptus leaves and pink oleander in ice,
like white arteries covered by a brown shell.
Their green leaves falling frenzied into water;
the bodies of the fallen shout out and their leaves float above
like painted kerchiefs.

Year after year won't kill the cold,
never coming to a boil. Its shape is hard and sure;
hundreds of people and domesticated animals frozen-mouthed,
astonished, perched around it on rocks
with dry sand underneath, distorted in fear of the cold.
Until overcome by its magic,
clinging like chilly vapors to the river bank:
"Bring on the cold!" howling, cold, worshipping, "We'll get
used to it over the years."
Covering millimeters of their sweating bodies from the South,
drops of sense and quiet eternal living, from the river and its cold;
in this failure – they'll try to corrupt it;
its stones they'll turn to fevered human flesh,
at a forty-degree vulnerability; let's say blood, let's say that
the river will rise
and the sun will come closer and a thousand electric wires
will be thrown out like fishhooks and their circuits will work; and the
    cold water will bubble in the mire,
there will be no leaves, branches, twigs or floating flowers;
in the gushing stream will appear:
skeletal cans, dull stone knives, rotting wooden prongs,
tumbling they'll form rusting razor-blade
waterfalls.

The Heat and the Cold

The warriors were divided in two: half to cold half to heat.
I was in the cold, was conquered by cold, then
I was in the heat, was conquered by heat.
Before I was in the cold I was in the heat
and was conquered by both. (Because)
in the fortress of heat and the fortress of cold, all is crushed
to perfect a new material compound
for a proper casting in a construct of senses.
Drops of the masons' sweat turned to ice pearls,
the blue limbs of those trapped in frost melted to
the color of the oleander yellow pink natural and soft.
The women swim the river in a shining of brilliant hair.
The darkness of face and belly of the warm ones sway in a dance.

The warm wind chilled in the eyes of those who come from the cold
as they saw: then it happened
that in some marvellous cryptic way,
the cold tolerated the heat in it,
the heat tolerated the cold in it,
and so it is for many years
in the heat, in the cold

Ostrich was translated by Lisa Fliegel.
Data-Processing no. 15, Gainsborough, Salammbô and Tibetan Princess were
translated by Linda Zisquit and Barbara Harshav.
Data-Processing 48: The Heat and the Cold was translated by Lisa Fliegel,
Lea Hahn and Jay Shir.
All translations are from the Hebrew.

Asher Reich

Three Poems

Desire is Long-Distance Running

Desire is long-distance running,
crossing pits, breaking barriers
clearing hurdles,

sometimes over a sweet landscape,
– flashing open, closing behind –
somersaulting like a gymnast over the horse.
Soul and thought run in parallel tracks

and dream in long leaps,
land on quicksand and vanish
while our swimming blood comes, finishes the race
with a butterfly stroke,
sometimes passing the shade of ancient records.
Desire is long-distance running,

sometimes daydreaming
of words on the promised summit,
passing without knowing over the holy love,
that even an Olympic soul cannot touch.
Suddenly she grabs me like a long pole
and vaults.

Cards and Love

I

Good cards speak for themselves
like poems, like love, I say.
Everything I didn't know to tell
in the bleating of youth
when I had a clean cardboard face,

I said now
when my calloused life takes to itself –
every sign of a sign, when all is still hidden,
the senses long for what is not yet here to long for
and late blooming is already in the air.

II

Wherever you go take five cards of your life.
Those chestnut eyes are the first card that caught me:
Healing springs where angels wash what they will tell of me to your
    heart.
Your lips are the second card that roused me: ripe berries for eating
what will they whisper in my ear before the kiss?
Nobility of hands, softness of palms – Is my fate etched in their lines?
Those majestic hands of yours when you move them they are
the third card that warms me and in them you will move my body to
    sing in time.
The fourth card is your breasts butterfly baskets in their slumber when
    will they
flower to me in your love – the fifth card – hidden from my eyes.

III

These days I pass in the skin of the thinking animal –
How was I trapped in terminal love, how did I wake from it?
An orphan of the storm, with the carrion of pain or odor of its memory.
And yearning still preys on me from every organ and distant smell of
    flesh
even if the sanity of my flesh says no with a clear shudder
still I am sick of thought of a robust girl.
She whose heart, muscular heart, pounds as if in another's body.
With the slowness of Young Werther's loading the gun
I load myself a longing: A wind brought you to me –
Let some wind come to take you away.

Haifa in Winter

Haifa in winter is a Japanese woodcut.
There the silk of rain awaits me, the softest of rains.
The shadow moth sleeps in the damp of the bushes

and variegated illusions rise from the misty waters.
With the delight of clouds Haifa in winter floats in the air
and the horizon is sometimes a rice paper sail.
Then like a wound in the city's stomach
comes the sun-stained evening.

Translated from the Hebrew by Karen Alkalay Gut.

Ronny Sommeck

Nine Poems

The Wonder of the Yarkon*

By and by the city of Tel Aviv will be drawn like a pistol.
What comes from the sea's direction will begin with hot winds
and in the streets it will be spoken in the silence of an aftershot.
Pity there is no circus in this town,
pity there is no sword-swallower, no magician, no elephants, no dragon,
pity only one boat passes by, now when I show a foreign girl
the wonder of the Yarkon.

A Touch

Like a segment of a Palestinian fire-bird's flight
tonight's touch shall be,
belly to belly,
navel to navel,
and the tits, strawberry tits forever.

*) A small river that runs to the sea at Tel Aviv.

The Gunslinger Harold S. Makes Love with the Land of Israel

You can live for years just from the smell of loaves
which the women leave for the cowboys.
There is a great forbearance in the fingers which tie an electric pole to
    the reins,
and after the first rain, by the horseshoes, weeds goad themselves,
    doubled-over, green.
'Oh why should I take it to heart,' sings the citrus grove watchman
in the morning on the way to Kalkilya,
the wind in this season is like a valley a-sliding, like a Tell a-leaping,
and from the night watchman's transistor blends even now Arab music
    with jackals' howls.
You can live for years just from the smell of loaves
which the women leave for the cowboys,
after three hours on horseback with barely a stop on the way,
barely by the kiosk, by the faucet,
barely by the shorts of the girls who turn their silk pleats up at the end
    of their thighs.

How to Know the Age of a Horse:
A Love Poem

The usual way to know the age of a horse is to look at its teeth.
At six months it has four molars.
At the age of two it has six, and these continue to grow until
the milk teeth are replaced by permanent ones.
At ten a crack appears in the back molars and it grows
to half the length of the tooth when the horse is fifteen.
Starting at twenty-five the crack slowly begins to disappear.
The usual way to know the age of love is to look at its milk teeth.
A small scar will mark what was extracted or left.

Speaking of a Guitar Hero

The exact curve of the spinal cord in jungle light,
and the fingers like dreadful animals glowing from string to string
in the wind that once shifted a dinosaur's body.
So what if somebody loses some sleep over a London girl
whose first name is Leila, and half a street over from
the store with the farm machinery,
another one plows the memory and her neck is a field.

Only fingernails are bitten still in *do re mi fa sol*
and the hand weighs heavy on the guitar neck as a cart full of sheaves.

Johnny

News of Johnny Weissmuller's death was broadcast in an army van
on the way to Beit Lid.
He who braved the jungles turned his head to the orchards of the
    Sharon.
In January '84 even an orchard is an attraction,
like a sprinkler or
a pitchfork.
What can you do, the Land of Israel doesn't live here anymore.
From the soul of Yehuda Halevi remains the flesh
and in some basement on a street bearing his name I can
say to a woman: you turn me on
and she: if you're turned on show me your motor.

What a wonderful world
with death defying leaps from limb to limb,
some winter birds hide in the horizon like in ladies' lingerie.

The Virgins

Virginity hangs like tarpaulin on the army truck.
This winter the Land-of-Israel-Wind can tousle
even night's gown.
Get dressed, I tell her, get dressed.
From over the belly of the hills
even the loveliest of anemones
shows like a splat of blood.

The Energy of a Single Line

What fruits will ripen tonight on the trees of life and knowledge
on the evergreen way from Tel Aviv to Petah Tikva,
what virginity will strike the thunder, strike the lightning
and what firebird will leave in her trail the energy of a single line.
I look into her eyes a moment before she is swallowed into the magic of
the central bus station,
on the last bus which never was her medium, and think
of the sky extinguished in a deep scarlet,
of the revolving sword
and of the love which is this night outside the law.

To Marilyn Monroe

So many sleeping pills are scattered
from Marilyn's torn eyes.
They cross her red lips' barrier like a train
and melt like gravel under the lines
in the warm stations of her body.
Only her breasts like tickets from a distant journey
thrown on the pavements, punched in the parts where
the old-time conductors used to love.

The Wonders of the Yarkon was translated by the poet.
A Touch and *To Marilyn Monroe* were translated by Assi Degani.
The Gunslinger Harold S. Makes Love With the Land of Israel was translated by
Gabriel Levin.
How to know the Age of a Horse: A Love Poem was translated by
Karen Alkalay Gut.
Speaking of a Guitar Hero was translated by Michel Opatowski.
Johnny was translated by Lisa Fliegel.
The Virgins was translated by Lisa Fliegel and Karen Alkalay Gut.
The Energy of a Single Line was translated by Mel Rosenberg.

Notes on Contributors

Dannie Abse, born in Wales, is one of the best-known poets in Britain. His poetry blends Celtic, English and Jewish elements. He has published several novels and an autobiography. A selection of his poems was translated into Hebrew by Moshe Dor, and was included in an anthology dedicated to Jewish-English poets.

Yehuda Amichai was born in Würzburg, and came to Eretz Israel as a child. He fought with the British Army in the Western Desert of Egypt, and participated in Israel's War of Independence. He lives in Jerusalem and is widely known in Israel and abroad as the outstanding modern Hebrew poet. Inheriting the mantle of major Hebrew poets, such as Bialik and Alterman, his work is distinguished by an extraordinary wealth of metaphor, blending a modernist poetics with an existentialist humanism that often recalls Auden. At the same time, his religious background as a child in Germany comes to expression even in the most secular of his poéms. He is also known as a novelist and playwright. The poems published in this issue are taken from his most recent collection, *From Man You Are and to Man You Shall Return.*

David Avidan is, from the point of view of language, the most prominent experimentalist among the members of the "State of Israel generation". When he began writing poetry in the 1950s, he combined the romantic influence of Russian Revolutionary poetry with Anglo-Saxon modernism. His later work is marked by a concern with extrapoetical sources, in which the notion of *text* replaces that of *poem.* What stands out in all his writing is a fascination with science fiction and futuristic themes. Avidan, Israel-born, is considered as the paradigmatic instantiation of the Tel Aviv avant-garde.

Isaac Bashevis Singer touches, in this interview, on a number of issues which recur in his tales.

Maya Bejerano is the best-known Israeli poet of her generation, which came to maturity after the Yom Kippur War. Her poetry is characterized by a neoclassicist approach, strong vitality and conceptual experimentation with didactic undertones. Her notion of self is at variance with the romantic existentialist vision of the poets of the 1950s. Maya Bejerano published most of her poems and collections of verse through *Ah'shav* and its publishing house.

Michael Benedikt is an American poet and lecturer. His main collections of verse and prose poems were published by the University of Pittsburgh Press and by the Wesleyan University Press.

Rachel Chalfi is a film maker and a teacher in the film and TV department in Tel Aviv University, in addition to her creative work as a poet. She presents programs and reads poetry on Israel Radio. Dominant in her lyric poetry are contemplative and legendary elements.

Amos Funkenstein is a historian of ideas with particular interest in theology and various fields of Jewish and general philosophy. He is professor at and co-chairman of the Institute for the History and Philosophy of Science at Tel Aviv University; he holds a simultaneous appointment at Stanford University. His most recent book, *Theology and the Scientific Imagination in Middle Ages to the 17th Century* (Princeton, 1987), discusses the relations between theology and the concepts of physical science against the background of continuity and change during the Renaissance.

Mordechai Geldman, born in a DP camp in Munich, was brought to Israel in his early youth. He is a clinical psychologist who also writes art criticism. His poetry is rich in aestheticist and contemplative elements. He belongs to the generation of poets which came to maturity in the 1960s. Like most of the Hebrew poets represented in this issue, Mordechai Geldman published his first works in the magazine *Ah'shav*.

Emil Habibi, one of the leaders of the Israeli Communist Party, is known as a spokesman for the Arabs in Israel. He is editor-in-chief of the party's Arabic daily, *al-Ittihad*. A well-known prose writer, he is the author of the satiric and picaresque novel *The Opsimist*.

Ya'ir Hurvitz, along with Yonah Wollach and Meir Wieseltier, is a well-known member of the poetic generation of the 1960s. He is a typesetter by profession. In spite of his allegiance to the mainstream of existentialist modernism in Hebrew poetry, he expresses most clearly the particular themes of his decade. In sharp contrast to the rather prosaic ironies of the previous generation, his work is distinguished by fantastic imagery and a highly rhetorical, almost baroque richness of expression that unites experimentation with an interest in earlier strata of Hebrew language.

Gabriel Josipovici is a well-known British novelist and critic, and Professor of English at Sussex University. His novels and criticism adhere to and comment on the tradition of existential modernism as outlined by Kafka, Proust, and other masters of 20th century fiction.

Yoram Kaniuk was wounded in Israel's War of Independence. Afterwards he worked as an artist and resided in New York from 1955 to 1965, where he began his novel-writing career. On his return to Israel he added political and journalistic activity to his literary work. His major works draw upon the sources of fantastic realism. Even though Kaniuk is a native-born Israeli, or *tzabar*, the Holocaust is a theme of several of his books. The story published here, *The Vultures*, is essentially autobiographical.

Abba Kovner (1918–1987), the leader of the Jewish Partisans in Ghetto Vilna and in the Lithuanian forests during the Holocaust, was a member of Kibbutz Ein Ha-Horesh, designer of the Diaspora Museum in Tel Aviv and winner of the Israel Prize for Poetry. He underwent surgery for the removal of his vocal chords at Memorial Sloan-Kettering Cancer Center in New York. The poems translated here are from his book *Sloan Kettering* (Tel Aviv, 1987). Abba Kovner died in Israel on Rosh Ha-Shana, September 1987.

K.Tzetnik (Yehiel De-Nur) is known as the most authentic representative of "Planet Auchwitz" in world literature. His books on the Holocaust have been translated into many languages and read by millions all over the world. The fragment appearing here is taken from his forthcoming book, a report on LSD therapy as applied to Holocaust survivors. It includes the hallucinations and memories which arose in the course of the therapy.

Nicholas de Lange is Instructor in Rabbinics at Cambridge University. He has translated into English various representative works of Hebrew literature. His translation of Ibn Gabirol in this number of the *TR* is, in our opinion, an important endeavour to transpose into a partly Elizabethan English the exquisite verse of the great Hebrew poet and philosopher of the eleventh century Spain.

Raphael Loewe is Professor of Hebrew and Jewish Studies at University College, London. When placed against the background of John Donne's Metaphysical poetry, his translations of Abelard from Latin into Hebrew, and of the twelfth-century poet Abraham Ibn Ezra from Hebrew into English, manifest affinities among the three poets which have not previously been made apparent.

Gabriel Moked was born in Poland, spent a part of his childhood in the Warsaw Ghetto, and arrived in Eretz Israel in 1946. He is a literary critic, and the founding editor of the magazine *Ah'shav*. Among his chief works of criticism are monographs on Kafka and Agnon. He completed his doctorate in philosophy at Hertford College, Oxford, and is at present senior lecturer at the Ben-Gurion University of the Negev. His philosophical works include a book on aesthetics (in Hebrew), and a book on Berkeley's philosophy of science, forthcoming from the Oxford University Press. He is the author of *Variations* (a philosophically oriented prose).

Alan Montefiore is a prominent British philosopher whose main work is done in the field of ethics. He is also active in bridging the gap between English and Continental schools of philosophy. He is Vice-Master of Balliol College, Oxford.

Ernst Neizvestny is a Russian-born sculptor, painter and engraver. His major works include the world's largest bass-relief and the tombstone of Nikita Khrushchev in Moscow, a monumental sculpture in the Aswan Dam in Egypt and another one dedicated to the cosmonauts' achievement. His recent project, called *The Tree of Life*, is envisioned by him as a gigantic monument to the spirit of Man. The full version of his encounter with Khrushchev and other members of the Politburo appears here for the first time in English.

Asher Reich was born into an ultra-orthodox Jerusalem neighborhood, and studied in a yeshiva. After leaving the orthodox community he came to live in Tel Aviv. He is, with Chaim Pessah, co-editor of *Moznaim*, the monthly journal of the Hebrew Writers Association in Israel.

Anthony Rudolf is a poet, critic and translator from French into English. He is also the founding editor and publisher of the Menard Press, London.

Harold Schimmel is a prominent member in the group of Jerusalem poets. An American by birth, he began writing in English. His Hebrew poetry still retains influence of the Anglo-Saxon tradition, while at the same time it is oriented to the landscapes of Israel. His work tends to minimalism and relies on reference to physical objects.

Dennis Silk, born in England, came to Israel as a young man. Although he writes in English, he is close to the Jerusalem group of modern Hebrew poets, which includes Yehuda Amichai, Harold Schimmel, Aharon Shabtai and Aryeh Sachs. Dennis Silk is well known to readers of poetry in English-speaking countries; among his books is a collection published by Viking and Penguin. He is also a puppeteer and a man of the theatre. The poems in prose published here exhibit a tendency to the fantastic, beside their being a critique of the contemporary political and social situation in Jerusalem and the West Bank.

Aryeh Sivan writes poetry whose fund of allusions is drawn from the experience of the native-born Israeli, and even has some "Canaanite" leanings. His work is partly characteristic of the "State of Israel generation", and recalls, for example, that of Moshe Dor and Moshe Ben-Shaul. Typical for his poetry are scenes of settlements of the Turkish and Mandatory period, scenes of sand and sea in the youthful Tel Aviv, and also biblical imagery. Nevertheless, his poetry also speaks with the voice of the individual. Sivan has written quasi-political poems as well, whose subjects include the Sinai war and Theodor Herzl's vision. He belongs among the founders of Hebrew literary magazines in the 1950s, including *Likrat* ('Toward'); he has also contributed regularly to *Ah'shav*.

Ronny Sommeck was born in Iraq, and has lived in Israel since early childhood. He is one of the youngest members of the "State of Israel generation" in poetry. He began writing in the early 1970s, mainly after the Yom Kippur War. He is considered a sort of modern troubadour by Israeli youth. His poetry has a collage-like structure, made of situations, concepts and visual elements taken partly from the world of pop and rock music. He has worked with juvenile delinquents in the Tel Aviv area, and at present is a highschool teacher.

Claude Vigée is a well-known French poet. Born in Alsace, he divides his time between Paris and Jerusalem. Claude Vigée has taught comparative literature in American and Israeli universities. His characteristic contribution to poetry and poetics is his endeavor to develop the concept and practice of typically 'Judaean' verse.

A.B. Yehoshua is known as one of the most important Hebrew prose writers of the "State of Israel generation". His abstract-*cum*-symbolical tales occupy a central position in the realm of style and experience which was opened up by Kafka, Camus and Agnon. In his later writings Yehoshua turned to psychological realism, also returning to the Sephardic and Levantine roots of his family.

List of Translators

Karen Alkalay Gut
David Avidan
Warren Bargad
Dalya Bilu
F.F. Chyet
Peter Cole
Assi Degani
Eliya Nina De-Nur
Lisa Fliegel
Myra Glazer Schotz
Lea Hahn
Barbara Harshav
Benjamin Harshav
Lisa Herman
Nicholas de Lange
Raphael Loewe
Gabriel Levin
Alexandra Meiri
Hanna Inga Moishezon
Michel Opatowski
Mel Rosenberg
Anthony Rudolf
Harold Schimmel
Jay Shir
Philip Simpson
Ronny Sommeck
Zvi Terlo
Linda Zisquit